A COMPLETE DIRECTORY OF
MILITARY VEHICLES

A COMPLETE DIRECTORY OF
MILITARY VEHICLES

FEATURES OVER 180 VEHICLES WITH 320 IDENTIFICATION PHOTOGRAPHS

An A–Z guide to logistics and troop carriers, wreckers, tankers, radio trucks, ambulances, missile transporters, amphibious cars and other specialized army vehicles of the world

PAT WARE

southwater

This edition is published by Southwater, an imprint of Anness Publishing Ltd, Blaby Road, Wigston, Leicestershire LE18 4SE; info@anness.com

www.southwaterbooks.com; www.annesspublishing.com

Anness Publishing has a new picture agency outlet for images for publishing, promotions or advertising. Please visit our website www.practicalpictures.com for more information.

Publisher: Joanna Lorenz
Senior Editor: Felicity Forster
Cover Design: Nigel Partridge
Production Controller: Christine Ni

Produced for Anness Publishing by JSS Publishing Limited, PO Box 6031, Bournemouth BH1 9AT
Editor: Jasper Spencer-Smith
Designer: Nigel Pell
Editorial Assistant: Lizzie Ware
Copy Assistant: Maree Brazill
Scanning: Reaction Ltd, Poole BH12 1DJ

Previously published as part of a larger volume, *The World Encyclopedia of Military Vehicles*

PUBLISHER'S NOTES
Although the information in this book is believed to be accurate and true at the time of going to press, neither the authors nor the publisher can accept any legal responsibility or liability for any errors or omissions that may be made.
    The nationality of each vehicle is identified in the relevant specification box by the national flag that was in use at the time of service.

PAGE 1: **MAN high-mobility cargo vehicle.**
PAGE 2: **MOWAG GW4500 ambulance variant.**
PAGE 3: **Mercedes-Benz G-Wagen.**
PAGE 5: **Alvis Stalwart Mk 2.**

Contents

Introduction

In 1879, Karl Benz had been granted a patent for his first internal combustion engine, and by 1885, Benz had designed and constructed the first recognizable motorized vehicle. He was awarded a patent for its invention in January 1886. Around 25 Benz vehicles were sold between 1888 and 1893, when his first four-wheeler was introduced. During the last years of the 19th century, Benz ran the largest motor company in the world, producing 572 units in 1899.

A handful of forward-thinking military officers in Europe and North America soon began to realize that the motor vehicle offered distinct advantages over the traditional horse or mule for carrying supplies, as well as being more adaptable in the prime mover role than teams of horses or steam traction engines. Within a decade, definite military roles had started to evolve for trucks, tractors, motor cars and motorcycles and, by the beginning of World War I, Germany, Britain, France, Belgium, Canada and the USA had all started the process of mechanization of their armies.

At the end of World War I, thousands of surplus military vehicles found their way into civilian hands. There was little appetite for military spending during the 1920s and, in most countries, there was little serious development in the military truck. Germany began a process of illegal rearmament in the 1930s, which included some attempts at producing a range of standardized military trucks. Britain was ill-prepared for another war and, having lost literally thousands of military vehicles during the retreat from northern France, the British motor industry spent much of the next two to three years catching up, and the War Office was forced to appeal to the USA and Canada for assistance.

US truck production during World War II reached a total of more than three million vehicles, and US trucks were supplied to all of the Allies under the Lend-Lease arrangements. Even Canada managed to build close to one million trucks, and the standardized Canadian Military Pattern (CMP) vehicles also became a familiar sight in all of the theatres of the war. By contrast, Germany and Japan struggled to provide sufficient logistics vehicles to their armies, and were frequently forced to use captured and impressed civilian vehicles.

By 1945, German industry was close to collapse and truck production had slowed to a trickle. Most of the trucks in the hands of the *Wehrmacht* were destroyed after VE Day, while Allied surplus vehicles were disposed of in their hundreds of thousands. The armies of the newly liberated European nations were equipped with surplus British, Canadian and American vehicles, many of which remained in service into the 1970s and '80s. In Britain and the USA, new vehicles were designed and produced which reflected the harsh lessons learnt in the six-year conflict. The Soviet Union also embarked on a rearmament

BELOW: **GMC 6x6 trucks leaving the D-Day beachhead. A number of amphibious DUKWS are on the beach, having ferried supplies from ship to shore.**

LEFT: **As in World War I, mud was often the greatest enemy, and without all-wheel drive it was all too easy for vehicles to be brought to a slithering halt. This column of *Wehrmacht* vehicles includes a standardized Auto-Union Horch Kfz 21 heavy personnel carrier (extreme left), a Ford V3000S or V3000A 3-ton truck (centre left), and a Zündapp KS750 heavy motorcycle combination (foreground, centre).**

programme, modelling the first generation of post-war military vehicles on the Lend-Lease trucks that had been supplied to them since 1941.

In the West, logistical military vehicles became ever more capable and sophisticated, while the Soviet Union opted for a more basic approach that relied heavily on quantity. All-wheel drive became commonplace, as did the use of diesel engines and multi-fuel units, and the availability of more powerful engines made it possible to design heavy equipment transporters which could carry tanks weighing up to 70 or 75 tons. The crossing of water obstacles remained an obsession on both sides, and the DUKW of World War II had shown that it was possible to design reliable amphibious vehicles, while many logistical vehicles were designed to be able to wade

through deep water with the minimum of preparation. Floating bridge and ferry equipment and sophisticated vehicle-launched bridges were developed that could be carried on regular trucks by both Western and Soviet forces.

By the end of the century, military vehicles had come a long way. Today's sophisticated trucks would be scarcely recognizable to the drivers and mechanics of the primitive machines known to the opposing sides between 1914 and 1918. But, curiously, many of the roles have remained unchanged.

This book explores the diversity of cargo trucks, artillery tractors, ambulances, ammunition carriers, gun trucks, and signals and reconnaissance vehicles which have always been vital to support the fighting men in every conflict across the world since the first such vehicle appeared.

LEFT: **The Bedford MK was introduced in 1970–71 as a replacement for the RL of 1951. In 1981, the MK was replaced by the near-identical, but turbocharged MJ. This example is one of those vehicles constructed by AWD after Bedford went into administration. The trailer mounts the Rapier 2000 with an Alenia Marconi "Dagger" 3D pulse doppler-radar search system.**

International Aust No 1, Mks 1-4

International Aust No 1, Mks 1-4

Type: Truck, 2¹/₂-ton, cargo, 4x4
Manufacturer: International Harvester Company of Australia; Melbourne
Production: 1959 to 1971
Powerplant: International AGD-282; six cylinders in-line; petrol; water-cooled; 4,621cc; overhead valves; power output, 148bhp at 3,800rpm
Transmission: 5F1Rx2; part-time 4x4
Suspension: Live axles on semi-elliptical multi-leaf springs; double-acting hydraulic shock absorbers
Brakes: Air-assisted hydraulic
Dimensions: Length – 6,375mm/244in
  Width – 2,438mm/96in
  Height – tilt in place, 2,896mm/114in
  Wheelbase – 3,683mm/145in
Weight: Unladen – 5,525kg/12,181lb
  Payload – 2,490kg/5,489lb
Performance: Maximum speed – 80kph/50mph

Launched in 1959, and remaining in production until 1971. A design project aimed at producing a tactical truck with a high national content of parts was initiated by the Army Design Establishment in 1953. International Harvester was the only company to show any interest, and prototypes were tested during 1955–59. The first 100 production vehicles were delivered in April 1959.

ABOVE: **The International 2¹/₂-ton truck was the Royal Australian Army's standard vehicle during the 1960s and 1970s.**

A further 600 were ordered in 1962 and by 1966 more than 1,500 examples were in service. More than 90 per cent of the components originated from Australia.

Aside from the use of glass-fibre mudguards on the steel cab, the design was thoroughly conventional, with a 4,621cc six-cylinder water-cooled petrol engine driving both axles through a five-speed gearbox and two-speed transfer box. The live axles were suspended on semi-elliptical springs.

Standard variants include cargo/ personnel, fire-tender, machinery, office/ stores, tipper, road-layer and water tanker.

International Aust No 1, Mk 5

With the 2¹/₂-ton variant of the Australian designed and produced military truck entering service in April 1959, work had begun in 1958 on a 6x6 variant. Launched in 1966, and rated at 5 tons, the larger vehicle shared many components with the earlier Mks 1–4 (4x4). Alongside the standard cargo body, there were dumper, tractor, pole-borer, and garbage-compactor variants. The two trucks formed the basis of the Army's logistics fleet and both were used widely during the Australian involvement in Vietnam.

Like the smaller truck, the Mk 5 was powered by the same 4,621cc International six-cylinder petrol engine, driving both axles through a five-speed gearbox and two-speed transfer box. The live axles were suspended on semi-elliptical springs. Prototypes had twin rear wheels, while the production trucks used singles of larger section.

LEFT: **Both versions of the Aust No 1 were assembled at the International Harvester plant at Dandenong, Victoria, alongside the company's civilian truck range.**

International Aust No 1, Mk 5

Type: Truck, 5-ton, cargo, 6x6
Manufacturer: International Harvester Company of Australia; Melbourne
Production: 1966 to 1971
Powerplant: International AGD-282; six cylinders in-line; petrol; water-cooled; 4,621cc; overhead valves; power output, 148bhp at 3,800rpm
Transmission: 5F1Rx2; part-time 4x4
Suspension: Live axles on semi-elliptical multi-leaf springs; double-acting hydraulic shock absorbers
Brakes: Air-assisted hydraulic
Electrical system: 12V
Dimensions: Length – 6,528mm/257in
  Width – 2,438mm/96in
  Height – tilt in place, 3,302mm/130in; minimum, 2,515mm/99in
  Wheelbase – 3,783mm/149in
  Bogie centres – 1,120mm/44in
Weight: Unladen – 6,624kg/14,604lb
  Payload – road, 6,804kg/15,000lb; cross-country, 4,990kg/11,000lb
Performance: Maximum speed – 80kph/50mph

Land Rover MC2 Perentie

From the early 1960s, the Royal Australian Army had used Series IIA and Series III Land Rovers produced by Leyland Australia (later Jaguar-Rover Australia (JRA)). During 1981, JRA started development work on a heavy-duty 3-ton 6x6 truck using components of the Land Rover 110, based on a

BELOW: The MC2 Perentie was based on the Land Rover 110, but was powered by an Isuzu 4BD1 diesel engine.

development vehicle produced by SMC Engineering. At the same time, the Army announced its intention to procure 25,000 1-ton and 400 2-ton vehicles under "Project Perentie". Seven companies submitted tenders, and three, including JRA and Jeep, were asked to provide vehicles for trials. At the conclusion of the trials, JRA received contracts for both types of vehicle, with deliveries taking place between 1987 and 1990.

The 1-ton vehicle was designated the MC2 4x4 Perentie. Based on standard Land Rover 110, the chassis was galvanized, and lengthened at the rear to allow the spare wheel to be carried under the body. The vehicle was powered by an Isuzu four-cylinder diesel engine driving through the four-speed transmission of the early Range Rover.

Land Rover MC2 Perentie

Type: Truck, 1-ton, cargo, 4x4
Manufacturer: Jaguar-Rover (Australia); Sydney
Production: 1987 to 1990
Powerplant: Isuzu 4BD1; four cylinders in-line; direct-injection diesel; water-cooled; 3,856cc; overhead valves; power output, 84bhp at 3,200rpm
Transmission: 4F1Rx2; full-time 4x4
Suspension: Live axles on dual-rate coil springs; hydraulic double-acting telescopic shock absorbers
Brakes: Servo-assisted hydraulic
Electrical system: 12V
Dimensions: Length – 4,877mm/192in
　　Width – 1,778mm/70in
　　Height – tilt in place, 2,057mm/81in
　　Wheelbase – 2,794mm/110in
Weight: Unladen – 2,250kg/4,960lb
　　Payload – 950kg/2,094lb
Performance: Maximum speed – 115kph/72mph

Standard variants included a soft-top cargo vehicle, hardtop and soft-top communications vehicles.

Land Rover MC2HD Perentie

In the early 1980s, Jaguar-Rover Australia (JRA) announced a heavy-duty 3-ton 6x6 civilian truck, based on developments from SMC Engineering, Bristol in the UK. When the Royal Australian Army announced it was planning to procure 400 2-ton vehicles under "Project Perentie", JRA submitted an upgraded version of this 6x6 vehicle for consideration. Following trials, the vehicle was accepted for production.

Known as the MC2HD 6x6 Perentie, the vehicle was built on a purpose-designed heavy-duty galvanized-steel chassis, with a fabricated rear section of rectangular tube to support the rear bogie. Power came from an Isuzu 4BD1 four-cylinder diesel engine, driving through Range Rover transmission. Drive to the rearmost axle was by a separate propeller shaft from the transfer box power take-off. The front and rear axles were fitted with lower ratio gears and were wider than standard to accommodate the increased weight.

Production variants included a pick-up truck, personnel carrier,

LEFT: Work on the MC2HD began in March 1989. The vehicle was also offered worldwide, with an option to fit the 3,500cc Range Rover V8 petrol engine.

Land Rover MC2HD Perentie

Type: Truck, 2-ton, cargo, 6x6
Manufacturer: Jaguar-Rover (Australia); Sydney
Production: 1989 to 1998
Powerplant: Isuzu 4BD1; four cylinders in-line; turbocharged direct-injection diesel; water-cooled; 3,856cc; overhead valves; power output, 115bhp at 3,200rpm
Transmission: 4F1Rx2; full-time 4x4, selectable 6x6
Suspension: Live axles; dual-rate coil springs at front; dual-rate semi-elliptical multi-leaf springs and cranked rocker beam at rear; hydraulic double-acting telescopic shock absorbers
Brakes: Servo-assisted hydraulic
Electrical system: 12V, 24V
Dimensions: Length – 6,147mm/242in
　　Width – 2,057mm/81in
　　Height – tilt in place, 2,083mm/82in
　　Wheelbase – 3,048mm/120in
　　Bogie centres – 1,500mm/35in
Weight: Unladen – 3,660kg/8,069lb
　　Payload – 2,000kg/4,409lb
Performance: Maximum speed – 100kph/62mph

water tanker, air-defence vehicle, gun tractor, four-stretcher ambulance, box body and shelter carrier. A long-range patrol vehicle was also produced for Australian special forces.

MACK RM600 Series MC3

Mack Trucks (Australia) is a wholly owned subsidiary of the US company, and has been supplying heavy-duty military vehicles to the Australian Defence Force (ADF) since 1981. The company also refurbishes all Australian military vehicles regardless of origin.

The RM600 Series is a bonneted truck with the front axle set well back, and with a centre cab. It is powered by an 11,000cc Mack six-cylinder turbocharged diesel engine driving all three axles through a Maxitorque five-speed gearbox and two-speed transfer box. The first three prototype vehicles were supplied for a two-year evaluation in 1979. Following successful performance in a range of

conditions, from the tropical climate found in the north-west of the continent, to the dry, searing heat of the central desert. The first order, for 906 vehicles, was placed in 1981 with deliveries scheduled for the following year.

The standard 8-ton cargo vehicle is fitted with a drop-side body manufactured by Walsh Engineering. Some vehicles were fitted with an Abbey hydraulic loading crane mounted between the cab and the body. Other standard variants include a heavy recovery vehicle, artillery tractor, fuel tanker, water distributor, dump truck, concrete mixer, bitumen layer and bridge laying/recovery vehicle. In the typical style of Australian road trains,

the vehicle is often required to tow two 12.2m/40ft container trailers. More than 1,000 of the vehicles have now been supplied to the ADF. In 2003, Mack were contracted to convert 158 trucks to the heavy-recovery and fuel-tanker roles.

Some RM600s were fitted with a front-mounted 10-ton Ateco winch. Mack Trucks was taken over by Volvo in 2001.

ABOVE: **An Australian Army Mack RM600 fitted with a heavy recovery body.** LEFT: **The standard 8-ton cargo vehicle is fitted with a drop-side body manufactured by Walsh Engineering. This example has had the drop-down sides removed to carry a container.**

MACK RM600 Series

Type: Truck, 8-ton, cargo, 6x6
Manufacturer: Mack Trucks Australia; Wacol, Queensland
Production: 1981 to date
Powerplant: Mack EM6-285 Maxidyne; six cylinders in-line; water-cooled; turbocharged diesel; 11,000cc; overhead valves; power output, 285bhp at 1,800rpm
Transmission: 5F1Rx2; full-time 6x6 (6x4 for bitumen layer and fuel tanker variants)
Suspension: Live axles on semi-elliptical multi-leaf springs; some trucks retro-fitted with rear air-bag suspension
Brakes: Air-pressure
Electrical system: 24V
Dimensions: Length – 9,601mm/378in
Width – 2,490mm/98in
Height – 3,150mm/124in
Wheelbase – 5,461mm/215in
Bogie centres – 1,397mm/55in
Weight: Unladen – 13,413kg/29,570lb
Payload – 8,000kg/17,637lb
Performance: Maximum speed – 90kph/56mph

LEFT: **The Austro-Daimler ADGR was a development of the earlier ADG. Some 361 were built for the Romanian Army between 1936 and 1940. Vehicles were used by the *Wehrmacht* during World War II. The truck featured independent rear suspension by swing axles and leaf springs, and was powered by a 3,915cc six-cylinder engine.**

Austro-Daimler ADGR

In 1899, the German manufacturer Daimler Motoren Gesellschaft, made an agreement with Bierenz-Fischer to build 100 Daimler cars in Austria. Meanwhile, Österreichische Automobil Gesellschaft, which had been founded during 1906 in Wien, had commissioned Daimler to build Maja cars. When Österreichische Automobil Gesellschaft went into receivership, the design was adopted by Daimler. In 1911, all contact with the German company was severed and the enterprise adopted the name Austro-Daimler.

During World War I, Austro-Daimler supplied cars, 1½- and 3-ton 4x2 trucks, and all-wheel-drive artillery tractors to the Austro-Hungarian Army. In 1928, the company merged with Puch-Werke and started to produce both cars and trucks using Puch designs, some of which were used in military service. First of these was the 2-ton 6x4 ADG – the initials stood for Austro-Daimler *Geländewagen* (command car) – based on a heavy car chassis dating from 1931. Less than 200 were supplied to the Austrian Army during 1935–36, built as trucks, ambulances, tankers, and command vehicles. The ADG was developed into the more numerous 2½-ton 6x4 ADGR of which 361 examples were built for the Romanian Army between 1936 and 1940. Both also saw service with the *Wehrmacht* during World War II.

The truck was unusual for the period in featuring independent rear suspension by means of swing axles and leaf springs. The engine was a 3,915cc six-cylinder unit driving through a seven-speed gearbox which included two reverse gears. Although the drive-line was a conventional 6x4, there were front rollers as well as free-running spare wheels mounted either side, to help prevent the chassis from grounding when driven cross-country. Standard variants included a cargo/personnel, ambulance, tanker and command car.

In 1934, Austro-Daimler-Puch merged with Steyr-Werke and the company became known as Steyr-Daimler-Puch. New products introduced after this date were generally badged "Steyr".

LEFT: **The twin spare wheels were mounted in such a way as to permit them to revolve freely, which helped to prevent the truck grounding. The two front rollers were an aid for crossing ditches.**

Austro-Daimler ADGR

Type: Truck, 2½-ton, cargo, 6x4
Manufacturer: Steyr-Daimler-Puch; Wien
Production: 1936 to 1940
Powerplant: Austro-Daimler M640; six cylinders in-line; petrol; water-cooled; 3,915cc; overhead valves; power output, 72bhp at 3,800rpm
Transmission: 7F2R; 6x4
Suspension: Live axle on semi-elliptical multi-leaf springs at front; independent suspension by swing axles on semi-elliptical multi-leaf springs at rear
Brakes: Mechanical at front; hydraulic at rear
Electrical system: 6V
Dimensions: Length – 6,500mm/256in
Width – 2,135mm/84in
Height – tilt in place, 2,230mm/88in
Wheelbase – 3,720mm/146in
Bogie centres – 1,200mm/47in
Weight: Unladen – 4,420kg/9,744lb
Payload – 3,000kg/6,614lb
Performance: Maximum speed – 68kph/42mph

LEFT: **Manufactured by Steyr-Daimler-Puch from 1937 to 1941, the Steyr 640 was not dissimilar in appearance to the Austro-Daimler ADGR although it was actually a replacement for the Steyr Model 440. The front axle was suspended on semi-elliptical leaf springs, at the rear were swinging half-axles which helped to maintain ground contact; twin spare wheels were provided to help prevent bellying on rough ground.**

Steyr 640

Originally established in 1864 as an arms manufacturer, Österreichische Waffenfabriks Gesellschaft started producing trucks under the name Steyr in a former weapons factory in a town of the same name near Wien in 1922. Four years later, the company name was changed to Steyr-Werke. In 1934, Steyr merged with Austro-Daimler-Puch to form Steyr-Daimler-Puch. The company produced a range of light trucks including many which were intended for military use.

The 1¹/₂-ton 6x4 Model 640 was introduced in 1937 as a replacement for the earlier, and very similar, Model 440. It was powered by a 2,260cc Steyr six-cylinder engine, driving the rear wheels through a four-speed main gearbox and two-speed auxiliary box. At the front, there was a live axle suspended on semi-elliptical leaf springs. At the rear, there were swinging half-axles, again using semi-elliptical leaf springs. Free-running spare wheels were fitted alongside the cab, to prevent grounding on rough terrain.

Standard variants included a cargo/ personnel carrier, an open four-door heavy command car, with a coach-built body and an all-steel four-stretcher ambulance (Kfz 31 *Krankenkraftwagen*).

The 640 remained in production until 1941, with most of the total of 3,780 being built during 1940–41. Almost all of the vehicles produced were supplied to the *Wehrmacht*, although the command car was also used by the Austrian Army.

Steyr 640

Type: Truck, cargo, 1¹/₂-ton, 6x4
Manufacturer: Steyr-Daimler-Puch; Wien
Production: 1937 to 1941
Powerplant: Steyr M640; six cylinders in-line; petrol; water-cooled; 2,260cc; overhead valves; power output, 55bhp at 3,800rpm
Transmission: 4F1Rx2; 6x4
Suspension: Live axle on semi-elliptical multi-leaf springs at front; swinging half-axles on semi-elliptical multi-leaf springs at rear
Brakes: Hydraulic
Electrical system: 12V
Dimensions: Length – 5,330mm/210in
  Width – 1,730mm/68in
  Height – tilt in place, 2,330mm/92in
  Wheelbase – 3,030mm/119in
  Bogie centres – 1,060mm/42in
Weight: Unladen – 2,400kg/5,291lb
  Payload – 1,500kg/3,307lb
Performance: Maximum speed – 70kph/44mph

ABOVE AND RIGHT: **Some 3,780 examples of the Steyr 640 were produced, with many supplied to the *Wehrmacht*. Most were bodied as standard cargo carriers.**

Steyr 270 1500A

Steyr 270 1500A

Type: Car, heavy, personnel, 4x4
Manufacturer: Steyr-Daimler-Puch; Wien.
Auto-Union; Siegmar
Production: 1941 to 1944
Powerplant: Steyr 1500A; eight cylinders in
V configuration; petrol; air-cooled;
3,517cc; overhead valves; power output,
85bhp at 3,000rpm
Transmission: 4F1Rx2; part-time 4x4
Suspension: Independent at the front using
wishbones and torsion bars; live axle at the
rear on semi-elliptical multi-leaf springs
Brakes: Hydraulic
Electrical system: 12V
Dimensions: Length – 5,080mm/200in
Width – 2,030mm/80in
Height – tilt in place, 2.320mm/91in;
minimum, 2,032mm/80in
Wheelbase – 3,250mm/139in
Weight: Unladen – 2,485kg/5,478lb
Payload – 1,675kg/3,693lb
Performance: Maximum speed – 90kph/56mph

Designed by Ferdinand Porsche, the Steyr 270 4x4 was in production between 1941 and 1944 for the *Wehrmacht*. The vehicle was co-produced by Steyr in Austria, who made 12,450 and by Auto-Union in Germany. The chassis was designated 1500A/01 and 1500/A2, and the most numerous of the three variants produced was an eight-seater utility-bodied personnel carrier (Kfz 70), which largely replaced the *Wehrmacht*'s

ABOVE: **Auto-Union and Steyr produced almost 12,500 examples of the 1500A heavy cross-country car chassis for the *Wehrmacht* between 1941 and 1945.**

earlier assortment of heavy cross-country cars. There was also a convertible staff/command car (Kfz 21) and a light cargo truck.

The engine was a 3,517cc V8 air-cooled unit, coupled to both axles via a four-speed gearbox and two-speed transfer box. A differential

lock was fitted in the rear axle. Suspension was independent with torsion bars at the front. At the rear there was a live axle suspended on semi-elliptical multi-leaf springs.

Steyr-Puch 700AP Haflinger

Steyr-Puch 700AP Haflinger

Type: Truck, light, cargo, 4x4
Manufacturer: Steyr-Daimler-Puch; Graz
Production: 1959 to 1973
Powerplant: Puch 700AP; horizontally opposed
two cylinders; petrol; air-cooled; 643cc;
overhead valves; power output, 24bhp
(27bhp from 1967) at 4,800rpm
Transmission: 4F1R (5F1R from 1966);
part-time 4x4; differential locks in both axles
Suspension: Independent suspension by
swing arm half-axles with coil springs
Brakes: Hydraulic
Electrical system: 12V
Dimensions: Length – 2,845mm/112in
Width – 1,350mm/53in
Height – 1,740mm/69in
Wheelbase – 1,500mm/59in, 1,800mm/71in
Weight: Unladen – 635kg/1,400lb
Payload – 515kg/1,135lb
Performance: Maximum speed – 75kph/47mph

Launched in 1959, the Steyr-Puch Haflinger was designed by Erich Ledwinka, son of the famous Tatra designer Hans Ledwinka. The vehicle incorporated the designer's trademark tubular backbone chassis on to which were attached the coil-sprung independent swing-arm axles. Despite being small, the Haflinger offered an extremely high level of off-road performance. The basic vehicle was little more than a flat platform to which was attached a front panel and windscreen. Both two- and four-door canvas hoods were available. A glass-fibre cab was also offered. Variants included rocket-launcher, communications vehicle and mount for a recoilless anti-tank gun. A longer wheelbase variant was introduced in 1962.

Power was provided by a rear-mounted 643cc horizontally opposed

two-cylinder air-cooled engine driving through a five-speed gearbox. Manual differential locks were fitted in both axles and final drive was through step-down spur gears in the hubs.

The Haflinger saw service with the armies of Austria, Indonesia, Italy, the Netherlands, Nigeria, South Africa, Sweden and Switzerland.

LEFT: **Despite its small size, the Ledwinka-designed Haflinger was an agile performer off the road.**

Steyr-Daimler-Puch Pinzgauer 710M, 712M

LEFT: **This armoured variant of the 712M was originally intended for New Zealand, but has subsequently been trialled by a number of other nations.**

During the UK trials in 1993, the company Automotive Technik was established, in Aldershot, Surrey, to provide trials support and to handle deliveries into the UK. However, when commercial production in Austria ceased in June 2000, Automotive Technik acquired the rights to the design and the production line was moved to the company's new premises in Guildford.

Alongside the basic cargo/personnel vehicles, the Pinzgauer has been produced for the command, cargo and shelter carrier, weapons carrier, special forces, radio, workshop, fire-tender and ambulance roles. Automotive Technik have also produced armoured and so-called "extreme mobility" variants with electronic traction control.

In 1965, Steyr-Daimler-Puch showed a prototype of the Model 710 Pinzgauer 4x4, intended to replace the Haflinger. This was soon followed by the 6x6 Model 712. By 1971 both models were in production. Both were initially offered with either a fully enclosed steel body or a military-type cargo body with a folding windscreen. The cargo area has removable top hoops, and bench seats fitted down both sides of the body for either eight men (Model 710) or 12 men (Model 712).

The vehicle is assembled around a torsion-resistant tubular backbone chassis on which are mounted independent swing axles with coil springs (rocking beam leaf springs at the rear of 6x6 variants). Early examples used a 2,460cc Steyr four-cylinder petrol engine but, from 1983, the petrol-engined versions were joined by 2,499cc six-cylinder turbocharged diesel engine. Subsequently, a Volkswagen five-cylinder turbocharged diesel engine has also been specified. The engine is coupled to a five-speed ZF gearbox and two-speed transfer box, with lockable differentials, front and rear. A four-speed ZF automatic gearbox is also available.

More than 20,000 Pinzgauer vehicles are in use by the armed forces of more than 15 countries including Austria, Ghana, Nigeria, Oman, Sudan, Switzerland, Tunisia, the former Yugoslavia and the UK. Also other nations in the Middle East and South America.

LEFT: **Although the design is now more than 40 years old, the Pinzgauer remains in production and is in service with 15 countries. The combination of a tubular backbone chassis combined with swinging half axles gives the vehicle a formidable off-road performance, further enhanced by traction control.**

Steyr-Daimler-Puch Pinzgauer 710M, 712M

Type: Truck, 1-ton, cargo/personnel, 4x4; or 1¹/₂-ton, cargo/personnel, 6x6

Manufacturer: Steyr-Daimler-Puch; Graz. Automotive Technik; Guildford

Production: 1965 to date

Powerplant: Steyr; four cylinders in-line; petrol; water-cooled; 2,460cc; overhead valves; power output, 92bhp at 4,000rpm. Five- and six-cylinder turbocharged 2,499cc diesel engines also offered.

Transmission: 5F1Rx2, or 4F1Rx2 automatic; part-time 4x4

Suspension: Independent suspension at all wheels using swing axles and coil springs; rocking beam at rear of 6x6 variants with semi-elliptical multi-leaf springs; dual-action hydraulic shock absorbers

Brakes: Hydraulic with vacuum servo-assistance; late models have ABS and electronic brake distribution

Electrical system: 24V

Dimensions: Length – (4x4 variants) 4,528mm/178in; (6x6 variants) 5,308mm/209in
Width – 1,800mm/71in
Height – tilt in place, 2,045mm/80in
Wheelbase – 2,400mm/95in
Bogie centres – (6x6 variants) 980mm/39in

Weight: Unladen – (4x4 variants) 2,450kg/5,401lb; (6x6 variants) 2,600kg/5,732lb

Performance: Maximum speed – 120kph/75mph

MZKT 74135 *Volat*

First seen in the early 1990s, the Minsk Wheel Tractor Plant (MZKT) *Volat* (Hero) 74135 is a massive 8x8 tractor designed for use with a 70-ton semi-trailer or a 60-ton drawbar trailer. MZKT's vehicle heritage includes such monsters as the MAZ-535, 537 and 547 which were used as missile "Transporter-Erector-Launcher" (TEL) rigs by the army of the former Soviet Union.

Weighing more than 26 tons, the *Volat* is powered by a 21,600cc Deutz-MWM V12 turbocharged inter-cooled diesel engine producing 788bhp. Alternatively, a 21,930cc Daimler-Chrysler 780bhp engine may be specified. The transmission is a joint US-Belarus project, a fully automatic Allison six-speed hydro-mechanical gearbox coupled to a two-speed Minsk transfer box which incorporates a lockable inter-axle differential. Each of the axles includes automatic and manual differential locks. There is also an automatic "Central Tyre-Inflation System" (CTIS) that operates on both the tractor and the three-axle MWTP-99941 semi-trailer.

The spacious four-door seven-man cab incorporates a full-width bonnet and a reverse-raked, divided windscreen. A 25-ton German-manufactured ITAG winch is mounted on the chassis behind the cab.

RIGHT: **The huge bonnet conceals either a Deutz-MWM V12 turbocharged diesel engine producing 788bhp, or a 780bhp Daimler-Chrysler OM 444LA. Transmission is by a fully automatic Allison six-speed hydro-mechanical gearbox and a two-speed Minsk transfer box.**

ABOVE: **Produced by the Minsk Wheel Tractor Plant, the *Volat* 74135 is a massive 8x8 tractor which can be coupled to either a 70-ton semi-trailer or a 60-ton drawbar trailer and is rated for a gross train weight of more than 200 tons.**

There is also a crane for handling the spare wheels.

The standard MWTP-99941 semi-trailer is rated at 70 tons and has a load-bed length of 13.9m/45.5ft. Loading is carried out via hydraulic ramps which are raised and lowered by an auxiliary power unit carried on the trailer. The trailer is large enough to accept a main battle tank or two armoured personnel carriers or infantry fighting vehicles. Other Soviet and East European semi-trailers may also be used and the tractor has been demonstrated coupled to both a semi-trailer and a drawbar trailer, with a gross train weight in excess of 200 tons.

MZKT describe this monster vehicle in their dual-language sales literature as being a "heavy-duty autotrain – suitable for the transportation of heavy caterpillar rigs".

MZKT *Volat* 74135

Type: Truck, 60- to 70-ton, tractor, 8x8
Manufacturer: Minsk Wheel Tractor Plant (MZKT); Minsk
Production: 1998 to date
Powerplant: Deutz-MWM TBD-234; 12 cylinders in V configuration; turbocharged diesel; water-cooled; 21,600cc; overhead valves; power output, 788bhp at 2,000rpm. Daimler-Chrysler OM 444LA; 12 cylinders in V configuration; turbocharged diesel; water-cooled; 21,930cc; overhead valves; power output, 780bhp at 1,800rpm.
Transmission: 6F2Rx2, automatic; full-time 8x8 with central and axle differential locks
Suspension: Independent suspension, front and rear, using torsion bars
Brakes: Air-pressure
Electrical system: 24V
Dimensions: Length – 9,700mm/382in
　　Width – 3,070mm/121in
　　Height – 3,670mm/145in
　　Wheelbase – 6,650mm.262in
　　Bogie centres – 2,200mm/87in + 1,700mm/67in
Weight: Unladen – 26,000kg/57,319lb
　　Gross train weight – 205,400kg/452,822lb
Performance: Maximum speed – 90kmph/55mph

LEFT: The FN 4RM/62C, manufactured between 1952 and 1954, was also co-produced by the Belgian companies Brossel Frères and Auto-Miesse. The standard variant was a steel-bodied canvas-covered cargo truck. There was also a quadruple anti-aircraft gun mount and a tipper. BELOW: The vehicle was powered by an FN 4,275cc six-cylinder unit with either overhead or side valves.

FN 4RM/62C

Based in the city of Herstal, near Liége, the Belgian armaments company FN (originally established as Fabrique Nationale des Armes de Guerre) started producing bicycles in 1895, progressed to trucks in 1900, with motorcycles following a year or so later. Trucks, artillery tractors and motorcycles

FN 4RM/62C

Type: Truck, cargo, 4½-ton, 4x4
Manufacturer: Fabrique Nationale Herstal; Herstal. Auto-Miesse; Brussels. Etablissements Brossel Frères Bovy et Pipe; Brussels
Production: 1952 to 1954
Powerplant: FN62C; six cylinders in-line; petrol; water-cooled; 4,275cc; side valves (overhead valves available as an option); power output, 92–134bhp at 2,400rpm
Transmission: 4F1Rx2; part-time 4x4
Suspension: Live axles on semi-elliptical multi-leaf springs
Brakes: Hydraulic
Electrical system: 12V
Dimensions: Length – 5,670mm/239in
　　　　Width – 2,300mm/90in
　　　　Height – tilt in place, 2,950mm/116in;
　　　　minimum, 2,150mm/85in
　　　　Wheelbase – 2,870mm/113in
Weight: Unladen – 3,185kg/7,022lb
　　　　Payload – 4,500kg/9,921lb
Performance: Maximum speed – 73kph/45mph

were supplied to the Belgian Army during World War I and after the outbreak of World War II. The company resumed the production of military vehicles after 1945 and produced a number of excellent tactical truck designs that were used in large numbers by the Belgian Army.

The 4RM/62C was typical of these post-war types, many of which served in the British-occupied zones of Germany where the Belgian 1st Army Corps assisted the occupation. Designed and manufactured between 1952 and 1954, and also co-produced by Brossel Frères and Auto-Miesse, the 4RM/62C was a 4½-ton 4x4 truck powered by a

4,275cc six-cylinder petrol engine, with either side valves or overhead valves: the latter offered a near 50 per cent increase in power output. Power was transmitted to both axles via a four-speed gearbox and two-speed transfer box; the rear wheels were twinned. Suspension was by live axles on semi-elliptical multi-leaf springs.

Standard variants included a steel-bodied cargo/personnel carrier, quadruple anti-aircraft gun mount and a tipper. A winch was fitted under the chassis. The total number produced was between 3,700 and 4,050. The company remains involved in defence work, but truck manufacture ceased in 1970.

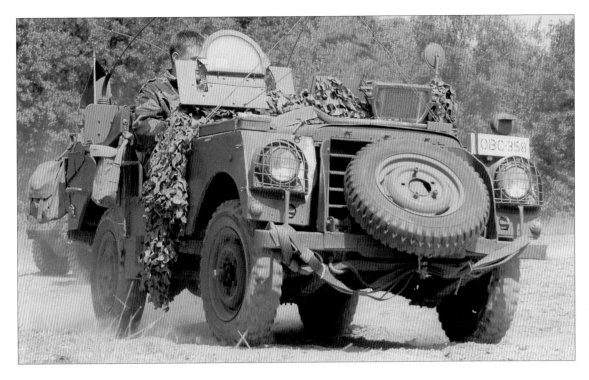

LEFT: **A superbly restored Minerva TT being displayed by its enthusiastic owner at a military vehicle show in Beltring, Kent.**

Minerva TT

The Belgian Minerva car company was established in 1899 by Sylvain de Jong, a Dutchman living in Antwerp. During World War I the company's large touring car chassis was used as the basis for a primitive armoured car. By the outbreak of World War II the company was producing commercial vehicles. Following a period when the works were used for aircraft repairs under German occupation, Minerva resumed commercial-vehicle production after the war.

At the end of the 1940s, the Belgian Army was seeking a replacement for the ageing US-supplied Jeeps. In 1951 they agreed to buy an initial 2,500 Land Rovers from a consortium established between Minerva and the British Rover Company.

Manufacture started on September 12, 1951. Rover supplied kits of parts

LEFT: **Even as late as 1985, some 2,500 Minervas remained in service, and many were sold from war reserve stock with very low mileage showing.**

to Belgium which were made up of the complete rolling chassis together with the vital bulkhead. The bodies were built locally. Lighting equipment, fuel tanks and upholstery were also sourced from Belgian manufacturers, with Minerva claiming that there was 60 per cent national content. At first, the vehicles used the 2,032mm/80in chassis but, in 1954, production changed to the 2,184mm/86in chassis. Some sources suggest that the chassis of late production vehicles were built in Belgium.

The body differed from that produced in the UK by mainly being manufactured from steel. It was fitted with non-standard flat-fronted mudguards which were easier to produce. There was also a fixed panel at the rear in place of the usual Land Rover-style tailgate.

Alongside the standard vehicle, there was a 24V "Fitted For Radio" (FFR) variant with a screened electrical system, and a two-stretcher field ambulance. A special forces model was

built with strengthened suspension, increased stowage and gun mounts. In 1980, 13 vehicles were converted to carry the MILAN anti-tank missile.

From October 1953, the type was also offered to civilians. Total military production was 5,921 vehicles, with a further 4,000 sold on the civilian market. Minerva went into liquidation in 1958.

Minerva TT

Type: Truck, ¼-ton, utility, 4x4
Manufacturer: Sté Nlle Minerva, Bruxelles
Production: 1951 to 1956
Powerplant: Rover; four cylinders in-line; 1,997cc; petrol; water-cooled; overhead inlet valves, side exhaust; power output, 52bhp at 4,000rpm
Transmission: 4F1Rx2; part-time 4x4
Suspension: Live axles on semi-elliptical multi-leaf springs; hydraulic double-acting shock absorbers
Brakes: Hydraulic
Electrical system: 12V, 24V
Dimensions: Length – 3,600mm/141in
　　Width – 1,550mm/61in
　　Height – tilt in place, 1,900mm/74in; minimum, 1,400mm/55in
　　Wheelbase – 2,032mm/80in, 2,184mm/86in
Weight: Unladen – 1,227kg/2,705lb
　　Payload – 600kg/1,323lb
Performance: Maximum speed – 89kph/55mph

Chevrolet C8, C8A

Dating from 1940, the 4x2 Chevrolet C8, and the very similar all-wheel drive C8A variant, was an 8cwt truck. It was designed to the same parameters as the equivalent British military types of the time, such as those produced by Humber, Morris-

BELOW: **Ford of Canada also built versions of both vehicles, designated F8 and F8A.**

Commercial and Ford. Although not strictly forming a part of the Canadian Military Pattern (CMP) programme, the vehicle was fitted with the standard CMP-type Number 11 cab.

The vehicle had a right-hand drive open-topped cab, and the standard body was a small welded-steel well-type design intended for general service use. A "wireless" body was also fitted, which could be dismounted and supported on internal folding legs to provide either an office or radio station in the field. The wireless vehicle was generally fitted with a "Chore-horse" generator mounted between the cab and the body.

Chevrolet C8, C8A

Type: Truck, 8cwt, cargo, 4x2
Manufacturer: GM Canada; Oshawa
Production: 1940 to 1941
Powerplant: Chevrolet; six cylinders in-line; petrol; water-cooled; 3,548cc; overhead valves; power output, 85bhp at 3,400rpm
Transmission: 4F1R; 4x2
Suspension: Live axles on semi-elliptical multi-leaf springs
Brakes: Hydraulic
Electrical system: 6V
Dimensions: Length – 4,216mm/166in
    Width – 2,108mm/83in
    Height – 2,286mm/90in
    Wheelbase – 2,565mm/101in
Weight: Unladen – 1,932kg/4,260lb
    Payload – 635kg/1,400lb
Performance: Maximum speed – 80kph/50mph

The vehicle was powered by a 3,548cc Chevrolet six-cylinder petrol engine driving the rear wheels through a four-speed gearbox. Suspension was by semi-elliptical multi-leaf springs.

Dodge T212-D8A

The Canadian-built Dodge T212-D8A could be regarded as something of an Anglo-American hybrid. Although fitted with right-hand drive, the chassis was similar to the US Army's ½-ton

Dodge T212–D8A

Type: Truck, cargo, 8cwt, 4x4
Manufacturer: Chrysler Corporation of Canada, Dodge Division; Windsor, Ontario
Production: 1941
Powerplant: Dodge T212; six cylinders in-line; petrol; water-cooled; 3,572cc; side valves; power output, 89bhp at 3,000rpm
Transmission: 4F1R; part-time 4x4
Suspension: Live axles on semi-elliptical multi-leaf springs
Brakes: Hydraulic
Electrical system: 6V
Dimensions: Length – 4,369mm/172in
    Width – 1,930mm/76in
    Height – tilt in place, 2,108mm/83in; minimum, 1,880mm/74in
    Wheelbase – 2,946mm/116in
Weight: Unladen – 2,337kg/5,152lb
    Payload – 702kg/1,548lb
Performance: Maximum speed – 88kph/55mph

T207-engined series of 1941, albeit the Canadian variant used a smaller engine. The open-topped rear body was typical of British War Office style of the period. Standard variants included cargo, personnel and wireless bodies.

The engine was a 3,572cc six-cylinder side-valve unit, driving all four wheels through a four-speed gearbox and single-speed transfer

box. The live axles were mounted on semi-elliptical leaf springs.

Although there is some controversy concerning the number of vehicles actually produced, the WD registration numbers indicate that the production total was 3,002.

BELOW: **The T212 was used extensively by Allied forces during the campaign in North Africa.**

Chevrolet and Ford CMP series

During World War II, the Canadian motor industry manufactured what was probably the most successful standardized truck designs. Almost identical vehicles were produced in a range of capacities and drive configurations by Ford and GM-Chevrolet throughout the war. Described as Canadian Military Pattern (CMP) vehicles, the design, co-developed by the two companies from 1936, managed to combine British War Office specifications with US automotive manufacture.

The major difference was in the power unit. The Ford-produced vehicles were powered by that company's ubiquitous V8 side-valve petrol engine. The Chevrolet trucks used a General Motors (GM) straight-six engine, but in other respects the trucks were virtually identical, with standard cab and body designs. The smallest of the series was the 8cwt chassis, designated C8 when produced by Chevrolet, and F8 for Ford. The "A" suffix indicated all-wheel drive. Next was the $^3/_4$-ton C15/F15 and C15A/F15A. Both companies also produced a $1^1/_2$-ton 4x4 truck, designated C30 and F30. Also a 3-ton 4x2 designated CC60 or FF60. There was also a 4x4 variant of the 3-ton chassis, on either long or short wheelbase, designated C60S/F60S and C60L/F60L. These were specialized versions for gun tractor and portee applications. Ford also produced a 3-ton 6x4, designated F60H and Chevrolet produced a 3-ton 6x6 identified as C60X.

Standard types included a heavy utility, general-service cargo truck, dump, van, water and fuel tanker, signals and communications vehicles, artillery tractor, ambulance, stores, machinery workshop and office. There were also armoured variants.

In total, more than 390,000 Canadian Military Pattern trucks were produced between 1940 and 1945, of which the majority were of the 3-ton 4x4 configuration. CMP vehicles were used by all of the Allies.

ABOVE: **The majority of the CMP trucks produced were the 3-ton 4x4 type, with a total of around 209,000. This Ford F60L, with a Number 13 cab, dating from 1942–43, has been fitted with Gar Wood twin-boom recovery gear.** LEFT: **The 1^1/2-ton chassis was designated C30 or F30, according to manufacturer. This Chevrolet C30 truck has the earlier Number 11 cab and carries a British-built timber cargo body.**

Chevrolet C60S, Ford F60S CMP

Type: Truck, 3-ton, cargo, 4x4

Manufacturer: Ford Motor Company of Canada; Windsor, Ontario. General Motors Products of Canada; Oshawa, Ontario

Production: 1940 to 1945

Powerplant: Ford variants – Ford 239; eight cylinders in V configuration; petrol; water-cooled; 3,917cc; side valves; power output, 95bhp at 3,600rpm GM-Chevrolet variants – GM 216; six cylinders in-line; petrol; water-cooled; 3,548cc; overhead valves; power output, 85bhp at 3,400rpm.

Transmission: 4F1Rx2; part-time 4x4

Suspension: Live axles on semi-elliptical multi-leaf springs

Brakes: Hydraulic with vacuum servo-assistance

Electrical system: 6V

Dimensions: Length – 5,182mm/204in
Width – 2,134mm/84in
Height – tilt in place – 2,946mm/116in; minimum, 1,905mm/75in
Wheelbase – 3,404mm/134in

Weight: Unladen – 3,558kg/7,845lb
Payload – 2,994kg/6,600lb

Performance: Maximum speed – 80kph/50mph

Beijing Jeep BJ212

Beijing Automobile Works was established in 1940. The company produced its first motor car in 1958. Production of the BJ212 light utility vehicle started in 1965. Described variously as the Peking or Beijing Jeep and occasionally as the Shanghai Jeep or Overlander, the BJ212 was initially produced with minor detail differences at several locations in China, before production finally settled at the Beijing Jeep Corporation. Aside from the front of the vehicle it could easily be mistaken for the Soviet UAZ-469.

The BJ212 was a light four-wheel drive vehicle intended for both military and civilian use. It was fitted with a four-door body with seating for five. The vehicle was also available as a 600kg/1,323lb two-door truck with transverse seats for six in the rear, designated BJ212A. Both types had a removable canvas top and a folding windscreen. In military service, the BJ212A could also be equipped with a NORINCO 105mm recoilless anti-tank rifle. Other variants subsequently produced included the BJ212F, which was the same as the BJ212A but fitted with a hard-top. The BJ211 was a long-wheelbase 1-ton truck, also available with rear-wheel drive only as the BJ121.

The original engine, which remained available to the end of the production run, was a Chinese-produced 2,445cc four-cylinder petrol unit, driving both axles through a three-speed gearbox and two-speed transfer box. In 1986, the BJ-212E variant was trialled with a US-built AMC four-cylinder petrol engine and a new transmission. The vehicle was finally offered with a 2,520cc Perkins four-cylinder diesel engine.

Aside from its service with the Chinese People's Liberation Army, the vehicle was in service in Chad, Pakistan and elsewhere. Export sales were handled through the State-owned China National Machinery & Equipment Import & Export Corporation.

By the mid-1990s when the BJ212 was superseded by the much-improved BJ2020S and BJ202SA variants, some 460,000 examples had been built.

LEFT: **The truck version of the Beijing Jeep BJ212 was also exported under the name Shanghai and Peking. Aside from the design of the radiator grille, the BJ212 was very similar in appearance to the Soviet-built UAZ-469.**
BELOW: **In utility vehicle or field-car form, the BJ212 was fitted with an open-topped four-door body with seating for five. The vehicle was powered by a 2,445cc four-cylinder water-cooled petrol engine.**

Beijing Jeep BJ212

Type: Truck, light, 4x4
Manufacturer: Beijing Jeep Corporation; Beijing
Production: 1964 on
Powerplant: Beijing; four cylinders in-line; petrol; water-cooled; 2,445cc; overhead valves; power output, 75bhp at 4,000rpm. Perkins 4.154; four cylinders in-line; diesel; water-cooled; 2,520cc; overhead valves; power output, 67bhp at 3,600rpm
Transmission: 3F1Rx2; part-time 4x4
Suspension: Live axles on semi-elliptical multi-leaf springs; double-acting telescopic shock absorbers
Brakes: Hydraulic
Electrical system: 12V
Dimensions: Length – 3,860mm/152in
Width – 1,750mm/69in
Height – tilt in place, (BJ212) 1,870mm/74in; (BJ212A) 2,105mm/83in
Wheelbase – 2,300mm/91in
Weight: Unladen – (BJ212) 1,530kg/3,373lb; (BJ212A) 1,520kg/3,351lb
Payload – 600kg/1,323lb
Performance: Maximum speed – 98kph/61mph

LEFT: **A Chinese-built Jiefang CA30 truck photographed during a military parade in Phnom Penh, Cambodia, May 1983.**

Jiefang CA30

During the 1950s, the Soviet Union helped the Communist regime in China to establish a motor industry and, as part of this aid, established the Tse Fan "Number 1 Automobile Plant" at Ch'ang-Ch'un, at first building virtual copies of Soviet vehicles. The first product of the factory, introduced in 1956, was the Jiefang ("Liberation") – sometimes, Jay-Fong or Chieh'Fang – CA10, a licence-built

ABOVE: **The Jiefang CA30 "Liberation" truck was effectively a licenced copy of the Soviet ZiL-157K, identifiable by the flattened front mudguards.**

version of the Soviet ZiL/ZIS-151 truck. This was followed in 1958–59 by the Jiefang CA30, based on the more-powerful 2¹/₂-ton ZiL-157K. Although broadly similar, the Chinese truck can easily be identified by squared-off front mudguards, sometimes fitted with integral headlamps.

Like the ZiL the truck was powered by a 5,550cc six-cylinder side-valve petrol engine producing 95bhp, driving all wheels through a five-speed gearbox, with overdrive top gear and two-speed transfer box. The suspension was of the live-axle type on semi-elliptical leaf springs. Large-section cross-country tyres were fitted all round, twinned on the rear wheels.

Production continued for some 28 years, and the truck was widely used by the Chinese People's Liberation Army until well into the 1990s, as well as seeing service with other friendly

nations, including Albania. Standard variants included cargo/personnel carrier, shop van, command post, communications vehicle, compressor, tanker, decontamination vehicle and rocket carrier. Some variants were fitted with a front-mounted winch. There was also a crew-cab variant, and a tractor for semi-trailers.

LEFT: **The standard variant was a cargo/personnel carrier. There was also a crew-cab variant, and a tractor for semi-trailers.**

Jiefang CA30

Type: Truck, 2¹/₂-ton, cargo, 6x6
Manufacturer: Tse Fan "Number 1 Automobile Plant"; Ch'ang-Ch'un, Jilin
Production: 1958 to 1986
Powerplant: Jiefang 120; six cylinders in-line; petrol; water-cooled; 5,550cc; side valves; power output, 95bhp at 2,800rpm
Transmission: 5F1Rx2; part-time 6x6
Suspension: Live axles on semi-elliptical multi-leaf springs; double-acting hydraulic shock absorbers on front axle
Brakes: Air-pressure
Electrical system: 12V
Dimensions: Length – 6,684mm/263in
    Width – 2,320mm/91in
    Height – tilt in place, 2,740mm/108in; minimum, 2,320mm/91in
    Wheelbase – 4,225mm/166in
    Bogie centres – 1,120mm/44in
Weight: Unladen – 5,340kg/11,773lb
    Payload – road, 4,500kg/9,921lb; cross-country, 2,500kg/5,511lb
Performance: Maximum speed – 65kph/40mph

Tatra T128

Tatra was originally established as Nesseldorfer Wagenbau-Fabriks-Gesellschaft in 1899, in what was then Austria. The town of Nesseldorfer came under Czech control following the end of World War I. The company name was changed to Tatra in 1923. Two years later, Tatra introduced an innovative tubular backbone chassis fitted with independently sprung swinging half-axles. This subsequently become something of a company trademark.

Dating from 1951, the Tatra T128 was the Czech Army's standard load carrier for many years. Power is provided by a 9,883cc V8 air-cooled diesel engine driving both axles through a four-speed gearbox and two-speed

Tatra T128	
Type: Truck, 3-ton, cargo/prime mover, 4x4	
Manufacturer: Ringhoffer Tatra; Národni Podnik	
Production: 1951 to 1954	
Powerplant: Tatra T108; eight cylinders in V configuration; diesel; air-cooled; 9,883cc; overhead valves; power output, 125bhp at 2,800rpm	
Transmission: 4F1Rx2; part-time 4x4	
Suspension: Independent suspension, front and rear, using swing axles and quarter-elliptical multi-leaf springs	
Brakes: Air-pressure	
Electrical system: 24V	
Dimensions: Length – 6,540mm/257in Width – 2,270mm/89in Height – tilt in place, 2,910mm/115in; minimum, 2,580mm/102in Wheelbase – 3,950mm/156in	
Weight: Unladen – 6,020kg/13,272lb Payload – road, 5,500kg/12,125lb; cross-country, 3,000kg/6,600lb	
Performance: Maximum speed – 60kph/37mph	

transfer box. Independent suspension is provided all round, by means of quarter-elliptical leaf springs. As well as the standard cargo vehicle, there were tanker and shop van variants.

LEFT: **Over a four-year period some 4,000 Tatra T128 vehicles were built, including winch-equipped T128Ns.**

Tatra T805

Despite having been designed in 1953, the steel-cabbed 1¹/₂-ton Tatra T805 did not enter production until two years later, when it was intended to replace the earlier Praga A150 as the Czech Army's standard light truck. However, maintenance difficulties meant that its service career was short-lived.

In typical Tatra fashion, off-road performance was excellent even if the design was far from straightforward. The truck was assembled around a tubular backbone chassis, which enclosed the propeller shafts. Suspension was by torsion bars to all four axles. Power was by a 2,545cc Tatra 603A eight-cylinder air-cooled petrol engine linked to with a four-speed gearbox and two-speed transfer box. All four wheel hubs were fitted with reduction gears.

The T805 was produced in cargo, ambulance and mobile repair variants and saw service with the Czech Army.

Tatra T805	
Type: Truck, 1¹/₂-ton, cargo, 4x4	
Manufacturer: Ringhoffer Tatra; Národni Podnik	
Production: 1955 to 1960	
Powerplant: Tatra 603A; eight cylinders in V configuration; 2,545cc; petrol; air-cooled; overhead valves; power output, 75bhp at 4,200rpm	
Transmission: 4F1Rx2; part-time 4x4	
Suspension: Swing axles front and rear, with independent suspension using torsion bars	
Brakes: Hydraulic	
Electrical system: 12V	
Dimensions: Length – 4,720mm/186in Width – 2,190mm/86in Height – tilt erected, 2,600mm/102in; minimum, 2,420mm/95in Wheelbase – 2,700mm/106in	
Weight: Unladen – 2,750kg/6,063lb Payload – road, 2,250kg/4,960lb; cross-country, 1,500kg/3,307lb	
Performance: Maximum speed – 78kph/48mph	

LEFT: **Total production for the T805 was 7,214 vehicles built over a five-year period from 1955.**

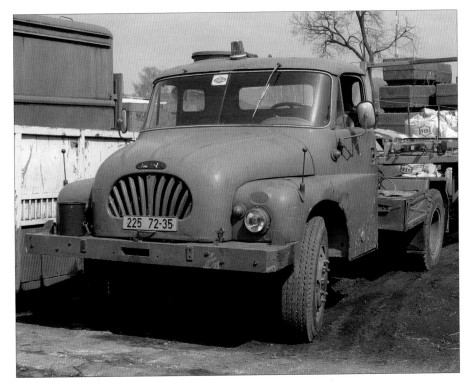

Tatra T138

The Tatra 8-ton T138 6x6 military truck was put into production in 1961 as a replacement for the 10-ton T111, which dated from 1945. Although the rounded three-seat steel cab was somewhat "civilian" in appearance, the T138 was nevertheless an extremely versatile and reliable military vehicle. Many remained in service for two or more decades. The truck was powered by an 11,762cc Tatra V8 air-cooled diesel engine in combination with a remotely mounted five-speed gearbox and two-speed transfer box. This combination provided excellent on-road performance. Off the road, the independent front suspension and lockable rear differentials ensured

BELOW: **The T138 was initially intended for the Czech Army, but was also exported to the Middle East, and to other friendly Soviet Bloc states, including East Germany (DDR). The truck was powered by a typical Tatra air-cooled V8 diesel engine and was produced in a wide range of variants.**

LEFT: **T137VT tractor for semi-trailers. Production continued from 1959 to 1978.**

that the Tatra would not become bogged down in difficult conditions. Most were fitted with a winch mounted under the chassis for self-recovery.

Standard variants included long- and short-wheelbase cargo trucks (designated T138VN and NT, respectively), hydraulic crane carrier (AJ6, AV8), dragline shovel (D013A), 12,000-litre/2,640 gallon tanker (C12 and C) and tipper (S1, S3). There were also 6x6 (T138NT) and 4x4 (T137VT) tractor versions for semi-trailers. Initial production went to the Czech Army, but there were subsequent exports to a number of Middle Eastern nations, as well as to other Soviet satellite states, including East Germany (DDR).

There were 4x2, 4x4, 6x4 and 6x6 versions for commercial use produced between 1961 and 1971. The civilian version could be identified by the absence of the roof hatch that was fitted to the military cab. A total of 48,222 examples of all models were produced. In 1972 the T138 was superseded by the upgraded T148.

Tatra T138

Type: Truck, 8-ton, cargo, 6x6
Manufacturer: Ringhoffer Tatra; Národni Podnik
Production: 1961 to 1972
Powerplant: Tatra T928-12; eight cylinders in V configuration; diesel; air-cooled; 11,762cc; overhead valves; power output, 180bhp at 2,000rpm; also available with a Tatra T928K supercharged diesel engine producing 220bhp
Transmission: 5F1Rx2; part-time 6x6
Suspension: Independent front suspension using swing axles and torsion bars; live axles at rear on semi-elliptical inverted multi-leaf springs
Brakes: Air-pressure
Electrical system: 24V
Dimensions: Length – 8,565mm/337in
Width – 2,450mm/97in
Height – tilt in place, 3,200mm/126in; minimum, 2,440mm/96in
Wheelbase – 4,260mm/168in (T138N); 3,690mm/145in (T138NT)
Bogie centres – 1,320mm/52in
Weight: Unladen – 8,740kg/19,268lb
Payload – road, 12,000kg/26,455lb; cross-country, 8,000kg/17,637lb
Performance: Maximum speed – 70kph/43mph

Tatra T813 *Kolos*

Dating from 1967, the Tatra T813 *Kolos* (Colossus) was an enormous 8-ton 8x8 cargo/prime mover produced primarily for the Czech Army, but also offered on the commercial market. The first prototype, built in 1960, was a 4x4 developed from elements of the company's ubiquitous T138 truck. This was subsequently developed into a powerful and very capable heavy 8x8 forward-control design which offered excellent off-road performance.

Typical of Tatra trucks of the period, the engine was a 17,640cc T930-3E V12 air-cooled direct-injection multi-fuel unit. In effect it was a T928 engine with four cylinders added and was capable of running on diesel fuel, petrol and aviation jet fuel (kerosene). The engine was coupled to a five-speed gearbox and two-speed auxiliary gearbox. There was also a single-speed transfer box and two-speed planetary step-down gearbox mounted between the front and rear axles. A total of 20 forward gears and four reverse were available.

The chassis was of backbone design, with independent suspension at all wheels using swing half-axles and longitudinal semi-elliptical leaf springs. Differential locks were provided in all axles, planetary reduction gears at the hubs and lockable inter-axle differentials. Both front axles were used for steering. There were options

LEFT: The massive Tatra T813 *Kolos* was a cargo/prime mover originally intended for the Czech Army, but was also available on the commercial market. The backbone chassis, a feature of most Tatra designs, was fitted with independent suspension front and rear by means of swing half-axles and longitudinal semi-elliptical leaf springs.

for a rear power take-off and winch drive. "Central Tyre-Inflation System" (CTIS) was fitted. Two- and four-door cabs were available, the latter providing seating for seven. The cab was fitted with a circular roof hatch and, for certain applications, could also be armoured. A fuel-burning cab heater was fitted which could also be used to warm the engine.

Standard variants included a cargo/prime mover which could be used as an artillery tractor, crane carrier, 122mm multiple rocket launcher and fire-tender. There was also a 4x4 tractor for semi-trailers. A 6x6 civilian type with tandem front axles and a single rear axle was produced.

A total of 11,751 were completed over a 16-year production period. The vehicle was superseded by the T815 in 1982. Tatra was taken over by the US-based Terex Corporation in 2003, and subsequently sold to the Czech-owned Blue River group in 2006.

Tatra T813 *Kolos*

Type: Truck, cargo/prime mover, 8-ton, 8x8
Manufacturer: Ringhoffer Tatra; Národni Podnik
Production: 1967 to 1982
Powerplant: Tatra T930-3E; 12 cylinders in V configuration; diesel; air-cooled; 17,640cc; overhead valves; power output, 257bhp at 2,000rpm
Transmission: 5F1Rx2x2; full-time 8x8
Suspension: Independent suspension at all wheels using swing half-axles and semi-elliptical multi-leaf springs
Brakes: Air-pressure
Electrical system: 24V
Dimensions: Length – 8,800mm/346in
    Width – 2,500mm/98in
    Height – tilt in place, 3,180mm/125in; minimum, 2,780mm/109in
    Wheelbase – 5,400mm/213in
    Bogie centres – 1,650+1,450mm/65+57in
Weight: Unladen – 14,000kg/30,864lb
    Payload – 8,000kg/17,637lb
Performance: Maximum speed – 91kph/56mph

LEFT: The cargo/prime mover variant could be used as an artillery tractor. There were also crane carrier, multiple rocket launcher and fire tender versions, as well as a 4x4 tractor for semi-trailers. A 6x6 version was sold on the civilian market.

Praga V3S

In 1948, the motor industry in Czechoslovakia was nationalized, with truck production divided between Tatra, Škoda and Praga, the latter being responsible for the design and production of vehicles in the medium weight class.

The Praga V3S was launched in 1952 and was intended for both military and civilian use. The military variants were identified by being fitted with a roof hatch. Despite being odd in appearance, due to the shortened bonnet and semi-forward-control layout, it was a technically interesting and versatile truck rather in the mould of the US-built GMC CCKW of World War II.

Production started in 1953 at the company's Prague factory. During the period 1960 to 1964, this was gradually transferred to the former Avia aircraft works at Letňany. The vehicle remained in production until the mid-1980s.

The engine was a 7,412cc six-cylinder direct-injection air-cooled diesel of typical Tatra design, producing 98bhp. Drive to all axles was through a four-speed gearbox and two-speed transfer box. In 1981, the engine was upgraded for more power. For maximum ground clearance, the axles were of the portal design, incorporating step-down final drive. Differential locks were fitted in both rear axles. Suspension was by semi-elliptical multi-leaf springs, inverted at the rear.

Aside from the standard wooden-bodied cargo vehicle, variants included a fuel tanker, shop van, rear three-way tipper, twin-boom recovery vehicle, fire-tender and 130mm rocket launcher. A number of vehicles were fitted with a mechanical winch. The chassis was also used to produce an armoured personnel carrier and a 30mm anti-aircraft gun carriage.

The Praga V3S was widely used by Warsaw Pact nations and was supplied to a number of Middle Eastern nations.

Praga V3S

Type: Truck, 3-ton, cargo, 6x6
Manufacturer: Praga, Praha; and Avia Zavody, Letňany
Production: 1953 to mid-1980s
Powerplant: Tatra licence T912, T912-2; six cylinders in-line; direct-injection diesel; air-cooled; 7,412cc; overhead valves; power output, 98bhp (110bhp for T912-2) at 2,100rpm
Transmission: 4F1Rx2; part-time 6x6; differential locks in both rear axles
Suspension: Live portal axles on semi-elliptical multi-leaf springs, inverted at rear
Brakes: Air-pressure
Electrical system: Hybrid 12V/24V
Dimensions: Length – 7,150mm/281in
　Width – 2,320mm/93in
　Height – 2,920mm/115in
　Wheelbase – 3,580mm/141in
　Bogie centres – 1,120mm/44in
Weight: Unladen weight (with winch) 5,470kg/12,059lb
　Payload – road, 5,300kg/11,684lb; cross-country, 3,000kg/6,614lb
Performance: Maximum speed – 60kph/37mph

RIGHT: **Standard variants included a wooden-bodied cargo vehicle, fuel tanker, shop van, rear and three-way tipper, twin-boom recovery vehicle, fire-tender and rocket launcher. This surplus tanker has been used as a commercial vehicle.**

Škoda RSO-175

In 1859, Emil Škoda established an engineering business in Prague and began truck production in 1924. Early products were based on the British Sentinel steam wagon but, following the acquisition of Laurin & Clement in 1925, the Škoda name began to appear on conventional trucks. The first diesel-powered vehicle was introduced in 1932.

Following the occupation of Czechoslovakia by the Germans in 1939, Škoda was forced to supply trucks to the German war effort. Notable among these was the RSO-175 (*Radschlepper Ost*), a heavy wheeled artillery tractor designed by Porsche for use on the Eastern Front where the roads became impassable either from mud or from being frozen solid. The first prototype was ready by October 1942, with several changes made during the trials period.

It was intended to replace the sophisticated half-tracks which had been produced by Germany since the mid-1930s, but which were proving unreliable under harsh combat conditions. By contrast, the RSO-175 was a straight-forward and somewhat utilitarian machine designed to be produced at minimum cost and in large numbers.

Aside from ungainly height, the main identifying feature was the use of large-diameter (1,500mm/59in) steel wheels with diagonal strakes, but not fitted with conventional rubber tyres. Although lacking a good top speed and satisfactory traction on frozen ground, it was a powerful machine almost in the style of the Austro-Daimler artillery tractor of World War I. The crew were accommodated in a closed, three-seat all-steel cab. A drop-side timber body was mounted at the rear with a removable canvas

cover. A V-shaped blade plough could be attached to the truck for digging trenches.

The vehicle was powered by a 6,024cc Porsche four-cylinder engine, either diesel or petrol, driving both axles through a five-speed gearbox. A 565cc auxiliary engine (half of a VW "flat-four") was fitted to assist with engine starting in the extreme cold of the Russian Front. Suspension was by semi-elliptical springs. The use of steel wheels and no tyres made it sensible to reduce the vehicle's maximum speed to 15kmh/10mph.

Between 100 and 200 examples were manufactured between 1942 and 1943. Vehicle production was cancelled in favour of heavy half-tracks also built by Škoda and the lower-cost *Maultier* half-tracks which were based on standard wheeled trucks.

Although Škoda continued to produce trucks after the war, the company was nationalized in 1945 and the vehicles badged as LiAZ (Liberecke Automobile Zavody).

ABOVE: **Dating from 1943, the French-built Latil FTARH was also produced for use on the Eastern Front.**
RIGHT: **The rounded cab gave the truck a modern appearance that was belied by the huge wheels.**

Škoda RSO-175

Type: Tractor, heavy, 4x4
Manufacturer: Škoda-Werke; Plzen
Production: 1942 to 1943
Powerplant: Porsche; four cylinders in-line; 6,024cc; petrol or diesel; air-cooled; overhead valves; power output, 90bhp at 2,000rpm
Transmission: 5F1R; full-time 4x4; centre locking differential
Suspension: Live axles on semi-elliptical multi-leaf springs
Brakes: Mechanical
Electrical system: 12V
Dimensions: Length – 6,220m/245in
Width – 2,300mm/91in
Height – 3,065mm/121in
Wheelbase – 3,000mm/118in
Weight: Unladen – 7,000kg/15,432lb
Towed load – 5,000kg/11,023lb
Performance: Maximum speed – 15kph/10mph

Sisu KB-45, A-45

Introduced in 1964, the Sisu KB-45 was a 3-ton 4x4 military tactical truck fitted with a high-pressure hydraulic system which could be used to drive the wheels of a suitable two- or four-wheel trailer. This provided significant advantages in mobility and cross-country performance, and allowed an increase in payload to 12 tons.

A Leyland six-cylinder diesel engine was mounted behind the cab, and was accessed via the cargo bay. The power was transmitted through a five-speed gearbox, with overdrive top gear, and a two-speed transfer box, and both axles included differential locks and planetary reduction gears in the hubs. There was a 6½-ton under-chassis winch, and a blowlamp-operated heating system was provided to warm the cooling water and engine oil.

Alongside the standard drop-side cargo/personnel carrier, other variants included artillery tractor, ambulance, fire-tender, radar or communications shelter, command vehicle and workshop. The vehicle could also be supplied as a crew-cabbed tractor for semi-trailers.

Sisu KB-45, A-45

Type: Truck, cargo, 3-ton, 4x4
Manufacturer: OY Suomen Autoteollisuus; Karjaa
Production: 1964 to 1982
Powerplant: Leyland 0.600; six cylinders in-line; diesel; water-cooled; 6,540cc; overhead valves; power output, 135bhp at 2,400rpm
Transmission: 5F1Rx2; part-time 4x4; hydraulic auxiliary trailer drive
Suspension: Live axles on semi-elliptical multi-leaf springs
Brakes: Air-pressure assisted hydraulic
Electrical system: 24V
Dimensions: Length – 5,700mm/240in
   Width – 2,300mm/90in
   Height – tilt in place, 2,800mm/110in; minimum, 1,753mm/69in
   Wheelbase – 3,400mm/134in
Weight: Unladen – 5,000kg/11,023lb
   Payload – road, 3,600kg/7,936lb; cross-country, 2,500kg/5,511lb
Performance: Maximum speed – 90kph/56mph

LEFT: **The Sisu KB-45, A-45 was in production from 1964 until 1982 and a total of 500 were delivered.**

Sisu E11T HMTV

Sisu has been producing trucks since 1931. During World War II, the company merged with Vanaja to concentrate on producing military vehicles under the name Yhteissisu. The two companies were de-merged in 1948, but Sisu took over Vanaja in 1967.

The Sisu E11T 6x6 15-ton truck was introduced in May 1998, as the first in a series of off-road vehicles

BELOW: **The Sisu E11T HMTV entered service with the Finnish Army in 1998 and remains in production.**

intended for both military and civilian use. Production began in September 1998 with the first 71 trucks delivered to the Finnish Army. The trucks have a Renault-designed tilt cab and were developed using as many components as possible from

Sisu's commercial-vehicle range. Power is provided by either an 11,000cc Cummins M380E or M405E six-cylinder diesel engine, driving all axles through a choice of manual or automatic seven-speed gearbox, linked to a two-speed transfer box.

Sisu E11T HMTV

Type: Truck, 15-ton, cargo, 6x6
Manufacturer: Sisu Auto; Karjaa
Production: 1998 on
Powerplant: Cummins M380E or M405E; six cylinders in-line; diesel; water-cooled; 11,000cc; overhead valves; power output, 380–405bhp at 1,900rpm
Transmission: Manual or automatic; 7F1Rx2; full-time 6x6
Suspension: Live axles on parabolic semi-elliptical springs
Brakes: Air-pressure
Electrical system: 24V
Dimensions: Length – 8,636mm/340in
   Width – 2,540mm/100in
   Height – minimum, 3,150mm/124in
   Wheelbase – 4,140mm/163in
   Bogie centres – 1,397mm/55in
Weight: Unladen – 10,500kg/23,148lb
   Payload – 15,000kg/33,069lb
Performance: Maximum speed – 90kph/56mph

LEFT: **Although originally produced as a private venture, some VLRAs have been supplied to the French Army. This example was previously in service with the Irish Defence Force (IDF) which used the VLRA as a tractor for the 105mm light gun. The IDF also had workshop, radio command and recovery versions.**

ACMAT VLRA

Although not particularly well known outside France, the Brittany-based company ACMAT (Ateliers de Construction Mécanique de l'Atlantique), has been producing military vehicles since 1958 when the first VLRA (*Véhicule Léger de Reconnaissance et d'Appui*) light reconnaissance and support vehicle was launched.

Superficially, the basic 4x4 vehicle has changed little since the first example was launched 50 years ago. The range has now been expanded to include 6x6 and 8x8 vehicles. The current product range includes 2½-, 5- and 7-ton trucks, in a range of some 40 variants, including

ambulance, crew bus, command car, tractor for semi-trailer, radio command vehicle, fuel and water tankers, dump truck and DROPS as well as recovery, personnel carrier, missile launcher and flat-bed shelter carrier. There are also armoured versions of both the 4x4 and 6x6 variants. The company boasts an 80 per cent commonality of parts across the product range, including items such as cabs, chassis components, engines and drive-trains.

Early examples used a Ford petrol engine, but this has now been superseded by a 4,390cc Perkins 6.354 diesel, driving all wheels through a four- or five-speed

gearbox (6x6 variants only), and two-speed transfer box which incorporates a lockable differential. The axles are suspended on semi-elliptical springs; these being inverted at the rear on the 6x6 and 8x8 variants, and rubber-mounted radius rods are used for axle location.

Almost in the style of the Dodge Power Wagon of the 1950s, the vehicle has an open cab with a folding windscreen; the cab on the 8x8 variant is a semi-forward control design. Enclosed cabs, with wind-up windows, are also available for all models.

The vehicle has appealed to mining and prospecting companies. The VLRA has been purchased by some armies of North Africa and Asia who could neither afford more expensive vehicles, nor had the maintainance ability. Some VLRAs have also been supplied to the French Army. The Irish Defence Force use the VLRA as a tractor for the 105mm light gun, also as a workshop vehicle, radio command vehicle and recovery vehicle. Since May 2006, ACMAT has been a wholly owned subsidiary of Renault Trucks.

ACMAT VLRA

Type: Truck, 2½-ton, cargo, 4x4
Manufacturer: Ateliers de Construction Mécanique de l'Atlantique (ACMAT); Saint-Nazaire
Production: 1958 on
Powerplant: Perkins 6.354; six cylinders in-line; diesel; water-cooled; 4,390cc; overhead valves; power output, 120–138bhp at 2,800rpm
Transmission: 4F1Rx2; part-time 4x4
Suspension: Live axles on semi-elliptical multi-leaf springs; hydraulic double-acting shock absorbers
Brakes: Air-assisted hydraulic
Electrical system: 24V
Dimensions: Length – 5,995mm/236in
  Width – 2,070mm/81in
  Height – minimum, 1,826mm/72in
  Wheelbase – 3,600mm/142in; also, 3,300mm/130in, 4,200mm/165in, 4,300mm/169in
Weight: Unladen – 4,300kg/9,480lb
  Payload – 2,500kg/5,511lb
Performance: Maximum speed – 100kph/62mph

LEFT: **The VLRA was produced by the Brittany-based company ACMAT (Ateliers de Construction Mécanique de l'Atlantique), with early prototypes being tested during 1958–59. The basic concept of the vehicle, which was designed to appeal to mining and prospecting companies, as well as to armies which might lack the resources to maintain more sophisticated machinery, has changed little since the early days.**

ABOVE: **The open cab, with a canvas top and folding screen, is uncompromisingly angular in appearance.** LEFT: **The Berliet GBC8KT equipped as a basic 4-ton cargo truck.**

Berliet GBC8KT

The Berliet GBC8KT was a French replacement for the classic World War II "Jimmy". Development began in the 1950s with the GBC8 Gazelle, a commercial 4x4 truck rated at 3½-ton. Described as a *porteur moyen à adhérence totale* (all-wheel drive medium load carrier), the Gazelle was adopted by the French Army from 1958. However, the Army was keen to develop the Berliet Gazelle into a more-capable off-road military vehicle and, in late 1959, a militarized prototype was produced which evolved into the purely military 6x6 GBC8KT.

Rated at 4 tons, the GBC8KT may have been derived from the Gazelle, but little of the original vehicle remained. The original curved cab of the civilian vehicle was replaced by a very angular open cab, a canvas top and folding screen. The front mudguards were also angular in shape. The upright radiator grille provided cooling via a series of horizontal slots.

The vehicle was powered by a 5,180cc five-cylinder multi-fuel

(polycarburant) diesel engine, driving through a ZF six-speed manual gearbox. Selectable all-wheel drive was provided by a Herwaythorn two-speed transfer box. Suspension was by conventional semi-elliptical springs, inverted at the rear. The rear bogie mounted on an oscillating pivot. The front axle was a Berliet-Herwaythorn unit, while those at the rear were both Berliet products.

The standard variant was a steel-bodied cargo vehicle, but there were also fuel tanker, light recovery, light recovery, tipper and air-compressor variants. Also the TBC8KT tractor for semi-trailers and recovery vehicle. Some cargo vehicles were fitted with a 5- to 7-ton capacity under-chassis winch.

The GBC8KT quickly became the standard vehicle in its class and a total of almost 18,000 were produced before production came to an end in 1976. Alongside examples supplied to the French Army, the GBC8KT was purchased by Algeria, Austria, China, Iraq and Morocco. The 4x4 variant was supplied to Portugal. The French Army,

in collaboration with Renault, has recently refurbished some 6,000 of these trucks, designating them as the Renault TRM GBC180.

Berliet GBC8KT

Type: Truck, 4-ton, cargo/personnel, 6x6
Manufacturer: Société Automobiles M Berliet; Lyon
Production: 1961 to 1976
Powerplant: Berliet MK-520 or MDU-35MK; five cylinders in-line; multi-fuel diesel; water-cooled; 5,180cc; overhead valves; power output, 125bhp at 2,100rpm
Transmission: 6F1R; part-time 6x6
Suspension: Live axles on semi-elliptical multi-leaf springs, inverted at rear; hydraulic double-acting shock absorbers
Brakes: Air-pressure
Electrical system: 12V, 24V
Dimensions: Length (cargo vehicles) – 7,280mm/286in; (long-wheelbase) 8,205mm/323in
Width – 2,400mm/94in
Height – tilt in place, 3,300mm/130in; minimum, 2,700mm/106in
Wheelbase – 3,950mm/156in or 4,350mm/172in
Bogie centres – 1,280mm/50in
Weight: Unladen – 8,370kg/18,452lb
Payload – road, 5,000kg/11,023lb; cross-country, 4,000kg/8,818lb
Performance: Maximum speed – 73kph/45mph

LEFT: **The Berliet TBU-15 was a fifth-wheel tractor for use as a 36-ton tank transporter. The transmission for the vehicle was developed by Rochet-Schneider.**

Berliet GBU–15, TBU–15

The Berliet GBU/TBU series was a development of the 6-ton Rochet-Schneider T6 truck from 1951, the company having been absorbed by Berliet in the early 1950s. The innovative transmission which Rochet-Schneider had developed for the T6 was retained, whereby one differential in the forward axle of the rear bogie was used to drive all four rear wheels, but an air-actuated braking system in the second

axle was fitted to prevent relative rotation of the wheels on the two axles. In 1955, Berliet redesigned aspects of the truck, notably to accept a multi-fuel diesel engine, produced under licence from the German company MAN, and relaunched it as the T6-15.

BELOW: **The GBU-15 was a 6-ton cargo/prime mover. There was also a heavy recovery variant (TBU-15 CLD) fitted with an Austin-Western crane.**

Just 10 pilot models were produced before the truck went into series production in 1959 as a 6x6 NATO tactical truck. Three variants were produced. The GBU-15 was a truck/prime mover fitted with an 8-ton under-chassis winch. The vehicle was frequently used as a tractor for the 155mm howitzer. The TBU-15 was a fifth-wheel tractor for use as a 36-ton tank transporter; a 10-ton winch was fitted behind the cab. The TBU-15 CLD (*Camion Lourd de Dépannage*) was equipped as a heavy recovery vehicle, with an Austin-Western hydraulic crane. A 7-ton front winch and a 14-ton rear winch was also fitted.

All three variants used the same type of six-cylinder multi-fuel (polycarburant) engine, driving through a five-speed gearbox and two-speed transfer box. The suspension was by semi-elliptical springs front and rear. The TBU-15 could be specified with reinforced rear suspension which allowed use with a 46-ton trailer.

The GBU-15 CLD was also produced under licence by Alvis in the UK, under the name Alvis-Berliet. Total production was just two vehicles.

Berliet GBU-15, TBU-15

Type: Truck, 6-ton, heavy wrecker, 6x6
Manufacturer: Société Automobiles M Berliet; Lyon
Production: 1959 to 1968
Powerplant: MAN-licence Berliet MK640; six cylinders in-line; multi-fuel diesel; water-cooled; 14,750cc; overhead valves; power output, 2,00bhp at 1,800rpm
Transmission: 5F1Rx2; part-time 6x6
Suspension: Live axles on semi-elliptical multi-leaf springs
Brakes: Air-pressure
Electrical system: 24V
Dimensions: (TBU–15 CLD)
    Length – 8,880mm/349in
    Width – 2,500mm/98in
    Height – 3,000mm/118in
    Wheelbase – 4,200mm/165in
    Bogie centres – 1,450mm/57in
Weight: Unladen – 21,200kg/46,737lb
    Maximum load on crane – 10,000kg/22,046lb
Performance: Maximum speed – 68kph/42mph

Citroën Type 46F, 46F/T

Never a company to shy away from innovation, the Citroën Type 46F air-portable cargo truck is typical of the company's approach to design. Originally described as the *Transocéanic*, the first prototype was completed in 1957 and was based on the company's 5-ton Type 55U truck which had been converted to all-wheel drive by Herwaythorn. When production started in 1964, there were both 3-ton and 5-ton variants, the latter identifiable by twinned rear wheels.

Frequently designated "FOM" (*Forces d'Outre Mer*), the truck was designed to provide exceptional off-road performance, and was intended for use by the French Overseas Forces.

Power was provided by a 5,180cc six-cylinder engine, with both petrol and diesel versions available, driving through

BELOW: **The "FOM" demonstrates the vehicle's extraordinary axle articulation. The bumper is designed to move with the front axle.**

LEFT: **Often described as the "FOM" (*Forces d'Outre Mer* – Forces Overseas), the Citroën Type 46 was designed to provide exceptional off-road performance, and was intended for the French Army. The standard variant was fitted with a steel drop-side cargo/personnel body with bench seating for 16 troops.**

a five-speed manual gearbox and two-speed transfer box. Unusually for Citroën, who tended to favour unconventional suspension arrangements, the axles were hung on normal semi-elliptical springs with hydraulic shock absorbers. The suspension was capable of extremes of articulation, particularly at the front.

The Type 46F/T differed from the Type 46F by being equipped with a front-mounted 5-ton winch. The standard variant was fitted with a steel drop-side cargo/personnel body, which had bench seats for 16 fully equipped men, and was occasionally fitted with a machine-gun ring mount. Other variants included a container vehicle, refrigerator van, fuel/water tanker, flat-bed truck, recovery and communications vehicles. A long-range "Sahara" version was also built with larger fuel tanks to extend the operating range.

As well as being used by the French Army, the vehicle was supplied to Cameroon, Chad, Ivory Coast, Mauritania, Senegal and Upper Volta. Production ended in 1967.

Citroën Type 46F, 46FT

Type: Truck, 3- or 5-ton, cargo/personnel, 4x4
Manufacturer: Citroën; Paris
Production: 1964 to 1967
Powerplant: Citroën P38; six cylinders in-line; petrol or diesel; water-cooled; 5,180cc; overhead valves; power output, (petrol) 80–97bhp at 5,200rpm, (diesel) 85bhp at 2,600rpm
Transmission: 5F1Rx2; part-time 6x6
Suspension: Live axles on semi-elliptical multi-leaf springs; dual-action hydraulic shock absorbers
Brakes: Air-pressure assisted hydraulic
Electrical system: 24V
Dimensions: Length – 7,010mm/276in
   Width – 2,480mm/98in
   Height – tilt in place, 2,770mm/109in
   Wheelbase – 4,600mm/181in
Weight: Unladen – 6,340kg/13,977lb
   Payload – 3,000–5,000kg/6,614–11,023lb
Performance: Maximum speed – 100kph/62mph

Citroën Méhari

Citroën introduced the utilitarian 2CV in 1948 and the vehicle remained in production for more than 40 years. Originally described as the TPV (*Trés Petit Voiture*) the 2CV was the basis of a number of similar types,

all sharing the two-cylinder horizontally opposed engine and unique interlinked coil-spring swing-arm suspension. The most interesting of these was the Dyane-based Jeep-like Méhari dating from 1968, which was also produced as a special 24V military version for use in rear areas. There was also a four-wheel-drive version introduced in 1979, although these did not enter military service.

Sharing the chassis, 602cc engine, platform and transmission of the Dyane, the Méhari was fitted with a unique moulded body featuring inner and outer panels of ABS (Acrylonitrile Butadiene Styrene) plastic riveted to a tubular-steel

LEFT: **The Méhari was used in service by the French Army and the Irish Defence Force.**

space frame. The military version was produced as a two-seater with a load area at the rear, or as a four-seater.

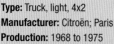

Citroën Méhari

Type: Truck, light, 4x2
Manufacturer: Citroën; Paris
Production: 1968 to 1975
Powerplant: Citroën AK-2; horizontally opposed two-cylinders; petrol; air-cooled; 602cc; overhead valves; power output, 26bhp at 5,500rpm
Transmission: 4F1R; 4x2
Suspension: Swing arms suspended on interlinked lateral coil springs, leading at front, trailing at rear; double-acting hydraulic shock absorbers
Brakes: Hydraulic
Electrical system: 24V
Dimensions: Length – 3,520mm/139in
  Width – 1,530mm/60in
  Height – tilt in place, 1,635mm/64in; minimum, 1,050mm/41in
  Wheelbase – 2,370mm/93in
Weight: Unladen – 585kg/1,290lb
  Payload – 405kg/893lb
Performance: Maximum speed – 100kph/62mph

Citroën-Kégresse P2

In 1910, the French engineer Adolphe Kégresse developed a traction system which allowed "travel at all speeds over deep snow and ice, or roads covered with lightly packed snow, or on dry or stony roads". Avoiding the standard crawler tractor approach, which used linked metal plates, Kégresse used an endless flexible-rubber belt track that offered a unique combination of performance, ride quality and reliability.

Returning to France from Russia after the Revolution, Kégresse made contact with André Citroën and sold him sole rights to the design. A Kégresse bogie was fitted to a Citroën B2 motor car to produce the Citroën-Kégresse P2. At military vehicle trials held at Satory (1923, 1924 and 1925) the P2 was the

BELOW: **The Citroën-Kégresse was also trialled by the British War Office.**

only vehicle in its class to be awarded a government subsidy. By 1927, the P2 had been replaced by the P7 with an improved positive drive system, and this led to the P107 of the late 1930s.

Citroën-Kégresse half-tracks were used by the French Army for a variety of roles up to 1940, including ambulance, field car, armoured car, tractor and anti-aircraft.

Citroën-Kégresse P2

Type: Car/tractor, 5-seat, half-track
Manufacturer: La Société Citroën-Kégresse-Hinstin; Paris
Production: 1921 to 1927
Powerplant: Citroën B2; four cylinders in-line; petrol; water-cooled; 1,452cc; side valves; power output, 20bhp at 2,000rpm
Transmission: 3F1R; drive to rear tracks
Suspension: Live axles on semi-elliptical multi-leaf springs
Brakes: Mechanical
Electrical system: 6V
Dimensions: Not available
Weight: Not available
Performance: Maximum speed – 40kph/25mph

Delahaye VLR-D

At the end of World War II, France received supplies of US-built Jeeps. Believing they could improve on the design, in 1947 the French Government began looking into developing a wholly French replacement. The Directorate of Armament Design and Manufacture prepared a specification for an advanced light 4x4 vehicle described as "*Voiture, Légère de Reconnaissance, 4x4, 4 hommes, 1 radio*". Following an approach to the French motor industry, only Delahaye, who were in financial difficulties, appeared willing to consider the proposal.

Delahaye's original prototype for the project, the VLR Delta (VLR-D), was based on a dual-purpose utility/agricultural vehicle that the company had launched immediately after the war. The vehicle had four seats, simple, open bodywork and a fold-flat windscreen. The engine was at the front; selectable four-wheel drive was fitted. In 1949, an example was delivered to the French Army and put through the usual military trials.

A second series of prototypes followed, at least one of which had a Renault 85 engine, the others being powered by Delahaye's new 1,992cc Type 182 four-cylinder engine fitted with wet-liners, an aluminium crankcase and dry sump lubrication. The gearbox was a four-speed unit with overdrive top gear. A single lever was used for selecting four-wheel drive and the low-ratio gears. The differentials

RIGHT: **The Delahaye VLR-D was a French attempt at improving on the American Jeep. Although it incorporated advanced features such as self-levelling independent suspension, it proved to be unreliable in service, with particular problems in the transfer box and in the general handling.**

could be locked manually by means of a separate lever. The suspension was independent all-round, using adjustable torsion bars and leading/trailing arms, with a self-levelling system on the rear axle.

Further modifications were made as a result of the second round of trials and, finally, on August 1, 1950, the vehicle was standardized. During 1951 production began as the VLR-D Model 51.

Problems arose as soon as the vehicle entered service. The independent suspension created handling difficulties, which resulted in numerous accidents. There were also problems with the locking differentials, which could lock unexpectedly, leading to a loss of control on bends, or causing complete transmission failure.

The French Army had this feature disconnected during the last few years of the vehicle's life.

A slightly improved VLR-D Model 53 was launched in 1953, but by this time, the French Army had begun the search for an interim solution. In 1955, the Delahaye started to be replaced by Hotchkiss licence-built Jeeps.

Total production between 1951 and 1954 was 9,326 of the 24V Models 51 and 53, plus 20 examples of a 12V Air Ministry variant. The civilian variant was designated VLR-C12.

LEFT: **More than 9,000 examples were built between 1951 and 1953 and a civilian version was available. Mechanical and handling problems were never solved and, within a few years, the VLR-D had been superseded by the Hotchkiss M201 – a licence-built version of the Jeep.**

Delahaye VLR-D

Type: Truck, ¼-ton, utility, 4x4
Manufacturer: Société Automobiles Delahaye; Paris
Production: 1951 to 1954
Powerplant: Delahaye Type 182; four cylinders in-line; petrol; water-cooled; 1,992cc; overhead valves; power output, 63bhp at 3,800rpm
Transmission: 4F1Rx2; part-time 4x4
Suspension: Independent suspension on leading/trailing arms, using adjustable torsion bars; self-levelling system on rear axle; telescopic shock absorbers
Brakes: Hydraulic
Electrical system: 12V, 24V
Dimensions: Length – 3,454mm/136in
　　Width – 1,626mm/64in
　　Height – tilt in place, 1,854mm/73in; minimum, 1,422mm/56in
　　Wheelbase – 2,150mm/85in
Weight: Unladen – 1,400kg/3,086lb
　　Payload – 990–1,100kg/2,182–2,425lb
Performance: Maximum speed – 110kph/65mph

Hotchkiss M201

Like most of the liberated European nations, France received supplies of surplus US-built Jeeps at the end of World War II. As the vehicles started to deteriorate through age, the Ministry of Defence initiated a largely unsuccessful attempt at producing an all-French replacement in the form of the Delahaye VLR-D. In 1955, a decision was taken to seek a licence from Willys-Overland to build the Jeep in France. Later that year, the Paris-based Hotchkiss company started work on manufacturing 465 examples of the MB, effectively a copy of the Willys MB using French parts wherever possible. This meant that the large proportion of war-surplus parts held by the French

Army for the original World War II Jeep could still be used on the French-built replacement.

In 1957, this was followed by the definitive Hotchkiss M201, a 24V version of the original Jeep in which every part was either retooled for manufacture in France or sourced from French manufacturers. Aside from an updated electrical system, this meant that there were no material design changes. The M201 was powered by the same 2,199cc Go-Devil four-cylinder engine as in the original, driving through a three-speed gearbox and two-speed transfer box to live axles which were suspended on semi-elliptical springs. The open bodywork was of the familiar Jeep design, although plastic-coated doors and side curtains were available to provide a full weatherproof enclosure.

Variants included a heavy-duty "Sahara" version, also the SS10, ENTAC and MILAN missile launchers. Another version mounted the US-built 106mm M40 recoilless anti-tank rifle.

Production continued until 1966, by which time 27,628 had been constructed. Hotchkiss also manufactured a civilian Jeep under various designations until 1969.

The M201 remained in service with the French Army and *Gendarmerie* (Police) until the late 1990s.

ABOVE: **The Hotchkiss M201 was a licence-built version of the World War II Jeep, differing only by the use of a 24V electrical system and screened ignition. Although the vehicle was French manufactured, virtually every part was interchangeable with the US original. A total of 27,628 were built.**

LEFT: **An M201 equipped with the M40 106mm recoilless anti-tank rifle. The split windscreen is similar to that on the similarly equipped US-built M38A1 Jeep.**

Hotchkiss M201

Type: Truck, 1/4-ton, 4x4
Manufacturer: Hotchkiss-Brandt; Paris
Production: 1957 to 1966
Powerplant: Licence-built Willys Go-Devil Type 442; four cylinders in-line; petrol; water-cooled; 2,199cc; side valves; power output, 52bhp at 3,600rpm
Transmission: 3F1Rx2; part-time 4x4
Suspension: Live axles on multi-leaf semi-elliptical springs; telescopic shock absorbers
Brakes: Hydraulic
Electrical system: 24V
Dimensions: Length – 3,372mm/133in
Width – 1,575mm/62in
Height – tilt in place, 1,772mm/70in; minimum, 1,302mm/51in
Wheelbase – 2,032mm/80in
Weight: Unladen – 1,160kg/2,557lb
Payload – 400kg/882lb
Performance: Maximum speed – 105kph/65mph

Hotchkiss-Laffly S15T

Hotchkiss-Laffly S15T

Type: Tractor, light, artillery, 6x6
Manufacturer: Etablissements Laffly; Billancourt. Etablissements Hotchkiss; St Denis
Production: 1936 to 1940
Powerplant: Hotchkiss 486; four cylinders in-line; petrol; water-cooled; 2,312cc; overhead valves; power output, 52bhp at 2,300rpm
Transmission: 4F1Rx2; part-time 6x6
Suspension: Live axle on semi-elliptical multi-leaf springs at front; independent suspension at rear using swing half-axles and semi-elliptical multi-leaf springs
Brakes: Mechanical
Electrical system: 12V
Dimensions: (artillery tractor variant)
Length – 5,550mm/219in
Width – 1,750mm/69in
Height – tilt in place, 2,550mm/100in
Wheelbase – 2,345mm/92in
Bogie centres – 1,000mm/39in
Weight: Unladen – 3,000kg/6,614lb
Payload – 1,500kg/3,307lb
Performance: Maximum speed – 50kph/31mph

LEFT: **Variants included a low-profile reconnaissance/prime mover (W15T). Also an ambulance (S15L), powered by a Peugeot engine.**

Laffly was founded in 1849 and started producing trucks at Billancourt in 1912. Although the company is probably best remembered for fire appliances, from the mid-1930s Laffly produced a range of six-wheeled military trucks fitted with an independently sprung rear bogie designed by the Hungarian engineer Hóllos Zsigsmond.

The lightest of these was the S15, for which development started in the mid-1930s, with the first examples entering service in 1936. The chassis was used for an artillery tractor (*auto caisson*), a recovery vehicle, and a personnel carrier, with production undertaken simultaneously by Laffly and Hotchkiss. Power came from a 2,312cc Hotchkiss four-cylinder petrol engine, connected to a four-speed gearbox and two-speed transfer box. There were also hub reduction gears. The front wheels were independently suspended using coil springs and double wishbones, while the rear suspension had swinging half-axles on semi-elliptical leaf springs.

The design featured an overhanging bonnet, with the front axle set back under the engine. Two small free-running wheels were fitted under the radiator to enable the crossing of ditches. Some 411 artillery tractors were in service in 1940 and were used to tow 75mm and 105mm field guns.

Latil TAR

In 1904, Charles Blum established what became Automobiles Industrielles Latil in Suresnes, near Paris to produce powerful four-wheel drive forestry tractors. It was almost inevitable that military vehicles would follow and several thousand of the company's 4x4 heavy trucks and artillery tractors were supplied to the French Army during World War I.

Looking rather like a Renault or a Mack by the shape of the bonnet, the TAR series dated from 1914 and was used for towing the heavy French guns such as the 155mm GPF, the Schneider 220L and the Schneider 280. The tractor was powered by a 4,200cc four-cylinder petrol engine driving through a five-speed gearbox, with separate drive shafts to gear wheels at the hubs. Twinned solid tyres were fitted all round. The truck was equipped with both four-wheel drive and four-wheel steering, and a heavy winch was fitted at the rear.

By 1918, 2,000 Latil tractors were in use, with many remaining in French service throughout the 1920s and into the 1930s. Despite the introduction of the updated TARH in 1932, a few of the originals even survived the opening years of World War II, being captured and used by the *Wehrmacht*. The TAR was also employed by the US Expeditionary Force in France. The last Latil artillery tractor was the low-profile M7Z1 dating from 1938. Latil was taken over by Saviem in 1955 and the name disappeared.

LEFT: **Some TAR tractors were equipped with tracked bogies in place of wheels.**

Latil TAR

Type: Tractor, heavy, artillery, 4x4
Manufacturer: Charles Blum, and then Automobiles Industrielles Latil; Suresnes
Production: 1913 to 1922
Powerplant: Latil; four cylinders in-line; petrol; water-cooled; 4,200cc; side valves; power output, 32bhp at 1200rpm
Transmission: 5F1R; full-time 4x4
Suspension: None
Brakes: Mechanical
Electrical system: Magneto only
Dimensions: Length – 5,900mm/232in
Wheelbase – 3,000mm/118in
Other dimensions not available
Weight: Unladen – 5,800kg/12,787lb
Payload – 2,000kg/4,409lb
Maximum towed load – 3,750kg/8,267lb
Performance: Maximum speed – 10kph/6mph

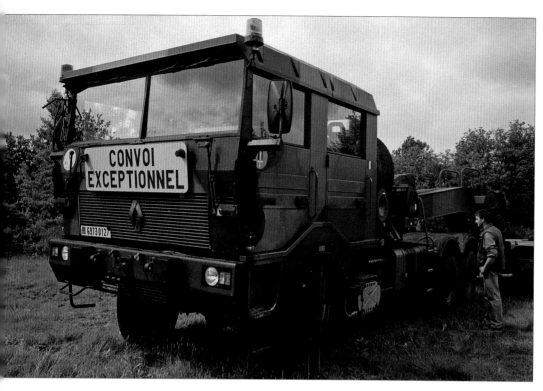

LEFT: **Powered by a 16,400cc Mack V8 turbocharged water-cooled diesel engine, the Renault TRM 700-100T was designed as the heavy equipment transporter for the French Army's Leclerc main battle tank.**

All three axles were equipped with double-reduction gears. Suspension was by semi-elliptical multi-leaf springs, inverted at the rear and located by torque reaction arms. An auxiliary equalizer spring was fitted at the front, together with hydraulic double-acting shock absorbers.

The truck was fitted with a tiltable four-door crew cab, broadly derived from that used on the TRM 10000 truck, but lengthened to provide seating for a driver and a crew of four. The fifth wheel was placed across the centreline of the rear bogie at a height of 1,640mm/65in. A pair of 15-ton hydraulic winches could be specified for installation behind the cab to assist with loading disabled tanks.

Following an extended period of evaluation, an initial 179 vehicles were ordered for the French Army in March 1994, with deliveries due to begin the following year. A second order was subsequently placed for a further 121 vehicles for delivery in the years 2000 to 2002.

Renault TRM 700-100T

The Renault TRM 700-100 tractor was first shown at the annual Satory defence equipment exhibition in 1987. It was designed to be used as the transporter for France's Leclerc main battle tank in conjunction with a Nicolas SFD A6 70-ton semi-trailer.

In 1987, Renault Véhicules Industriels (RVI) had also acquired a 40 per cent stake in the US company Mack Trucks.

This led to the TRM 700-100 being powered by a 16,400cc Mack E9 V8 diesel, driving through a hydraulic torque converter and six-speed automatic gearbox with electronic control. The transfer case, which provided permanent all-wheel drive in the ratio of 33 per cent to the front and 67 per cent to the rear, was integral with the gearbox. Cross-axle and inter-axle differential locks were also fitted.

Renault TRM 700-100T

Type: Truck-tractor, 70-ton, 6x6
Manufacturer: Renault Véhicules Industriels; Suresnes
Production: 1987 to 2001
Powerplant: Mack (RVI) E9; eight cylinders in V configuration; turbocharged diesel; water-cooled; 16,400cc; overhead valves; power output, 700bhp at 2,500rpm
Transmission: Automatic 6F1R; full-time 6x6; lockable centre and axle differentials
Suspension: Live axles on semi-elliptical multi-leaf springs with auxiliary equalizer spring and hydraulic double-acting shock absorbers at the front
Brakes: Air-pressure
Electrical system: 24V
Dimensions: Length – 8,045mm/317in
Width – 2,680mm/106in
Height – 3,283mm/129in
Wheelbase – 4,325mm/170in
Bogie centres – 1,350mm/54in
Weight: Unladen – 12,848kg/28,324lb
Gross train weight – 106,000kg/233,686lb
Performance: Maximum speed – 76kph/47mph

ABOVE: **Two 15-ton capacity hydraulic winches are installed behind the crew cab to assist with the recovery and loading of immobilized or damaged tanks.**

Simca F594WML

Simca F594WML

First produced in 1956, the Simca F594WML was derived from a militarized version of the French-built Ford F59WM truck. Dating from four years earlier, the F294WM had been fitted with a Marmon-Herrington front axle and transfer box in order to provide

four-wheel drive. Ford France was absorbed by Simca in 1954 and truck production was moved from Poissy to the Unic plant at Suresnes. The trucks were then known as Simca-Unic.

The F594WML was powered by a 3,923cc Simca-Ford V8 petrol engine, driving through a four-speed gearbox and two-speed Marmon-Herrington transfer box. The axle and suspension assemblies were thoroughly conventional, with live axles, front and rear, suspended on semi-elliptical springs. The standard body was a composite steel/wood cargo/personnel unit. Other variants included a container body, workshop, compressor, end tipper and fuel tanker. Some vehicles were fitted with a front-mounted winch. There was also a short-wheelbase variant, designated F594WMC.

Simca F594WML

Type: Truck, 3-ton, cargo, 4x4
Manufacturer: FFSA Division Camions Unic; Suresnes
Production: 1956 to 1961
Powerplant: Ford-Simca Type F6CWM; eight cylinders in V configuration; petrol; water-cooled; 3,923cc; side valves; power output, 100bhp at 3,800rpm
Transmission: 4F1Rx2; part-time 4x4
Suspension: Live portal axles on semi-elliptical multi-leaf springs; hydraulic double-acting telescopic shock absorbers
Brakes: Hydraulic with vacuum servo-assistance
Electrical system: 24V
Dimensions: Length – 6,806mm/268in
    Width – 2,286mm/90in
    Height – tilt in place, 3,200mm/126in; minimum, 2,550mm/100in
    Wheelbase – 3,655mm/144in
Weight: Unladen – 4,800kg/10,582lb
    Payload – road, 5,000kg/11,023lb; cross-country, 3,200kg/7,055lb
Performance: Maximum speed – 80kph/50mph

LEFT: **There was also a very similar 4x2 variant, designated F569WML. This example is in French Army service.**

SUMB MH600BS

SUMB MH600BS

The SUMB – Simca-Unic-Marmon-Bocquet – MH600BS was developed in France in the late 1950s to replace the ageing Dodge WC63. Designed by Arthur Bocquet of Marmon-Herrington, the design closely followed the specification of the German-built Unimog. Dating from 1957–58, the first prototypes were powered by a 4,184cc Ford-Simca V8 petrol engine but, in 1960, there were trials with a Panhard-built four-cylinder air-cooled engine.

In 1962, after extended trials and modification, the original Ford-Simca powered version was adopted as the French Army's standard 1½-ton tactical cargo truck. Off-road performance was enhanced by a manual differential lock in the rear axle.

Production started in 1962, with an initial order for 2,150 vehicles, but by the time production ended in 1965, a total of 9,000 examples had been built. Almost all were bodied as cargo/personnel trucks. Other variants included a vehicle-servicing truck, fire tender and light mobile digger. Some examples were

SUMB MH600BS

Type: Truck, 1½-ton, cargo, 4x4
Manufacturer: FFSA Division Camions Simca-Unic; Suresnes
Production: 1962 to 1965
Powerplant: Ford-Simca Type F7CWM; eight cylinders in V configuration; petrol; water-cooled; 4,184cc; side valves; power output, 100bhp at 3,200rpm. Late production – fitted with 5,184cc six-cylinder Fiat 8060 diesel engine; in 1996, 564 examples were fitted with a 3,600cc Renault 720-SPC diesel
Transmission: 4F1Rx2; part-time 4x4
Suspension: Live portal axles on coil springs; hydraulic double-acting telescopic shock absorbers
Brakes: Air-pressure assisted hydraulic
Electrical system: 24V
Dimensions: Length – 5,195mm/205in
    Width – 2,305mm/91in
    Height – tilt in place, 2,880mm/113in; minimum, 2,770mm/109in
    Wheelbase – 2,900mm/114in
Weight: Unladen – 3,670kg/8,091lb
    Payload – 1,500kg/3,307lb
Performance: Maximum speed – 85kph/53mph

LEFT: **The MH600BS is a popular vehicle with military enthusiasts.**

fitted with removable shelter bodies equipped for the communications role.

A 3-ton long-wheelbase variant was produced from 1974.

LEFT: **The three-cylinder two-stroke Auto-Union DKW MUNGA was one of the first generation of West German military vehicles, and was used by the *Bundeswehr* and the *Grenzschütz*, as well as by the Indonesian and Netherlands armies.**

RIGHT: **A MUNGA 4 leading a convoy of *Bundeswehr* M41 Bulldog tanks.**

Auto-Union DKW F91 MUNGA

In the mid-1950s, the Government of the newly formed West German Federal state was permitted to establish a defence force – the *Bundeswehr*. No money was available to buy foreign vehicles. Similarly, insufficient funds were available to pay the high maintenance costs of US war-surplus stock. The State authorities approached their automotive industry seeking a range of German designed logistics vehicles in the 1/2-ton, 1-ton, 3-ton, 6-ton and 10-ton weight classifications.

Goliath, Porsche and Auto-Union all provided prototypes in the 1/4-ton category. Porsche produced what they described as the Type 597, Goliath-Werk of Bremen developed the Model 31, and Auto-Union/DKW produced the F91/4, more usually described as the MUNGA (*Mehrzweck Universal Geländewagen mit Allradantrieb*). After a period of initial testing, contracts were placed with Porsche and Goliath for 50 vehicles each. Auto-Union/DKW received an order for 5,000. The success of Auto-Union was

apparently down to their ability to promise a very short lead time into production.

The MUNGA was an innovative and unusual vehicle with several features setting it apart from the military-vehicle mainstream of the period. For example, the 897cc engine was a three-cylinder two-stroke unit featuring triple coils and contact breaker sets. The engine was upgraded twice during the production of the vehicle. From 1957, the vehicle featured permanent all-wheel drive, with a four-speed gearbox and two-speed transfer box. The front and rear axle units were interchangeable. Independent front and rear suspension by means of transverse leaf springs was standard. The basic model was the four-seat F91/4, or MUNGA 4. There was also the F91/6 MUNGA 6, and F91/8 MUNGA 8. Standard variants included an ambulance,

BELOW: **The angular nose was all its own, but the inspiration for the MUNGA clearly came from the World War II Jeep.**

radio-command vehicle and a mount for the Cobra anti-tank missile. In the autumn of 1957, the vehicle was launched on the commercial market at the 38th International Motor Show, Frankfurt.

The MUNGA served in West Germany with the *Bundeswehr* and the *Grenzschütz* (Border Guard), as well as with the armies of Indonesian and the Netherlands.

Production began in 1955 and ended in December 1968. A total of 46,750 vehicles were delivered. Approximately 25,000 F91/4 and 3,000 F91/8s were supplied to the *Bundeswehr*.

Auto-Union DKW F91 MUNGA

Type: Field car, 4-seat/6-seat/8-seat, 1/4-ton, 4x4
Manufacturer: Auto-Union DKW; Ingolstadt
Production: 1955 to 1968
Powerplant: Auto-Union AU1000; three cylinders in-line; 897cc, 974cc, or 980cc; two stroke petrol; water-cooled; power output, 38bhp at 4,000rpm, 40bhp at 4,250rpm, or 44bhp at 4,250rpm, respectively
Transmission: 4F1Rx2; full-time or part-time 4x4 (1955–56 only)
Suspension: Independent suspension using transverse semi-elliptical multi-leaf springs
Brakes: Hydraulic
Electrical system: 24V
Dimensions: Length – 3,429–3,581mm/135–141in
Width – 1,702–1,778mm/67–70in
Height – tilt in place, 1,753–1,930mm/69–76in; minimum, 1,321mm/52in
Wheelbase – 2,000mm/79in
Weight: Unladen – 1,200–1,810kg/2,645–3,990lb
Payload – 365kg/805lb
Performance: Maximum speed – 93kph/58mph

Auto-Union Horch 108

Introduced in 1937, the Auto-Union 108 was one of two chassis types used for the *Schwere Geländegängige Einheits Personenkraftwagen* (sglEPkw) – standardized heavy cross-country car. The other was the Ford EG. All *Typ* A chassis variants were fitted with four-wheel steering, while the *Typ* B had conventional front-wheel steering only. Standard body types included personnel carrier *Kraftfahrzeug* (Kfz) 18, Kfz 70, command car, ambulance (Kfz 31), amplifier van (Kfz 24), gun mount (Kfz 81) and telephone vehicle (Kfz 23).

Early examples were fitted with a 3,500cc Horch V8 petrol engine, driving through a five-speed gearbox and single-speed transfer box to provide permanent all-wheel drive. Both axles had lockable differentials. The engine was subsequently replaced by a 3,823cc unit. Free-running twin spare wheels were fitted on each side to assist in ditch and trench crossing. Suspension was

LEFT: **A Horch 108; note the spare wheel mounting in the body side.**

by independent coil springs. In 1940, the Horch 108 was replaced by the very similar Horch 40, fitted with a wider body but without the side-mounted spare wheels.

Auto-Union Horch 108

Type: Car, heavy, 4x4
Manufacturer: Auto-Union Horch-Werke; Zwickau
Production: 1937 to 1940
Powerplant: Horch 108; eight cylinders in V configuration; petrol; water-cooled; 3,500cc, 3,823cc; side valves; power output, 80–81bhp at 3,600rpm
Transmission: 5F1R; full-time 4x4; lockable differentials
Suspension: Independent suspension by wishbones and coil springs
Brakes: Hydraulic
Electrical system: 12V
Dimensions: Length – 4,850mm/191in
    Width – 2,000mm/79in
    Height – tilt in place, 2,040mm/80in
    Wheelbase – 3,000mm/118in
Weight: Unladen – 2,300kg/5,070lb
    Payload – 2,000kg/4,409lb
Performance: Maximum speed – 80kph/50mph

Borgward B3000

Having already been producing motorcar components, Carl F. Borgward took over Goliath, manufacturers of commercial vehicles under the name Hansa-Lloyd, in 1927. Two years later, Borgward-Goliath took over the car manufacturing side of Hansa and in 1937, renamed the companies Carl F. Borgward Automobil & Motoren-Werke. During the 1930s, Borgward co-produced the *Einheits* 2½-ton,

standardized 6x6 truck (leglELkw) for the *Wehrmacht*. Between 1939 and 1944 some 30,000 military trucks under the designation B3000 were built.

There were four chassis variants – the 4x2 B3000S/O and B3000S/D were powered by either a 3,745cc petrol or 4,962cc diesel engine, respectively. The equivalent 4x4 chassis were designated B3000A/O and B3000A/D. The engine was attached to a five-speed gearbox and two-speed transfer box. Suspension was by semi-elliptical multi-leaf springs.

In late 1944 the Borgward factory was virtually destroyed by Allied bombing.

LEFT: **A B3000 on the Russian Front in 1942.**

Borgward B3000

Type: Truck, cargo, 3-ton, 4x2, 4x4
Manufacturer: Carl F. Borgward Automobil & Motoren-Werke; Hemelingeny
Production: 1939 to 1944
Powerplant: Borgward D6M5; six cylinders in-line; diesel; water-cooled; 4,962cc; overhead valves; power output, 75bhp at 2,000rpm.
    Borgward B3000; six cylinders in-line; petrol; water-cooled; 3,745cc; overhead valves; power output, 78bhp at 3,000rpm
Transmission: 5F1Rx2; part-time 4x4
Suspension: Live axles on semi-elliptical multi-leaf springs
Brakes: Hydraulic
Electrical system: 12V (petrol engine), 24V (diesel engine)
Dimensions: Length – 6,450mm/254in
    Width – 2,300mm/91in
    Height – tilt in place, 2,930mm/115in; minimum, 2,220mm/87in
    Wheelbase – 3,700mm/146in
Weight: Unladen – 6,190–6,646kg/13,618–14,572lb
    Payload – 3,125kg/6,889lb
Performance: Maximum speed – 80kph/50mph

Faun SLT50-2 *Elefant*

In the late 1960s, West Germany and the USA embarked on a joint development project for a new main battle tank to be known as MBT-70. At the same time, a joint project was also initiated for the development of a heavy equipment transporter, designated HET-70 or SLT-70. The German partner in the project was Faun-Werke, while work in the USA was entrusted to the Chrysler Corporation. Both projects were eventually cancelled but, in Germany, Faun continued to develop the HET-70 for the *Bundeswehr* and the result was the LH70/420-8 tractor, described by them as the SLT50-2, but often known as *Elefant* (Elephant).

Low and wide, with a huge flat windscreen, the SLT50-2 was a low-profile eight-wheeled tractor powered by a 29,920cc Mercedes-Benz MTU V8 turbocharged diesel engine mounted immediately behind the cab. The transmission was by a four-speed automatic gearbox, having two reverse gears, linked to a two-speed transfer box with a lockable differential. Additionally there were lockable differentials in all four axles. Two 17-ton capacity Rotzler hydraulic winches were installed between the engine compartment and the fifth-wheel coupling; the winches were subsequently upgraded to 18.6-ton capacity. The

ABOVE: **Produced for just four years (1976–79), the Faun *Elefant* was intended as the tractor for towing a Leopard, the main battle tank of the *Bundeswehr*. The four-axle trailer was produced by Krupps.**

vehicle went into production in 1976, with 324 produced over a three-year period. A major upgrade programme was initiated in 1984.

A compatible four-axle 52-ton steered semi-trailer was developed by Krupp. The trailers were manufactured under licence by Kassbohrer. A V12-engined "austerity" 8x6 version of the tractor, designated FS42.75/42, was launched in 1981.

ABOVE LEFT AND LEFT: **The Faun SLT50-2 was originally designed as a joint project with the Chrysler Corporation in the USA. Although the project was cancelled, Faun carried on the development of their vehicle resulting in the *Elefant*.**

Faun SLT50-2 *Elefant*

Type: Heavy equipment transporter, 8x8
Manufacturer: Faun-Werke Karl Schmidt; Lauf
Production: 1976 to 1979
Powerplant: Mercedes-Benz MTU MB837Ea-500; eight cylinders in V configuration; turbocharged diesel; water-cooled; 29,920cc; overhead valves; power output, 730bhp at 2,100rpm
Transmission: Automatic 4F2Rx2; cross-axle differential locks
Suspension: Live axles on semi-elliptical multi-leaf springs with equalizing beams
Brakes: Air-pressure
Electrical system: 24V
Dimensions: (tractor only)
  Length – 8,830mm/348in
  Width – 3,070mm/121in
  Height – 3,000mm/118in
  Wheelbase – 5,700mm/224in
  Bogie centres – 1,500+2,700+1,500mm/ 59+106+59in
Weight: Unladen – 22,800kg/50,265lb
  Gross train weight – 92,000kg/202,822lb
Performance: Maximum speed – 70kph/44mph

Ford G198TS, G398TS

Ford-Werke was founded in Berlin in 1925 to import US-built Ford vehicles. Demand for the vehicles was such that a new assembly plant was built the following year, and within five years, this had been replaced by a new factory in Köln (Cologne), manufacturing cars and trucks for the German market.

When the US-based Ford company introduced a new 3-ton 4x2 truck in 1940, Ford Köln produced the same a year later. The German truck, designated G198TS, was powered by a 3,923cc V8 petrol engine, driving the rear wheels through a five-speed gearbox. In 1943, the G198TS was superseded by the G398TS, with a deeper radiator and cooling slots in the front. From October that year, shortages of steel saw the standard steel replaced by the utility *Wehrmacht Einheits* cab of compressed cardboard and timber. At the same time, the front mudguards were simplified in shape.

The *Wehrmacht* described the truck as the V3000S. Between 1941 and 1945, some 25,000

LEFT: **A Ford truck with *Einheits* cab and gas generator equipment.**

were built, 14,000 as the half-track *Maultier* (Mule). During the latter stages of the war, shortages of fuel often led to the use of a wood-gas generator. This system burned air-dried wood or anthracite to produce carbon monoxide gas that was used in place of petrol.

Ford G198TS, G398TS	

Type: Truck, 3-ton, cargo, 4x2
Manufacturer: Ford-Werke; Köln
Production: 1941 to 1945
Powerplant: Ford; eight cylinders in V configuration; petrol; water-cooled; 3,923cc; side valves; power output, 95bhp at 3,500rpm
Transmission: 5F1R; 4x2
Suspension: Live axles on semi-elliptical multi-leaf springs
Brakes: Hydraulic
Electrical system: 12V
Dimensions: Length – 6,390mm/252in
  Width – 2,250mm/89in
  Height – 2,180mm/86in
  Wheelbase – 4,013mm/158in
Weight: Unladen – 2,540kg/5,600lb
  Payload – 3,300kg/7,275lb
Performance: Maximum speed – 85kph/53mph

Ford G398SAM

Dating from 1956, the Ford G398SAM was designed for the German *Bundeswehr* to comply with NATO specifications for medium-weight multi-terrain trucks. It had been developed from a post-war 3-ton 4x4 chassis that Ford had produced for the British and US occupying forces. Like these, and the wartime G198TS/G398TS, the truck was powered by the reliable 3,923cc Ford V8 side-valve engine, driving all four wheels through a four-speed gearbox and two-speed transfer box.

Frequently nicknamed "Sam" for obvious reasons, it was a curiously angular truck, produced with both open and closed steel cabs. Most were fitted with a steel cargo/personnel body. Other variants included vehicles bodied for the office (*Kofferbau*), field kitchen, ambulance, radar, tipper, workshop, and communications roles.

A chassis variant (G398SAM-S3) was also available for special bodywork. Some examples were

LEFT: **A small number of the Ford G398SAM were supplied to the armies of Greece, Turkey and Israel.**

fitted with a winch. The truck remained in production from 1956 to 1961.

Ford G398SAM

Type: Truck, 3- to 4-ton, cargo, 4x4
Manufacturer: Ford-Werke; Köln
Production: 1956 to 1961
Powerplant: Ford G29T; eight cylinders in V configuration; petrol; water-cooled; 3,923cc; side valves; power output, 92bhp at 3,500rpm
Transmission: 4F1Rx2; part-time 4x4
Suspension: Live axles on semi-elliptical multi-leaf springs
Brakes: Hydraulic with air servo-assistance
Electrical system: 24V
Dimensions: Length – 7,250mm/285in
  Width – 2,250mm/89in
  Height – tilt in place, 3,180mm/125in; minimum, 2,130mm/84in
  Wheelbase – 4,013mm/158in
Weight: Unladen – 3,970kg/8,752lb; with winch, 4,270kg/9,414lb
  Payload – road, 5,000kg/11,023lb; cross-country, 3,500kg/7,716lb
Performance: Maximum speed – 80kph/50mph

Henschel *Einheitsdiesel*

In 1934, the Nazi party proposed that the German motor industry should be financially supported by the Army to ensure that military interests were adequately represented in the design of motor vehicles. Two years later, the Government announced the implementation of an economic Four Year Plan, under Hermann Göring, designed both to promote the development of key heavy industries, and to encourage increased domestic production of strategic materials such as steel, rubber and petroleum. The Germans believed that an increase in the production of motor vehicles would boost the domestic economy and, at the same time, provide a valuable source of foreign exchange income through export sales. If the vehicles were also suitable for use by the military, then this would be a bonus.

By the middle of the decade there were 36 motor manufacturers in Germany producing military vehicles, or vehicles which could be used by the military should the need arise. This led to a multiplicity of types being available to the

Reichswehr, which obviously presented technical problems. In 1936, in an attempt to rationalize the situation, plans were drawn up for a series of standardized vehicle chassis (*Einheitsfahrgestell*) which were to be developed in conjunction with the *Heereswaffenamt* (Ordnance Department). The plan covered light, medium and heavy cars/personnel carriers, as well as the light, medium and heavy trucks. All of these vehicles were to be provided with all-wheel drive, featuring two, three or four independently sprung and driven axles, according to weight classification.

Curiously, the specifications only laid down broad parameters and did not include any detailed aspects of design. Participating manufacturers were free to interpret the requirements in their own way, and to fit their own engines. As a result, there was little real benefit, and the only truly standardized military truck produced as a result of this programme was a 2½-ton 6x6 cross-country load carrier, production of which started in 1937.

ABOVE: **Pre-dating the** *Einheitsdiesel* **by two years, Henschel and Magirus also produced a similar-looking medium 6x4 truck (1934 to 1943), designated 33G1. The two vehicles are not easy to differentiate.**
RIGHT: **The side access door to the rear of the body suggests that this is an engineers' vehicle.**

Described as the *Leicht Geländegängig Einheits Lastkraftwagen* (light cross-country standardized truck), the vehicle was effectively a product of Henschel, who developed the chassis, and the *Heereswaffenamt*. It was eventually produced by seven manufacturers including Borgward, Büssing-NAG, Daimler-Benz, Faun, Henschel, Magirus (Klöckner-Humboldt-Deutz after 1937), and MAN. VOMAG may also have been involved.

The chassis featured independent front and rear suspension by means of swing arms and coil springs as well as permanent six-wheel drive. Power was provided by a 6,234cc six-cylinder diesel engine, based on a design produced by MAN in collaboration with Henschel, driving the wheels through a four-speed gearbox and a two-speed transfer box. Three self-locking differentials were fitted which, in combination with the independent suspension, gave excellent off-road performance.

Most chassis were fitted with an open cab and a steel or timber drop-side cargo body. Different types of standardized body were also available for specific roles including signals,

recovery, field kitchen, snow-blower and others. Until 1943, these body types were indicated by a Kfz (*Kraftfahrzeug*) number. The permitted gross weight of the vehicle was 7,500kg (15,500lb) with an open cargo body and 7,420kg (16,324lb) with a closed body. Production of what was often referred to as the *Einheitsdiesel* continued until 1940. The total number of vehicles produced was around 10,250, with the majority (3,200) built by Büssing-NAG.

Medium (*mittler*) and heavy (*schwere*) standardized vehicles were also planned along similar lines but never made it into production.

ABOVE: **Although it was designed and built by Henschel, the *Einheitsdiesel* was also produced by Borgward, Büssing-NAG, Daimler-Benz, FAUN, Magirus, and MAN.**

LEFT: **The vehicle was large with what was a relatively small payload. It was also bodied for the signals, recovery, field kitchen and as a fire tender. The all-wheel drive and independent suspension on all wheels was standard equipment.**

Henschel *Einheitsdiesel*

Type: Truck, cargo, light, 6x6
Manufacturer: Borgward (Hansa-Lloyd & Goliath Werke); Bremen. Büssing-NAG; Braunschweig. Daimler-Benz; Stuttgart. Faun; Nürnberg. Henschel & Sohn; Kassel. Klockner-Humboldt-Deutz (Magirus); Ulm. Maschinenfabrik Augsburg-Nürnberg (MAN); Augsburg.
Production: 1937 to 1940
Powerplant: HWa526D; six cylinders in-line; 6,234cc; diesel; water-cooled; overhead valves; power output, 85bhp at 2,400rpm
Transmission: 4F1Rx2; full-time 6x6
Suspension: Independent at all six wheels using swing axles and coil springs
Brakes: Air-pressure
Electrical system: Hybrid 12V/24V
Dimensions: Length – 5,850mm/230in
Width – 2,200mm/87in
Height – tilt in place, 2,400mm/94in
Wheelbase – 3,650mm/144in
Bogie centres – 1,100mm/43in
Weight: Unladen – 5,000kg/11,023lb
Payload – 2,500kg/5,511lb
Performance: Maximum speed – 70kph/44mph

Krauss-Maffei KM-m-10, 11

Type: Tractor, medium, 8-ton, half-track

Manufacturer: Carl F. Borgward; Bremen.
Krauss-Maffei; München

Production: 1936 to 1944

Powerplant: Maybach HL57 TU; six cylinders
in-line; petrol; water-cooled; 5,698cc;
overhead valves; power output, 135bhp
at 2,600rpm.
Maybach HL62 TUK; six cylinders in-line;
petrol; water-cooled; 6,191cc; overhead
valves; power output, 140bhp at 2,600rpm

Transmission: 4F1Rx2

Suspension: Pivoting front axle suspended on
transverse semi-elliptical multi-leaf spring;
paired leaf springs for each road wheel at rear

Brakes: Hydraulic

Electrical system: 12V

Dimensions: Length – 8,100mm/319in
Width – 1,940mm/76in
Height – 1,750mm/69in
Track length on ground – KM-m-10,
1,400mm/55in; KM-m-11, 2,235mm/88in

Weight: Unladen – 9,500kg/20,943lb
Payload – 1,500kg/3,307lb
Maximum towed load – 8,000kg/17,637lb

Performance: Maximum speed – 50kph/31mph

Krauss-Maffei KM-m-10, 11

During World War II, the *Wehrmacht* tended to favour large numbers of half-tracked vehicles, particularly for use as prime movers. Following common design principles, the machines were produced in six weight classes ranging from 1–18 tons. First into production was the 8-ton *SonderKraftfahrzeug* (Sd Kfz) 7 "medium" tractor designed for towing heavy artillery including the 17cm and 15cm guns; other variants were fitted with a wooden load-carrying body or were used to mount a 2cm FlaK38 or 43 gun.

Work started in 1933, with early prototypes built by both Krauss-Maffei (KM-m-7) and Büssing-NAG (BN-m-8). Krauss-Maffei was authorized to begin production of the KM-m-8 variant in May 1934. The vehicle was powered by a 5,184cc Maybach HL52 six-cylinder petrol engine driving through a four-speed main gearbox and two-speed auxiliary box. The open coach-type body

had seating for up to 11 men on three rows of bench seats. Stowage for ammunition was at the rear. The vehicle was rated to tow 8,000kg/8 tons. A powerful horizontal-spindle winch was fitted at the rear of the chassis. The winch was eventually superseded by a vertical spindle with a drum design.

In 1935, the KM-m-8 was followed by the KM-m-9, with the definitive KM-m-10 dating from 1936. The original engine gave way to the higher-powered 5,698cc Maybach HL57, followed by the 6,191cc HL62. The final variant dates from March 1938 when Krauss-Maffei and Borgward produced the KM-m-11 (and HL-m-11), which featured longer tracks.

The Sd Kfz 7 was the only one of the German half-tracks to retain the paired leaf-spring suspension for the road wheels a feature from the original prototypes. Torsion-bar suspension was incorporated for the idler wheels. A solid beam axle was

fitted at the front, suspended on a transverse semi-elliptical spring, pivot-mounted on the front cross-member and retained by radius rods.

The KM-m-11 remained in production until 1944, with Krauss-Maffei producing 5,026 examples. In all some 12,000 of these vehicles were built by six manufacturers, including licensed production by Breda of the Type 61 in Milan, Italy. A proposed KM-m-12 of 1939, which was to have been powered by a Maybach HL80 engine was not produced.

ABOVE AND RIGHT: **The medium (8-ton) Sd Kfz 7 tractor was produced by Krauss-Maffei and Borgward. The vehicle was bodied as a personnel carrier/prime mover, gun mount and cargo carrier.**

Krupp L2H, L2H43, L2H143

Originally established in November 1811, Friedrich Krupp Motoren & Kraftwagen Fabrieken started building trucks, locomotives and agricultural machinery in 1919, the first vehicle being a chain-driven 5-ton truck. Shaft drive was offered in 1925 and, by 1930, Krupp was producing 4x2 and 6x4 forward-control trucks. The company's most significant contribution to the *Wehrmacht* was the Protze (Poseur) light truck, which originated as the L2H in 1933, and entered production the following year as the L2H43, which was also sold commercially. This was eventually superseded by the uprated 1½-ton L2H143 in 1937.

It was an innovative design of 6x4 light truck with independent rear suspension using horizontal coil springs, and was powered by a 3,308cc Krupp M304 air-cooled flat-four engine which allowed the adoption of a distinctive sloping bonnet. The rear wheels were driven through a four-speed gearbox and two-speed transfer box. Although there was no front-wheel drive, a self-locking differential gave excellent cross-country performance.

The most common role was that of a light artillery tractor (Kfz 69), but many were bodied as a cargo vehicle or personnel carrier (Kfz 70). Others were fitted with a searchlight (Kfz 83) or FlaK gun (Kfz 81), or carried a closed signals telephone body (Kfz 68). Production continued until 1941, by which time some 7,000 examples had been built.

The company also produced 3-ton and 6½-ton trucks until the factory was affected by heavy bombing in September 1942. In December 1943, the company Friedrich Krupp AG reverted back to sole ownership being transferred to the eldest son, Alfried Krupp von Bohlen und Halbach. The company's manufacturing activities were then relocated to areas less vulnerable to bombing.

LEFT: **A column of *Wehrmacht* troops in Krupp L2H143 vehicles pass through a village in Poland, September 1939. The vehicle was used extensively by troops of the *Legion Kondor* (Condor Legion) during the Spanish Civil War from July 17, 1936 to April 1, 1939.**

Krupp L2H, L2H43, L2H143

Type: Truck, light, 6x4
Manufacturer: Friedrich Krupp Motoren & Kraftwagen Fabrieken; Essen
Production: 1933 to 1941
Powerplant: Krupp M304; four cylinders, horizontally opposed; petrol; water-cooled; 3,308cc; side valves; power output, 60bhp at 2,500rpm
Transmission: 4F1Rx2; 6x4
Suspension: Live front axle on semi-elliptical multi-leaf springs; independent rear suspension using trailing arms and horizontal coil springs
Brakes: Hydraulic
Electrical system: 12V
Dimensions: Length – 5,100mm/201in
  Width – 1,960mm/77in
  Height – tilt in place, 1,620mm/64in; minimum, 1,485mm/58in
  Wheelbase – 2,905mm/114in
  Bogie centres – 910mm/36in
Weight: Unladen – 2,450kg/5,401lb
  Payload – 1,150kg/2,535lb
Performance: Maximum speed – 70kph/43mph

Magirus-Deutz M178D15A

In 1938, the Köln (Cologne) based Klöckner-Deutz Motoren company, which manufactured tractors, took over Conrad Dietrich Magirus, a fire appliance manufacturer based in Ulm. Although the company's origins went back to 1903, Magirus had not started manufacturing trucks until 1916. In 1933, Magirus launched a range of specialized military vehicles powered by a 7,500cc diesel engine. Subsequent diesel engines included a 12-cylinder horizontally opposed unit, but the distinctive Deutz air-cooled engines started to be used from the middle years of World War II. Between 1937 and 1940, Magirus was one of the manufacturers commissioned to build the standardized 6x6 *Einheits* truck, but the company's most significant *Wehrmacht* vehicles included some 18,000 examples of the 3-ton A3000/S3000 as both 4x2 and 4x4.

The company's factory was badly damaged during the latter years of the war. In 1946, production resumed and the company continued to prosper,

specializing in heavy vehicles, including tank transporters. The A6500 Jupiter was announced in 1951. Conservatively rated at 7 tons, it was powered by a 10,644cc Deutz F8L V8 air-cooled multi-fuel diesel engine driving through a six-speed gearbox and two-speed transfer box. In 1958, the original engine was replaced by a more-powerful 12,667cc unit, and the designation was changed to A7500. The 4x4 was replaced by a 6x6 variant in 1962. In 1964, the name Jupiter was deleted and the truck carried the designation M178D15A.

On all models, the suspension was by semi-elliptical multi-leaf springs, inverted at the rear. There were both open- and closed-cab designs. Standard variants included a steel drop-side cargo body, dump, workshop, crane carrier and multiple rocket launcher; also as a snow plough,

ABOVE: **The Magirus Jupiter (M178D15A) was introduced in 1951 and was widely used by the *Bundeswehr*. Aside from the multiple rocket launcher, standard variants included cargo, dump, workshop, crane carrier, snow plough, airfield fire tender, fuel tanker, recovery and tractor for semi-trailer.**

airfield fire tender, fuel tanker, recovery and tractor for semi-trailer. A total of 7,800 were produced, and widely used by the *Bundeswehr*. Many were also used by the British Army in Germany. The M178D15A was widely exported. In 1975, Magirus-Deutz AG was merged into the Fiat Iveco Group.

BELOW: **A winch-equipped M178D15A recovery tractor fitted with a World War II-style canvas-covered cab.**

Magirus-Deutz M178D15A

Type: Truck, cargo, 7-ton, 4x4, 6x6

Manufacturer: Klöckner-Humboldt-Deutz; Ulm

Production: 1951 to 1967

Powerplant: Deutz F8L-614; eight cylinders in V configuration; multi-fuel diesel; air-cooled; 10,644cc; overhead valves; power output, 170bhp at 2,300rpm.
Deutz F8L-714A; eight cylinders in V configuration; diesel; air-cooled; 12,667cc; overhead valves; power output, 178bhp at 2,300rpm

Transmission: 6F1Rx2; part-time 4x4

Suspension: Live axles on semi-elliptical multi-leaf springs, inverted at the rear

Brakes: Air-pressure assisted hydraulic

Electrical system: 24V

Dimensions: Length – 7,520mm/296in, 8,000mm/315in
Width – 2,500mm/98in
Height – tilt in place, 3,240mm/128in; minimum, 2,500mm/98in
Wheelbase – 4,410mm/174in, 4,820mm/190in
Bogie centres (6x6 variant only) – 1,280mm/50in

Weight: Unladen – typical, 14,600kg/32,187lb
Payload – 10,000kg/22,046lb

Performance: Maximum speed – 75kph/47mph

LEFT: **The diesel-powered MAN ML4500 was produced as a 4x4 (ML4500A) and also the 4x2 (ML4500S) variant. The vehicle was among the largest trucks used by the** *Wehrmacht* **during World War II. It was also manufactured by ÖAF in Austria.**

MAN ML4500A, ML4500S

In 1897, Maschinenfabrik Augsburg-Nürnberg (MAN) worked with Dr Rudolf Diesel on the design and development of the compression-ignition engine which was to bear his name. The company began building Saurer trucks under licence from 1915, before production of trucks under the MAN badge began in 1920. The name was changed to Kraftwagenwerke MAN-Saurer in 1916, with Saurer trucks being built until 1918. MAN produced the first diesel-engined truck in 1923 and the company's products manufactured during the 1930s were generally available with either diesel or petrol engines. MAN was also responsible for the design of the diesel engine which powered all of the light 6x6 German military vehicles.

Since the 1930s the company had tended to specialize in heavier trucks, becoming a major supplier to the

Wehrmacht. Typical of these were the 4$^{1}/_{2}$-ton ML4500S (4x2) and ML4500A (4x4), both of which were built in relatively large numbers between 1940 and 1945. The truck was of conventional design and was powered by a 7,980cc six-cylinder direct-injection diesel engine driving through a five-speed gearbox with overdrive top gear. The 4x4 variant was also fitted with a two-speed transfer box. The suspension was by semi-elliptical springs carrying live axles.

Production was at MAN in Nürnberg (until the factory became too busy building submarine engines) and at the ÖAF factory in Wien, Austria. The ÖAF company was purchased in 1936. Some 10,000 were built, with most bodied as cargo vehicles. The ML4500A was discontinued in 1944 and the ML4500S continued until 1945.

MAN ML4500A, ML4500S

Type: Truck, heavy, 4$^{1}/_{2}$-ton, 4x2, 4x4
Manufacturer: Maschinenfabrik Augsburg-Nürnberg (MAN); Nürnberg. Österreichische Automobil-Fabriks (OAF); Wien
Production: 1940 to 1945
Powerplant: MAN D1040G; six cylinders in-line; direct-injection diesel; water-cooled; 7,980cc; overhead valves; power output, 1,10bhp at 1,900rpm
Transmission: (ML4500A) 5F1Rx2; part-time 4x4. (ML4500S) 5F1R; 4x2
Suspension: Live axles on semi-elliptical multi-leaf springs
Brakes: Air-pressure
Electrical system: 12V
Dimensions: Length – 7,500mm/295in
  Width – 2,350mm/93in
  Height – tilt in place, 3,350mm/132in; minimum, 2,610mm/103in
  Wheelbase – 4,600mm/181in
Weight: Unladen – 5,050–5,550kg/11,113–12,235lb
  Payload – road, 4,950kg/10,890lb; cross-country (ML4500A only), 4,350kg/9,590lb
Performance: Maximum speed – 63kph/39mph

MAN HX2000, SX2000

In the mid-1960s, the German truck manufacturer Maschinenfabrik Augsburg-Nürnberg (MAN) started work on the second generation of logistics trucks for the *Bundeswehr*. Assistance came from Klöckner-Humboldt-Deutz (KHD), Rheinstahl-Henschel, Krupp and Büssing. By late 1965, vehicles had been demonstrated in the 4-, 7- and 10-ton weight classes, using what was basically an identical chassis. Following extensive trials, the series was officially accepted for production in April 1975. The first production vehicle was the 10-ton cargo truck, designated Kat 1. Deliveries began in January 1977, with the last of almost 9,000 vehicles delivered on May 18, 1983.

In 1985, work started on an improved version in collaboration with the US Army. Designated Kat 2, some were delivered to the USA, France and Canada. At the same time, work was in progress building the Kat 3 variant, and a total of 1,594 of these were purchased by Algeria, Ireland, Oman, Peru, Singapore and Venezuela. The Kat 1-A1 variant entered production in 1987, and was an improvement on the original Kat 1 with a wider, tilting cab and improved performance. In 1989, drawing on the experience gained in service since the launch of the original Kat 1 trucks, the range was rationalized into what MAN described as the improved medium-mobility SX, the medium-mobility HX and LX, and the militarized civilian FX. The trucks were available with a choice of power units, and with 4x4, 6x6 and 8x8 drive configurations. The range also included tractor variants. All shared the MAN-originated modular three-man tilting cab. An appliqué armour kit was available for fitting when operating in hazardous areas.

ABOVE: **British Army high-mobility 8x8 recovery vehicle.** RIGHT: **In 2001, the British Ministry of Defence awarded a contract to MAN for 4,851 high-mobility cargo vehicles in three drive configurations. The bodies were to be built by Marshall Specialist Vehicles Ltd., Cambridge.**

LEFT: **The four-wheel-drive cargo vehicle will replace existing Leyland-DAF and Bedford trucks in service with the British Army. All the trucks are fitted with the same low-profile cab first seen on the *Bundeswehr* Kat 1 trucks in the mid-1960s.**

MAN acquired ERF, a British company, in March 2000, forming MAN-ERF in 2004. A year later it was announced that the Ministry of Defence had awarded MAN-ERF a contract worth 1.5 billion Euros covering 4,851 4x4, 6x6 and 8x8 high-mobility cargo vehicles, plus 314 high-mobility recovery tractors. All were to use the HX and SX chassis. Deliveries began in 2007 and are scheduled to continue until 2014, replacing a variety of existing, in many cases ageing, vehicles including Leyland-DAF and Bedford MJ, Bedford TM4-4 and TM6-6 models, as well as Foden and Scammell recovery vehicles.

The trucks are powered by an 11,967cc MAN six-cylinder turbocharged diesel engine driving all wheels through an eight- or twelve-speed (8x8 variants) semi-automatic gearbox and two-speed transfer box. Suspension is by live axles suspended on coil springs, with radius rods.

Bodies and associated equipment for the UK trucks come from Marshall Specialist Vehicles (MSV), EKA, Fluid Transfer, Andover Trailers and Atlas Cranes.

BELOW: **The manufacturer's six-wheel drive demonstrator for the cargo-bodied truck. The vehicle is painted in the distinctive UN white livery.**

MAN HX2000, SX2000

Type: Truck, cargo, 8- to 10-ton, 4x4
Manufacturer: MAN Nutzfahrzeuge Altiengesellschaft; München
Production: 1989 on
Powerplant: MAN D2866; six cylinders in-line; turbocharged diesel; water-cooled; 11,967cc; overhead valves; power output, 400bhp at 2,000rpm
Transmission: Semi-automatic 8F2R; full-time 4x4
Suspension: Live axles on coil springs with axle location by radius rods; hydraulic double-acting shock absorbers at front
Brakes: Air-pressure
Electrical system: 24V
Dimensions: Length – 7,711mm/304in
   Width – 2,550mm/100in
   Height – top of cab, 3,308mm/130in
   Wheelbase – 4,500mm/177in
Weight: Unladen – 7,950kg/17,526lb
   Payload – 8,000-10,000kg/17,637-22,046lb
Performance: Maximum speed – 88kph/55mph

Type: Car, heavy, six-seat, 6x4, 6x6
Manufacturer: Mercedes-Benz; Stuttgart
Production: 1933 to 1939
Powerplant: Mercedes-Benz M24; eight cylinders in-line; petrol; water-cooled; 5,018, 5,252 or 5,401cc; overhead valves; power output, 110–115bhp at 3,400rpm
Transmission: 4F1Rx2; 6x4 (W31), 6x6 (W131)
Suspension: Live axles, front and rear on semi-elliptical multi-leaf springs; hydraulic vane shock absorbers
Brakes: Vacuum servo-assisted hydraulic
Electrical system: 12V
Dimensions: Length – 5,400mm/213in
Width – 1,890mm/74in
Height – top erected, 1,800mm/71in
Wheelbase – 2,530mm/100in
Bogie centres – 9,50mm/37in
Weight: Unladen – 3,566kg/7,826lb
Performance: Maximum speed – 60kph/37mph

Mercedes-Benz G4

Often described as "Hitler's Mercedes", the G4 was a six-seater heavy staff car (*schwere Personnenkraft-wagen*) built for senior ministers, military officers and officials of the Third Reich. Despite much evidence to the contrary, it was a product of the belief that three axles offered the best off-road performance. The design only remained in production because it was favoured by the *Führer*.

ABOVE: **The Mercedes-Benz G4 6x4 heavy motor car was much favoured by Hitler and his senior staff. Just 57 examples were produced between 1933 and 1934. Although equipped for the purpose, the vehicle was hardly ever used for cross-country travel.**

The G4 had a Mercedes-Benz M24 straight-eight cylinder petrol engine, coupled to a four-speed main gearbox and two-speed auxiliary transfer box.

The W31 was driven by the rear wheels only, while the W131 was fitted with six-wheel drive. Despite an impressive power output of 110–115bhp, the unladen weight of 3,566kg/7,826lb restricted top speed to 60kph/37mph. Just 57 were completed between 1933 and 1939.

Mercedes-Benz G5

Announced in 1937 the Mercedes-Benz G5 first appeared in public at the 1938 British Motor Show at Olympia. Based on the 200V passenger car, the G5 was not the company's first all-wheel-drive vehicle, nor was it an entirely new design. Mercedes-Benz built an all-wheel-drive vehicle in 1904.

The car was powered by a 2,006cc four-cylinder petrol engine, driving both axles via a unitary five-speed gearbox/transfer box, the fifth gear being an overdrive. The differentials were located so that the drive-shafts passed through the chassis side members for increased ground clearance. The suspension was independent at front and rear, using cast wishbones and heavy-duty coil springs, together with double-acting shock absorbers. In normal use, the vehicle was steered by means of the front wheels, with the rear wheels locked in the straight-ahead position. The driver could select all-wheel drive and steering.

Type: Car, medium, 4x4
Manufacturer: Mercedes-Benz; Stuttgart
Production: 1937 to 1940
Powerplant: Mercedes-Benz M149; four cylinders in-line; petrol; water-cooled; 2,006cc; overhead valves; power output, 48bhp at 3,700rpm
Transmission: 5F1R; part-time 4x4
Suspension: Independent front and rear, using coil springs; hydraulic vane shock absorbers
Brakes: Hydraulic
Electrical system: 12V
Dimensions: Length – 3,990mm/157in
Width – 1,680mm/66in
Height – 1,900mm/75in
Wheelbase – 2,530mm/100in
Weight: Unladen – 1,880kg/4,145lb
Performance: Maximum speed – 80kph/50mph

LEFT: **The prototype G5 Mercedes-Benz. Note the all-wheel steering.**

Three body styles were built – a strictly military *Kübelwagen* with steel half doors, a four-door convertible known as the *Kommandeurwagen*, and an open-sided vehicle with side curtains.

LEFT: **Like the 4¹/₂-ton MAN truck, the Mercedes-Benz L4300 was produced in 4x4 (L4500A) and 4x2 (L4500S) variants. There was also a half-tracked *Maultier* (Mule) conversion, designated L4500R. The truck was introduced in 1939 and produced until 1944. It was then was put back into production for the post-war commercial market.**

Mercedes–Benz L4500A, L4500S

The Mercedes-Benz L4500 was the standard heavy truck in the *Wehrmacht* during the later years of World War II and was produced in both 4x2 and 4x4 configurations. The road-going L4500S 4x2 variant was launched in 1939 and remained in production until 1944. The off-road L4500A 4x4 was introduced in 1941 and continued to be built until 1944. The Austrian company Saurer also produced the L4500A during 1944 and 1945, and the total number of both types built by the two companies was some 9,000.

Power was provided by a 7,274cc six-cylinder diesel engine driving the rear wheels through a five-speed gearbox with overdrive top gear. For the all-wheel drive variant, there was a two-speed auxiliary gearbox that included the transfer gears. Suspension was by semi-elliptical leaf springs.

In original form, the truck was fitted with an all-steel enclosed cab. But from around 1943, continued shortages of materials led to the adoption of the *Einheits* cab, made from pressed cardboard and timber. Most were bodied as cargo vehicles but there were also other body types, including shop vans. The chassis was used

as a mounting for 3-, 5- and 8-ton cranes. The vehicle was used as a self-propelled mount for the 37cm FlaK gun. Some 1,480 were adapted for use as a heavy *Maultier* (Mule) by fitting a tracked bogie at the rear. This was designated L4500R.

The L4500S was put back into production after the war for civilian customers and another 1,500 of the vehicle were manufactured.

BELOW: **The *Maultier* (Mule) Mercedes-Benz 4500R fitted with a 7,274cc six-cylinder diesel engine.**

Mercedes-Benz L4500A, L4500S

Type: Truck, cargo, 4¹/₂-ton, 4x4
Manufacturer: Daimler-Benz; Stuttgart
Production: 1939 to 1944
Powerplant: Daimler-Benz OM67/4; six cylinders in-line; diesel; water-cooled; 7,274cc; overhead valves; power output, 112bhp at 2,250rpm
Transmission: L4500S, 5F1R; 4x2. L4500A, 5F1Rx2; part-time 4x4
Suspension: Live axles on semi-elliptical multi-leaf springs, inverted at the rear
Brakes: Hydraulic front, air-pressure rear
Electrical system: 12V
Dimensions: Length – 7,860mm/309in
　Width – 2,350mm/93in
　Height – L4500S, 3,215mm/127in;
　L4500A, 3,345mm/132in
　Wheelbase – 4,600mm/181in
Weight: Unladen – L4500S, 4,930kg/10,846lb;
　L4500A, 5,715kg/12,573lb
　Payload – L4500S, 4,950kg/10,913lb;
　L4500A, road 4,685kg/10,328lb,
　cross-country 4,085kg/9,006lb
Performance: Maximum speed – 66kph/41mph

Mercedes-Benz G Class

The military vehicle that is universally known as the G-Wagen was first manufactured by the Austrian company Gelaendewagenfahrzeug Gessellschaft (GFG) in 1979. Although it was originally sold on the civilian market, the design had been inspired by proposals for a military vehicle by Shah Mohammad Reza Pahlavi of Iran in the early 1970s.

At the time, GFG was part-owned by Mercedes-Benz and Steyr-Daimler-Puch. When GFG closed down in the early 1980s, Steyr-Daimler-Puch continued to produce the vehicle under direct contract to Mercedes-Benz. In 1980, Peugeot entered the vehicle in a competition held by the French Army to find a replacement for the ageing Hotchkiss M201 Jeep. The Peugeot entry was selected against competition from Citroën and Renault, and entered service as the Peugeot licence-built P4 in 1982.

The Austrian-built original is generally now described as the Mercedes-Benz G Class and has undergone continuous development since it was first launched. The vehicle was originally produced in a choice of two wheelbases – 2,400mm/94in and 2,850mm/112in – but the original shorter wheelbase has been discontinued and a new 3,428mm/135in wheelbase has been added. There are currently four body variations: station wagon, van, open cargo vehicle (which can also be configured as a weapons mount) and chassis-cab for special body-work, including an ambulance for forward areas. A crew cab is also available, as are armoured variants. The engine is a 2,874cc five-cylinder turbocharged common-rail diesel driving both axles through a four-speed

ABOVE LEFT AND ABOVE: **The G-Wagen was introduced in 1979 as a commercial design and has remained in production ever since. Military users can choose between open and closed bodywork on a long- or short-wheelbase chassis.**

automatic gearbox and two-speed transfer box. Suspension is by live axles on coil springs located by longitudinal and transverse links. Both the front and rear axles include differential locks.

Since its launch, more than 60,000 Mercedes G Class have been supplied to more than 24 nations, including Germany, USA and Ireland.

The G Class is produced also under licence by the Hellenic Vehicle Industry in Greece as the 290GD.

LEFT: **Since 1979, more than 60,000 G-Wagen military vehicles have been produced and have been sold to more than 24 nations. A licence-built version was produced in France as the Peugeot P4. The G-Wagen is also manufactured by the Hellenic Vehicle Industry in Greece.**

Mercedes-Benz G Class

Type: Truck, personnel/cargo, 4x4
Manufacturer: Daimler; Stuttgart
Production: 1979 on
Powerplant: Mercedes-Benz OM602/DE29LA; five cylinders in-line; turbocharged diesel; water-cooled; 2,874cc; overhead valves; power output, 156bhp at 3,800rpm
Transmission: Automatic 5F1Rx2; part-time 4x4; differential locks front and rear
Suspension: Live axles on coil springs with longitudinal and transverse links; double-acting telescopic shock absorbers
Brakes: Vacuum servo-assisted hydraulic
Electrical system: 12V, 24V
Dimensions: Length – 4,165mm/164in
Width – 1,700mm/75in
Height – tilt in place, 2,005mm/86in
Wheelbase – 2,400mm/94in, 2,850mm/112in, 3,428mm/135in
Weight: Unladen – typical, 2,100kg/4,630lb
Payload – 500–2,000kg/1,102–4,409lb
Performance: Maximum speed – 138kph/86mph

Unimog U25, U402

The Unimog – the name is a contraction of *Universal Motor Gerät* (Universal Power Plant) – was designed by Albert Friedrich, former chief engineer of aviation engine research at Daimler-Benz. However, because Germany was not permitted to produce four-wheel drive vehicles, the pre-production models were assembled by Erhard & Söhn in Schwäbisch Gmünd. During 1949 and 1950

initial production was carried out by Gebr. Boehringer in Goppingen under a licence agreement. It was only in 1951 that Daimler-Benz received consent to build the Unimog and found space for a production line at Gaggenau.

Development had started in 1945 with the first prototype, powered by a 1,697cc petrol engine, ready by the end of 1947. The vehicle was unveiled to the public at Frankfurt am Main in August 1948, with deliveries beginning the following year. The first production model

was designated 70200 by Boehringer but by 1950 this had been changed to U25.

The vehicle was assembled around a steel channel-section ladder chassis. All production machines were diesel powered, at first utilizing the 1,697cc engine of the Mercedes-Benz 170. By 1951, there was a choice of either 1,720cc or 2,120cc engine.

The engine was coupled via an extended bell housing to a centre-mounted combined gearbox and transfer box. Short drive-shafts conveyed power to portal axles at front and rear. The axles incorporated self-locking differentials, and were suspended on coil springs. A power take-off on the side of the gearbox was used to drive a flat pulley situated on the right-hand side of the vehicle.

The intention was to produce a universal tractor/truck which could be used for industrial, agricultural and forestry work, but the Unimog was equally suitable for military usage. In 1950–51, the French Army became the first military customer, placing an order for 400 for use in the French-occupied zones of Germany. The *Bundeswehr* also acquired some early examples following the formation of the post-war German Army in 1955.

In 1953, the model designation was changed to U401 for the short-wheelbase model and U402 for the long-wheelbase. These models remained in production until 1956, by which time 16,250 had been built.

Unimog U25, U402

Type: Truck, 1-ton, prime mover, 4x4
Manufacturer: Daimler-Benz Unimog; Gaggenau
Production: 1949 to 1956
Powerplant: Mercedes-Benz; four cylinders in-line; diesel; water-cooled; 1,697cc, 1,720cc, 2,120cc; overhead valves; power output, 34–45bhp at 2,500rpm
Transmission: 6F2Rx2; part-time 4x4
Suspension: Live portal axles on coil springs; hydraulic shock absorbers
Brakes: Hydraulic
Electrical system: 12V
Dimensions: Length – 3,520mm/139in
　　Width – 1,630mm/64in
　　Height – tilt in place, 2,050mm/81in; minimum, 1,600mm/63in
　　Wheelbase – 1,720mm/68in
Weight: Unladen – 1,700kg/3,740lb
　　Payload – 1,000kg/2,240lb
Performance: Maximum speed – 65kph/40mph

ABOVE: **Following its formation in 1955, the West German Army (*Bundeswehr*) acquired some early Unimogs. Note how the portal-type axles provide high ground clearance. RIGHT: The original Unimog was designed as a dual-purpose universal tractor/truck for both industrial and agricultural use but was equally suitable for military usage. The first military versions were supplied to the French Army.**

Unimog S404

The 1½-ton Unimog Model S was effectively an enlarged and improved version of the original civilian-based U25/U402. The S404 was designed as a military machine, originally intended for the embryonic *Bundeswehr*, at that time restricted to the role of internal security. Daimler-Benz had started to produce development models as early as 1953, but the vehicle did not enter production until 1955, the first production variant being the military S404.

ABOVE: **The definitive military version of the Unimog is the S404 which was widely used by the *Bundeswehr* and by other armies in the NATO alliance.**

There were strong visual and technical similarities with the original U25/U402. However, where, for example, early prototypes for the Model S had retained the rather flat, angular front of the original U25/U402 models, extended to accommodate the larger engine, on the production version the windscreen was moved forward and the bonnet shortened. At the same time, the front was made more rounded with a stylized full-width radiator grille carrying the distinctive Mercedes three-pointed star.

Under NATO pressure, the diesel of the original design was removed in favour of the Daimler-Benz M180, a 2,195cc six-cylinder overhead-camshaft petrol engine. Although it was down-rated for use in this vehicle, specifically having a lower compression ratio and a single carburettor, it was essentially the same as that in the Mercedes-Benz 220 and 230 cars of the 1950s and 1960s. Transmission was by a six-speed all-synchromesh gearbox driving through a two-speed transfer box with selectable four-wheel drive. Both axles had manual differential locks and these, as well as the front-wheel drive, could be selected on the move in any gear. A crucial feature of the first Unimog design has always been the high ground clearance achieved by the use of portal-type axles and large wheels.

LEFT: **Unlike the original diesel-engined U25, the S404 was powered by a 2,195cc Mercedes-Benz M180 water-cooled petrol engine.**

The S404 was effectively hand-built and offered with a choice of engine, body and cab options as well as a wide range of additional equipment. The basic cab options included the open-cabbed S404 and the metal-cabbed S404.1. The latter was often fitted with a roof hatch. There were also single and crew-cab configurations. As regards the body, users could choose the standard 1¹/₂-ton cargo or box (*Kofferbau*) body, as well as special bodies such as ambulance, fire appliance, radio shelter and maintenance or decontamination unit. There was also a choice of engine-driven compressor, generator and winch, as well as auxiliary equipment, including a rear stabilizer bar, larger wheels and tyres, raised air-intake, sound insulation, power-assisted brakes, auxiliary fuel pump, steering-protection plate, larger generator and engine/battery heater. During the production run, the truck was made available in a choice of two standard wheelbase lengths – the S404, S416 and S421 had a 2,900mm/114in wheelbase, while the equivalent length for the S406 and S411 was 1,720mm/68in.

Once again, it seems that the French were the first military customers for the U404s, ordering 1,100. Throughout the life of the vehicle, the *Bundeswehr* was a dedicated user. Other military buyers included the British and US armies (for use in West Germany) as well as Argentina, Austria, Belgium, Finland, Greece, India, Jordan, Netherlands, Switzerland and Turkey. The Unimog was also a popular choice with the German civil authorities and was frequently equipped as a fire tender or rescue vehicle. In 1963, a steel-cabbed variant, the S406, was made available for civilian customers.

ABOVE: **The S404 was available with a choice of open and closed cabs and also cargo and box bodies. This example also has a front-mounted winch.**

An "Armoured-Personnel Carrier" (APC) variant was produced by the Swedish company Landsverk between 1956 and 1960 for the Belgian Army. In 1960, the Swedish Government stopped delivery of the last 15 when civil war erupted in the Belgian Congo. Following a period in storage, they were supplied to the Irish Defence Force in 1971–72.

With a production run of 64,242 units over nearly 20 years, the Unimog S was the most numerous and successful of the type.

LEFT: **Despite the use of live axles, suspended on nothing more sophisticated than coil springs, the Unimog was always capable of negotiating the most extreme terrain.**

Unimog S404

Type: Truck, 1¹/₂-ton, cargo, 4x4
Manufacturer: Daimler-Benz Unimog; Gaggenau
Production: 1955 to 1972
Powerplant: Mercedes-Benz M180; six cylinders in-line; petrol; water-cooled; 2,195cc; overhead valves; power output, 80bhp at 4,850rpm
Transmission: 6F2Rx2; part-time 4x4
Suspension: Live portal axles on coil springs; hydraulic shock absorbers
Brakes: Hydraulic
Electrical system: 12V
Dimensions: Length – 4,925mm/194in
Width – 2,141mm/84in
Height – tilt in place, 2,540mm/100in; minimum, 2,190mm/86in
Wheelbase – 2,900mm/114in
Weight: Unladen – 2,000kg/4,409lb
Payload – 1,500kg/3,307lb
Performance: Maximum speed – 95kph/60mph

Opel *Blitz S*

Opel was founded in Rüsselsheim in 1862, at first producing sewing machines and bicycles but moving into motor car production in 1899. The company's first trucks appeared in 1912. General Motors acquired all of the stock of Opel between 1928 and 1931. By 1937, GM-Opel was the largest German truck manufacturer. Three years later, Opel had built a total of one million vehicles and supplied 31,674 *Blitz* (Lightning) trucks to the *Wehrmacht*.

Launched in 1930, the original *Blitz* range was a family of trucks covering load ratings of 1, 1¹⁄₂ and 2 tons. In 1934, Opel started building a new factory at Brandenburg on the Havel river. The first new product of the factory was a replacement for the 1930 *Blitz*.

The new vehicle, known as the *Blitz S*, was a modern truck with an all-steel two-door cab, very much in the American style. It was powered by the original 3,417cc engine, driving the rear axle through a new five-speed gearbox. In 1937, the original engine was replaced by a new 3,626cc unit. By this time, the *Blitz* was being offered as the 3-ton Model 3.6-36, which was favoured by the *Wehrmacht* in the "medium" truck category, together with the Models 3.6-42 and 3.6-47. In 1938, the 1¹⁄₂-ton Model 2.5-32 was added to the range, remaining in

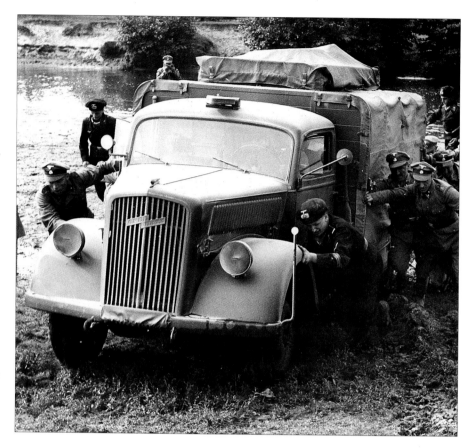

production until 1942, and used by the military in the "light" category.

Most military types were fitted a standard general-purpose wooden cargo body. There were other standardized variants including a fire-fighter, tanker, radio van, shop or office van and water-purification plant (*Wasseraufbereitungs*). A bus which could be used as a troop carrier or large ambulance was also built.

In 1940, a military all-wheel-drive variant was added to the range. Designated Model 3.6-6700 Typ A – or simply 6700A – the "A" indicating *Allradantreib* (all-wheel drive), the vehicle was fitted with a two-speed transfer box which used a single control to both select the low ratios and engage the front axle.

In 1940, the government took control of the Opel factories and all civilian production ceased, but the *Blitz* continued to be produced for the *Wehrmacht*. From October 1943, shortages of raw materials

led to the replacement of the steel cab with the utility *Einheits* cab made from pressed cardboard and timber.

More than 120,000 *Blitz* were built before production ceased in 1944. The chassis was also selected for conversion to the 2-ton half-tracked *Maultier* (Mule).

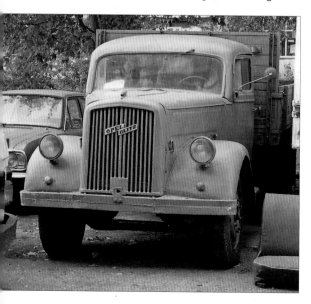

ABOVE AND LEFT: **More than 120,000 Opel *Blitz* were manufactured between 1937 and 1944, with 4x2 and 4x4 variants produced.**

Opel *Blitz S*

Type: Truck, medium, cargo, 4x2 or 4x4
Manufacturer: Adam Opel; Rüsselsheim
Production: 1937 to 1944
Powerplant: Opel; six cylinders in-line; petrol; water-cooled; 3,417cc (1936 only) or 3,626cc; overhead valves; power output, 75bhp at 3,000rpm
Transmission: Model 3.6-36, 5F1R, 4x2; Model 3.6-6700A, 5F1Rx2; part-time 4x4
Suspension: Live axles suspended on semi-elliptical multi-leaf springs
Brakes: Hydraulic
Electrical system: 12V
Dimensions: Length – 3,450mm/136in
Width – 2,265mm/89in
Height – tilt in place, 2,825mm/111in; minimum, 2,175mm/86in
Wheelbase – Model 3.6-36, 3,330mm/131in; Model 3.6-6700A, 3,450mm/136in
Weight: Unladen – 2,710kg/5974lb
Payload – road, 3,500kg/7,716lb; cross-country, 3,000kg/6,614lb
Performance: Maximum speed – 85kph/53mph

LEFT: **The Phänomen**
Granit **25H dates from**
the mid-1930s and
was essentially a
commercial truck
chassis. It was replaced
in 1940 by the updated
Granit **1500, built as**
a 4x2 and 4x4.

Phänomen *Granit* 1500S, 1500A

The Phänomen-Werke, Zittau, was established by Gustav Hiller in 1888, at first to produce bicycles and motorcycles. The Phänomobil motor car was launched in 1907. From 1927 onwards, when the company name was changed to Phänomen, only commercial vehicles were produced. The company specialized in lightweight trucks, at first powered by a 1,550cc V2 air-cooled petrol engine, but soon

BELOW: **The standard variant was fitted with a**
drop-side timber cargo body, but the chassis
was also often used for an ambulance or box van.

upgraded to 2,678cc. The trucks acquired a reputation for reliability and were widely used as mail vans and civilian ambulances, as well as being supplied to the German Army.

The updated *Granit* range, now with four-cylinder air-cooled engine, was introduced in 1940, replacing the earlier 25H. Rated at 1½ tons, it was available with two-wheel drive (1500S) and from 1942 and more rarely, with all-wheel drive (1500A). The two-wheel-drive variant was fitted with twinned rear wheels, but larger single wheels were used on the 1500A. Both types had a four-speed gearbox.

The all-wheel-drive variant was fitted with a two-speed transfer box.

Both cargo and box van types were procured by the *Wehrmacht* in relatively large numbers from 1940, the 4x2 and 4x4 van being widely used as a field ambulance (*Krankenwagen*).

After the end of World War II, Phänomen-Werke, Zittau, was in the Soviet Zone. But vehicles continued to be produced under the IFA Robur *Granit* name until 1956.

Phänomen *Granit* 1500S, 1500A

Type: Truck, 1½-ton, 4x2, 4x4
Manufacturer: Gustav Hiller,
   Phänomen-Werke; Zittau
Production: 1940 to 1944
Powerplant: Phänomen Granit 27; four cylinders
   in-line; petrol; air-cooled; 2,678cc; side valves;
   power output, 50bhp at 2,800rpm
Transmission: Model 1500S, 4F1Rx2; 4x2 (1500S);
   Model 1500A, part-time 4x4
Suspension: Live axles on semi-elliptical
   multi-leaf springs
Brakes: Hydraulic
Electrical system: 12V
Dimensions: Length – 5,490mm/216in
   Width – 1,980mm/78in
   Height – 2,160mm/85in
   Wheelbase – 3,270mm/129in
Weight: Unladen – 2,215kg/4,883lb
   Payload – 1,400–1,600kg/3,086–3,527lb
Performance: Maximum speed – 80kph/50mph

LEFT: **The Stoewer version of the *leichter Geländegangige Personenkraftwagen* for the *Wehrmacht* was introduced in 1936 as the R180 and remained in production until 1943. The designation was changed to R200 in 1938 then to R200 Typ AW2 in 1940.**

Stoewer R200 *Spezial*

Stoewer-Werke manufactured the R180 *Spezial* (Special) four- to five-seat cross-country car between 1936 and 1938, when it was replaced by the larger engined R200 which remained in production until 1940. Between 1937 and 1940, similar vehicles were also produced by BMW (*Typ* 325) and Hanomag (*Typ* 20B). Although the products of each manufacturer differed, both in detail and in the choice of power unit, the vehicle was designed on what was described as the *Einheits Leicht Geländegangige Personenkraftwagen* chassis – "standardized light field car".

Unfortunately, the intended interchangeability of power units was compromised by details such as differing fuel supply and exhaust outlet positions. From 1940, the introduction of the *Typ* 40 AW2 variant saw all production moved to the Stoewer factory and the adoption of the Stoewer 1,997cc engine as the standard power unit.

Regardless of origin, the engine was linked to the wheels via a five-speed gearbox and single-speed transfer box. Self-locking differentials were fitted in both axles as well as in the transfer box. Suspension was independent on all four wheels, using upper and lower wishbones and coil springs. The earliest examples had four-wheel steering and four-wheel drive, but this proved to offer no particular advantage in off-road use and was eventually abandoned as being dangerous.

Alongside the four- to five-seat field car (Kfz 1), standard variants included a communications vehicle (Kfz 2), maintenance/repair vehicle (Kfz 2/40) and surveillance vehicle (Kfz 3). In all cases, the bodies were built by Ambi-Budd Stanzerie, Berlin.

Some problems arose when the vehicle was operated under the extreme conditions encountered on the Eastern Front, but it was generally a useful and reliable vehicle. Total production amounted to some 13,000 vehicles over an almost eight-year period.

LEFT: **Early examples of the vehicle were fitted with a four-wheel steering system which was intended to be locked out at speeds above 25kph/16mph. The feature was eventually abandoned as being dangerous.**

Stoewer R200 *Spezial*

Type: Car, light, four seat, 4x2; Kfz 1
Manufacturer: Stoewer-Werke; Stettin
Production: 1936 to 1943
Powerplant: Stoewer AW2; four cylinders in-line; petrol; water-cooled; 1,997cc; overhead valves; power output, 48bhp at 3,600rpm. Up to 1940, alternative engines include BMW (six cylinders, 1,957cc), and Hanomag (four cylinders, 1,991cc)
Transmission: 5F1R; part-time 4x4; axle and inter-axle self-locking differentials
Suspension: Independent suspension at all four wheels using twin wishbones and coil springs
Brakes: Mechanical
Electrical system: 12V
Dimensions: Length – 3,900mm/154in
  Width – 1,690mm/67in
  Height – tilt in place, 1,900mm/75in
  Wheelbase – 2,400mm/94in
Weight: Unladen – 1,780kg/3,924lb
  Payload – 420kg/926lb
Performance: Maximum speed – 80kph/50mph

LEFT: **A G1200 built to** *Wehrmacht* **specifications. The vehicle was fitted with four-wheel drive and selectable all-wheel steering. A revolving spare wheel was mounted on each side to prevent gounding.**

Tempo G1200

Type: Car, light, four seat, 4x4
Manufacturer: Vidal & Söhn, Tempo-Werke; Hamburg
Production: 1936 to 1939
Powerplant: ILO; two cylinders in-line; 2x 596cc; petrol; two-stroke; air-cooled; power output, 2x 19bhp
Transmission: 4F1R; part-time 4x4
Suspension: Independent suspension front and rear, by swing axles and coil springs
Brakes: Mechanical
Electrical system: 6V
Dimensions: Length – 4,000mm/157in
Width – 1,680mm/66in
Height – minimum, 1,500mm/59in
Wheelbase – 2,830mm/111in
Weight: Unladen – 1,060kg/2,332lb
Performance: Not available

Tempo G1200

Tempo began manufacturing motorcycles in 1926. Following the acquisition of the manufacturing rights to the Vidal & Söhn three-wheeler in 1928, they turned to producing motor cars. Dating from 1936, the G1200 car designed by Ing Otto Daus was developed as a private venture for military use. By any standards, it was one of the most unusual vehicles of the period, by virtue of using two engines to provide four-wheel drive.

Each of the two axles was driven by a 596cc two-cylinder air-cooled engine through a four-speed gearbox. The drive could select to run one or both engines. There was also selectable four-wheel steering. The suspension was independent, front and rear, by means of swing axles and coil springs. Most of the vehicles were fitted with a four-seat open body, but a small number had doors. The G1200 was supplied to the *Wehrmacht* and to the armies of Sweden, Romania, Argentina and Mexico.

Tempo-Rover

Although Tempo stopped making motor cars in 1940, the company continued to produce light trucks after the war. In 1952, the West German Army's *Grenzschütz* (Border Guard) invited bids for a six-seat cross-country vehicle for patrolling the country's eastern border. The most satisfactory of the vehicles trialled for the role was the Land Rover Series I, but the service was obliged to purchase a German vehicle. Tempo approached Rover for a licence to assemble the Land Rover in Germany and the result was the Tempo-Rover.

Between April and August 1953, approximatley 100 to 189 vehicles were assembled at Tempo-Werke, Hamburg, using complete rolling 2,030mm/80in chassis and bulkheads supplied from the UK. Although broadly resembling the

Tempo-Rover

Type: Car, six seat, 4x4
Manufacturer: Vidal & Söhn, Tempo-Werke; Hamburg
Production: 1953 to 1954
Powerplant: Rover; four cylinders in-line; 1,997cc; petrol; water-cooled; overhead inlet valves, side exhaust; power output, 52bhp at 4,000rpm
Transmission: 4F1Rx2; part-time 4x4
Suspension: Live axles on semi-elliptical multi-leaf springs; hydraulic double-acting shock absorbers
Brakes: Hydraulic
Electrical system: 12V
Dimensions: Length – 3,700mm/147in
Width – 1,550mm/61in
Height – tilt in place, 1,930mm/76in; minimum, 1,420mm/56in
Wheelbase – 2,030mm/80in, 2,180mm/86in
Weight: Unladen – 1,422kg/3,138lb
Payload – 625kg/1,375lb
Performance: Maximum speed – 89kph/55mph

LEFT: **A radio-equipped Tempo of the** *Grenschütz*. **Storage lockers were also incorporated in the front wings.**

standard Land Rover, the bodies were built by Herbert Vidal & Söhn and differed in many respects, most notably in the use of steel rather than aluminium. In 1954, up to 187 further examples were assembled using the 2,180mm/86in wheelbase chassis which had replaced the original 2,030mm/80in in the UK.

Volkswagen *Typ 82 Kübelwagen*

The Volkswagen *Kübelwagen* – "Bucket" or "Cube" car because of its simple bodywork – was the closest vehicle the *Wehrmacht* had to the US-built Jeep during World War II. The *Kübelwagen* had independent suspension which ensured a high standard of road-holding and the vehicle's light weight meant that it could perform equally well on most surfaces. Despite the use of special balloon tyres, it was never particularly good on loose sand due to the lack of four-wheel drive. On the road fuel economy was very good.

The *Kübelwagen* or, the correct military designation, *leicht Kraftpersonenwagen*, Kfz 1, was effectively a militarized version of Ferdinand Porsche's iconic "Beetle". Work on the design of a military "Beetle" had begun in 1938 and the first prototype was ready by the end of the year. Early pre-production models were available in December 1939 in time for the invasion of Poland. The first standard production examples – described by Porsche as the *Typ 82* – were manufactured during February 1940, with the first 25 vehicles being built in Stuttgart. From May 1940 onwards, production took place at the Fallersleben factory. The vehicle was first used in action in Russia and North Africa in 1941, the air-cooled engine ensuring rugged reliability in either climatic extreme.

The *Kübelwagen* had a backbone-and-platform chassis used on the standard "Beetle" and, with some modification,

ABOVE: **Based on the backbone-and-platform chassis of the standard VW "Beetle" and sharing many mechanical components, the Porsche-designed *Typ 82 Kübelwagen* was the closest vehicle the *Wehrmacht* had to the US-built Jeep. Although the vehicle lacked all-wheel drive, the light weight and an air-cooled engine were distinct benefits in harsh conditions.**

most of the mechanical components from the same vehicle. Power came from a 985cc four-cylinder horizontally opposed air-cooled engine mounted in a fork between the chassis members, low down at the rear. The engine was bored out to 1,131cc in March 1943, increasing output from 23.5bhp to 25bhp. The drive from the engine was transmitted through a single dry-plate clutch to a four-speed non-synchromesh gearbox with an overdrive top gear. Drive to the rear wheels was through a limited-slip ZF differential. Reduction gears were used in the rear hubs.

Suspension was independent at all four wheels by means of laminated torsion bars; at the front these were contained within the tubular cross members.

The angular, flat-panelled four/five-seat open body was built by the American-owned company Ambi-Budd Stanzerie at their Johannesthall factory, Berlin. The body was little more than a rectangular tub of ribbed pressed steel, with curved projecting wings to cover the wheels at the four

ABOVE: **The simple, flat-panelled body that gave the vehicle its nickname** (*Kübelwagen* – "Bucket" or "Cube" car) **provided reasonably comfortable accommodation for four. Other variants were produced, including radio, survey and maintenance/repair vehicles.**

corners. A simple, top-hinged flat cover was provided for the engine compartment at the rear. The spare wheel was placed on top of the sloping front compartment, either in a recess or on a boss. Four un-trimmed steel doors, hinged on the centre pillar, provided access. The body was strengthened by means of a transverse beam across the door pillars which also served as a grab rail for the occupants. Small headlamps were mounted on the front wings, with the inevitable Notek blackout light on the front panel. Inside, there were four thinly upholstered seats covered with coated cloth, and wooden duckboards covered the floor.

Instrumentation was minimal. A canvas hood, supported on a folding frame, provided weather protection. Sidescreens were designed to be attached to the door tops to make a complete enclosure.

During its six years of production 48,454 were built. Along with the basic four-seat personnel car, standard variants included a three-seat command car (Kfz 3), radio communications vehicle (Kfz 2) and an automotive repair car (Kfz 2/40). There were experimental variants produced as a dummy tank. In the manner of the Jeep, there was also a field ambulance conversion. Some work was done on two four-wheel-drive prototypes (*Typ* 86 and *Typ* 87); also on an experimental half-tracked version (*Typ* 155). None entered production.

ABOVE: **Unlike the US-built Jeep, which was not provided with satisfactory weather protection, the *Kübelwagen* had shoulder-high doors fitted with sidescreens and a weatherproof roof.**

Volkswagen *Typ 82* Kübelwagen

Type: Car, light, four seat, 4x2; Kfz 1
Manufacturer: KDF Volkswagen; Wolfsburg
Production: 1940 to 1945
Powerplant: VW; four cylinders horizontally opposed; 985cc or 1,131cc; petrol; overhead valves; air-cooled; power output, 23.5–25hp at 3,000rpm
Transmission: 4F1R; 4x2; limited-slip differential
Suspension: Independent suspension by swing axles and torsion bars
Brakes: Mechanical
Electrical system: 6V
Dimensions: Length – 3,740mm/147in
Width – 1,600mm/63in
Height – tilt erected, 1,650mm/65in; minimum, 1,111mm/44in
Wheelbase – 2,400mm/96in
Weight: Unladen – 685kg/1,510lb
Payload – 450kg/992lb
Performance: Maximum speed – 80kph/50mph

RIGHT: **The VW** *Typ* **166** *Schwimmwagen* **was effectively a four-wheel drive amphibious version of the** *Kübelwagen.* **With all-wheel drive, the vehicle had excellent off-road performance.**

Volkswagen *Typ* 166 K2s

The *Schwimmwagen* – or, simply *Schwimmer* – was an amphibious version of the standard *Kübelwagen* light field car, sharing the same basic rear-engined layout as well as engine and suspension components. It was originally intended for use on the Eastern Front where, unlike the *Kübelwagen*, conditions called for four-wheel drive. Design work started in July 1940, with the first prototype – the *Typ* 128 – available for testing in September of that year. The inevitable teething problems meant that the vehicle was not approved for production until March 1942 but, by the end of the war, some 14,250 examples had been constructed.

As in the *Kübelwagen*, the engine was the familiar horizontally opposed

air-cooled four-cylinder unit of the VW "Beetle". Aside from the first 150 vehicles – designated *Typ* 138 – which were constructed by Porsche for extended field trials, all of the production *Typ* 166 *Schwimmwagen* used the more powerful 1,131cc version of the engine. There was a new five-speed gearbox, in combination with selectable all-wheel drive through a single-speed transfer box. With independent suspension at all four wheels using swing arms and torsion bars, combined with the use of self-locking differentials, the vehicle offered almost unstoppable cross-country performance even where amphibious operation was not required. However, the use of mechanical brakes was an oddly archaic touch.

The mechanical components were assembled into a boat-shaped welded-steel watertight hull fabricated by Ambi-Budd, which provided accommodation for a driver and three passengers. Access to the rear-mounted engine was via a horizontal hinged cover, and there were twin fuel tanks in the front. The windscreen could be folded forward and there was a simple canvas roof which could be erected to provide weather protection.

LEFT: **The** *Schwimmwagen's* **propeller was lowered manually to engage with a dog clutch attached to a power take-off from the engine.**

Propulsion in the water was achieved via a hinged propeller unit manually swung down and locked to engage with a drive dog on the front of the engine crankshaft. No reverse gear was available in the water, and when afloat the vehicle was steered by the front wheels.

Prototypes were initially produced by both Porsche and Volkswagen, but most of the production vehicles were produced by Volkswagen at Wolfsburg.

Volkswagen *Typ* 166 K2s

Type: Car, light, amphibious, 4x4
Manufacturer: KDF Volkswagen; Wolfsburg. Porsche; Stuttgart
Production: 1942 to 1944
Powerplant: VW; four cylinders horizontally opposed; 1,131cc; petrol; overhead valves; air-cooled; power output, 25hp at 2,500rpm
Transmission: 5F1R; part-time 4x4; self-locking differentials; amphibious operation by hinged propeller
Suspension: Independent suspension by swing axles and torsion bars
Brakes: Mechanical
Electrical system: 6V
Dimensions: Length – 3,825mm/151in
Width – 1,480mm/58in
Height – tilt erected, 1,615mm/64in; minimum, 960mm/37in
Wheelbase – 2,000mm/79in
Weight: Unladen – 910kg/2,006lb
Performance: Maximum speed – 74kph/46mph; in water – 12kph/7.5mph

VEB G-5, G-5/2

Produced by the Ernst Grübe factory of the East German VEB (Volkseigener Betriebe or People's Enterprises), the 3½-ton G-5 6x6 was introduced in 1957 and quickly became the standard truck of the East German Army.

The design was entirely conventional, with a front-mounted six-cylinder diesel engine driving all axles through a five-speed gearbox, with overdrive on top gear, and a two-speed transfer box. Suspension was by means of leaf springs all round. Early examples had an open cab, but this was replaced by an all-steel type in the G-5/2.

In the most numerous cargo form, the truck was fitted with a drop-side timber body but there were also many other variants.

The G-5 was superseded by the upgraded G-5/2 in 1958, but the planned air-cooled G-5/3 was not produced.

LEFT: **VEB G-5 trucks at an East German May Day parade.**

VEB G-5, G-5/2

Type: Truck, 3½-ton, cargo, 6x6
Manufacturer: VEB Kraftfahrzeugwerk Ernst Grübe; Sachsen
Production: 1957 to 1961
Powerplant: EMb W6 (G-5) or W6-20 (G-5/2); six cylinders in-line; diesel; water-cooled; 9,036cc (G-5) or 9,840cc (G-5/2); overhead valves; power output, 120–150bhp at 2,000rpm
Transmission: 5F1Rx2; part-time 6x6
Suspension: Live axles on multi-leaf semi-elliptical springs
Brakes: Air pressure
Electrical system: 24V
Dimensions: Length – 7,170mm/282in
 Width – 2,500mm/98in
 Height – tilt in place, 3,000mm/118in; minimum, 2,600mm/102in
 Wheelbase – 4,420mm/174in
 Bogie centres – 1,250mm/49in
Weight: Unladen – 7,850kg/17,306lb
 Payload – road, 5,000kg/11,023lb; cross-country, 3,500kg/7,716lb
Performance: Maximum speed – 105kph/65mph

Trabant P601A

After the end of World War II, the East German provinces came under Soviet control, and the former Auto Union factory at Zwickau, which had produced Horch and Audi cars, became part of the State-owned IFA (Industrie-Vereinigung Volkseigner

Trabant P601A

Type: Field car, four seat, 4x2
Manufacturer: VEB Sachsenring Automobilwerke; Zwickau
Production: 1964 to 1988
Powerplant: P60; two-cylinders in-line; two-stroke petrol; air cooled; 595cc; power output, 26bhp at 4,200rpm
Transmission: 4F1R; freewheel on top gear; 4x2
Suspension: Independent suspension using transverse leaf spring at front and swing axles with coil-over shock absorber struts at rear
Brakes: Hydraulic
Electrical system: 12V
Dimensions: Length – 3,480mm/137in
 Width – 1,498mm/59in
 Height – 1,498mm/59in
 Wheelbase – 2,006mm/79in
Weight: Unladen – 645kg/1,422lb
Performance: Maximum speed – 100kph/62mph

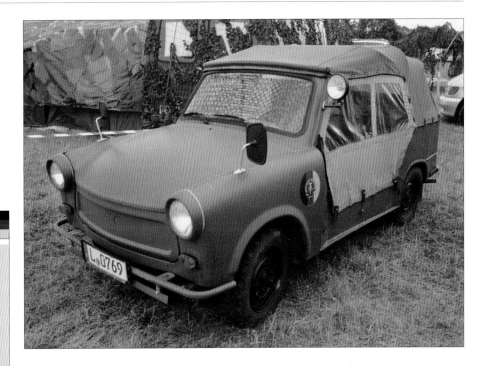

ABOVE: **An open field car, military designation P601A (known as the *Grentztrabant*), was used by the East German Border Police.**

Fahrzeugwerke), an administrative group of nationalized manufacturers.

In 1948, car production commenced with the two-cylinder two-stroke F8, later renamed P70. Shortages of steel meant that the body was moulded from a composite of phenolic resin reinforced with linen, wool or cotton fibres known as Duroplast. In 1959, the same technology was incorporated into the Trabant P50, a small four-seat car. In 1962, the design was modified and the vehicle was renamed P60. Two years later, the familiar Trabant P601 was launched, still with a Duroplast body.

Csepel 130

The Csepel Engineering Works was established in Budapest in 1950, to manufacture commercial and military vehicles for the domestic market. Exports were handled through the Hungarian state-owned Mogurt organization.

The 1-ton Csepel 130, which dates from 1951, was a purpose-designed military vehicle with more than a passing resemblance to the Dodge WC series. Standard variants included an open cargo vehicle, available with or without a winch, as well as a box-bodied van and ambulance.

Sharing mechanical components with the company's militarized D350 truck, the Csepel 130 used a petrol version of the company's D413

LEFT: **The Csepel 130 is very similar looking to the Dodge WC series of World War II.**

diesel engine, driving both axles through a five-speed gearbox. Suspension was by multi-leaf semi-elliptical springs. In the late 1970s, the company name was changed to Csepel Autogyar.

Csepel 130

Type: Truck, 1-ton, cargo, 4x4
Manufacturer: Csepel Engineering Works; Budapest
Production: 1951 on
Powerplant: Csepel; four cylinders in-line; petrol; water-cooled; 5,322cc; overhead valves; power output, 85bhp at 2,200rpm
Transmission: 5F1R; part-time 4x4
Suspension: Live axles on semi-elliptical multi-leaf springs; hydraulic double-acting telescopic shock absorbers
Brakes: Hydraulic
Electrical system: 12V
Dimensions: Length – 4,840mm/191in
　　Width – 2,150mm/85in
　　Height – minimum, 2,070mm/81in
　　Wheelbase – 3,000mm/118in
Weight: Unladen – 3,500kg/7,716lb
　　Payload – 1,300kg/2,867lb
Performance: Maximum speed – 80kph/50mph

Rába Botond

Rába Magyar Vagon és Gépgyár (MAVAG) started producing trucks in 1904, acquiring a licence to build the Praga 5-ton model in 1912. During World War I, the company built 2- and 3-ton 4x2 trucks under Praga licence and, by 1920, was licence-building Krupp models.

The Botond A was a 1¹/₂-ton 6x4 anti-aircraft gun tractor. It was designed by

Dezsö Winkler in 1936–37 and entered production at MAVAG and four other companies in 1938. The truck was powered by a 3,770cc engine driving two worm-gear axles at the rear, through a five-speed gearbox. It was replaced by

BELOW: **Production continued after the war, but only five vehicles were built between 1948 and 1950.**

the Botond B in 1942, which used a 4,330cc engine and had self-locking differentials but was otherwise similar.

The timber rear body provided accommodation for a two-man crew together with a gun crew of 14.

Rába Botond

Type: Truck, 1¹/₂-ton, tractor, 6x4
Manufacturer: Rába Magyar Vagon és Gépgyár (MAVAG); Györ
Production: 1938 to 1948
Powerplant: Rába; four cylinders in-line; petrol; water-cooled; 3,770cc, 4,330cc; overhead valves; power output, 65–70bhp at 3,800rpm
Transmission: 5F1Rx2; part-time 4x4
Suspension: Live front axle on semi-elliptical multi-leaf springs; independent suspension at rear using balancing beam and coil springs
Brakes: Hydraulic
Electrical system: 12V
Dimensions: Length – 5,746mm/226in
　　Width – 2,080mm/82in
　　Height – tilt in place, 2,550mm/100in
　　Wheelbase – 3,030mm/119in
Weight: Unladen – 3,950kg/8,708lb
　　Payload – 1,500kg/3,307lb
Performance: Maximum speed – 60kph/37mph

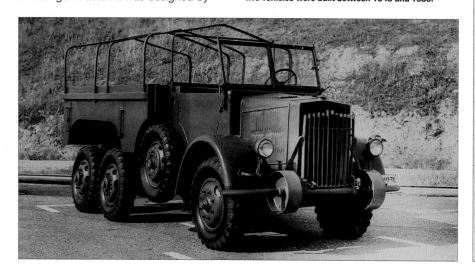

Mahindra CJ3B

In 1947, Mahindra began assembling Willys CJ2A Jeeps under licence at their Mumbai (Bombay) engineering works. By the early 1950s, they were manufacturing their own versions. The first of these was the CJ3B Universal Jeep which had been launched in the USA in 1953 and which Mahindra started to manufacture under licence from 1954. Both military and civilian versions were produced.

Although the CJ3B was probably Jeep's first really new post-war product, in truth, it differed little from the World War II original. The most significant change was the use of the Willys Hurricane F-head engine in place of the side-valve Go-Devil. The gearbox was a three-speed unit, installed in conjunction with a two-speed transfer box, and a 4x2 variant was also produced. There were live axles, front and rear, hung on multi-leaf semi-elliptical springs.

The vehicle was also used as a mount for the US-built 106mm M40 recoilless rifle. Mahindra continued to offer the CJ3B alongside the exclusively Indian CJ4 into the 1970s.

Mahindra CJ3B

Type: Truck, ¼-ton, utility, 4x4
Manufacturer: Mahindra & Mahindra; Mumbai
Production: From 1954 on
Powerplant: Licence-built Willys Hurricane; four cylinders in-line; petrol; water-cooled; 2,199cc; overhead inlet valves, side exhaust; power output, 72bhp at 4,000rpm. Diesel engine option also available
Transmission: 3F1Rx2; part-time 4x4, or 4x2
Suspension: Live axles on semi-elliptical multi-leaf springs
Brakes: Hydraulic
Electrical system: 12V
Dimensions: Length – 3,330mm/131in
Width – 1,750mm/69in
Height – minimum, 1,680mm/66in
Wheelbase – 2,030mm/80in
Weight: Unladen – 1,077kg/2,374lb
Payload – 545kg/1,201lb
Performance: Maximum speed – 100kph/62mph

LEFT: **An Indian Army CJ3B with a US-built 106mm M40 recoilless rifle.**

Shaktiman 415 L1AR

In 1958, the Indian State Ordnance Factory, Jabalpur acquired a licence to build MAN 415 L1AR 4-ton trucks. By 1963 a total of some 5,000 had been built. Early production used a high proportion of imported components, but this was gradually reduced until the trucks were almost entirely of Indian origin.

The vehicle was powered by a 5,880cc MAN multi-fuel engine, driving both axles through a five-speed gearbox and two-speed transfer box. A lockable torque-splitter was included in the transfer box, and the rear axle was fitted with a differential lock. Suspension was by multi-leaf semi-elliptical springs.

A simple, robust and reliable vehicle, it remained in service for more than four decades, eventually being replaced by Indian-built Ashok-Leyland and Tata vehicles.

BELOW: **The distinctive front of the Shaktiman 415 L1AR, powered by a 5,880cc MAN multi-fuel engine.**

Shaktiman 415 L1AR

Type: Truck, 3- to 5-ton, cargo, 4x4
Manufacturer: Indian State Ordnance Factory; Jabalpur
Production: 1958 to 2003
Powerplant: Licence-built MAN D0026M1; six cylinders in-line; multi-fuel diesel; water-cooled; 5,880cc; overhead valves; power output, 110bhp at 2,500rpm
Transmission: 5F1Rx2; part-time 4x4
Suspension: Live axles on semi-elliptical multi-leaf springs
Brakes: Air-assisted hydraulic at front, hydraulic at rear
Electrical system: Hybrid 12V/24V
Dimensions: Length – 7,163mm/282in
Width – 2,275mm/90in
Height – minimum, 2,413mm/95in
Wheelbase – 4,191mm/165in
Weight: Unladen – 2,540kg/5,600lb
Payload – road, 5,000kg/11,023lb; cross country, 3,000kg/6,614lb
Performance: Maximum speed – 72kph/45mph

Timoney 8x8

The Irish company, Timoney Technology, produced a series of technically advanced "Armoured Personnel Carriers" (APCs) for the Irish Defence Force in the 1970s, and has long been involved in the development of high-mobility suspension systems and related technology. Under the name Timoney High Mobility Vehicles, the company has also developed a high-mobility 8x8 truck as a demonstrator for a heavy-duty independent suspension system. The truck is effectively a front-engined development of an airfield crash/rescue truck, and was the first such vehicle with independent suspension to be supplied to the US Air Force.

Aside from the Timoney suspension system, the truck was of conventional design, using a Volvo six-cylinder turbocharged diesel engine driving through a Volvo six-speed automatic gearbox and Steyr two-speed transfer box. All-wheel steering was offered as an option. The cab was a Volvo commercial forward-control design with seating for a crew of two or three.

The use of independent suspension remains unusual for a truck of this size. The patented Timoney axle units, which were initially developed for the company's APC in 1972, were separate axle units rigidly attached directly to the chassis. The suspension is by double wishbones at each wheel, with twin variable-rate coil springs and concentric dampers allowing more than 400mm/16in of travel. A version of this system, which is also manufactured under licence in the US by Rockwell, was fitted to a high-mobility 6x6 carrier produced by the British Defence

ABOVE: **Timoney's heavy-duty suspension and chassis technology has been licensed to Volvo. Under this agreement the Swedish company took over manufacturing and marketing the Timoney high-mobility truck range.**

Equipment Research Agency (DERA). The same system was used on the TACOM 10x10 technology demonstrator, which was based on the Oshkosh 10x10 "Palletized Load System" (PLS) truck.

The standard body was a flat platform with removable drop-down side panels. The vehicle could also be equipped with a Multilift demountable rack (DROPS) load-handling system.

Other variants, none of which has progressed beyond the demonstrator stage, included 10x10, 6x6 and 4x4 truck chassis, and a 6x6 tractor.

ABOVE AND LEFT: **The Timoney independent suspension system is by double wishbones on each wheel, with twin variable-rate coil springs and concentric dampers. A version of this system was trialled on this 6x6 high-mobility cargo carrier produced by the British Defence Equipment Research Agency (DERA).**

Timoney 8x8

Type: Truck, cargo, 18-ton, 8x8
Manufacturer: Timoney High Mobility Vehicles; Navan, Co Meath
Production: 2000
Powerplant: Volvo D12A4220; six cylinders in-line; turbocharged diesel; water-cooled; 12,100cc; overhead valves; power output, 420bhp at 1,900rpm
Transmission: Automatic 6F2Rx2; cross-axle differential locks
Suspension: Independent at all eight wheels using double wishbones and twin variable-rate coil springs
Brakes: Air-pressure
Electrical system: 24V
Dimensions: Length – 9,155mm/360in
  Width – 2,500mm/98in
  Height – 3,200mm/125in
  Wheelbase – 7,898mm/311in
  Bogie centres – 1,524mm/60in
Weight: Unladen – 13,630kg/30,048lb
  Payload – 18,370kg/40,498lb
Performance: Maximum speed – 105kph/65mph

Alfa-Romeo 800RE

Although best known for sporting motor cars, (much favoured by Benito Mussolini) the Italian manufacturer Alfa-Romeo first started producing trucks in 1930. The earliest designs were based on German designs by Büssing-NAG, but by the end of the decade the company had developed its own vehicles. Alfa-Romeo became a significant supplier of military vehicles to the Italian Army during World War II. The 800RE was

BELOW: **Most examples were fitted with a wooden cargo body, but there was also a fire tender variant. The chassis was also used for an experimental half-track conversion.**

a 4x2 cargo truck introduced in 1940. It was allocated to the standardized 6¹/₂-ton "heavy" class (*Autocarro Unificato Pesante*), one of three standardized vehicle classes introduced in 1932 – light, medium and heavy – which laid down gross vehicle weights, payloads and basic dimensions.

Power came from an Alfa-Romeo six-cylinder diesel engine, driving the rear axle through a four-speed gearbox, together with a two-speed rear axle. Essentially a conventional road-going truck, it had live axles carried on semi-elliptical springs. Although the doors lacked windows, the all-steel cab and deep windscreen

were surprisingly modern in appearance for the period.

As well as the standard cargo variant, there was a fire appliance. The truck was also used as the basis for an experimental half-track conversion. There was also a medium version (430RE) of similar appearance.

The truck remained in production until 1944, and was reintroduced after the war in a slightly modernized form, notably with a window in the cab door. Designated CP48, it remained in production until 1950. Alfa-Romeo terminated truck production in 1967.

Alfa-Romeo 800RE

Type: Truck, 6¹/₂-ton, cargo, 4x2
Manufacturer: Alfa-Romeo (Societa Anonima Lombarda Fabbrica Automobili); Milano
Production: 1940 to 1944, 1950
Powerplant: Alfa-Romeo AR800; six cylinders in-line; diesel; water-cooled; 8,725cc; overhead valves; power output, 108–115bhp at 2,000rpm
Transmission: 4F1Rx2; 4x2
Suspension: Live axles on semi-elliptical multi-leaf springs
Brakes: Air-assisted hydraulic
Electrical system: 12V
Dimensions: Length – 6,840mm/269in
  Width – 2,350mm/93in
  Height – tilt in place, 2,850mm/112in
  Wheelbase – 3,800mm/150in
Weight: Unladen – 5,500kg/12,125lb
  Payload – 6,500kg/14,330lb
Performance: Maximum speed – 65kph/40mph

Alfa-Romeo 1900M *Matta*, AR51, AR52

The prototype for the Alfa-Romeo *Matta* (Crazy) field car was produced in 1950 under the designation 1900R. It went into production from 1951 as the 1900M, in two variants –

the AR51 was intended for the Italian Army, the AR52 for the Air Force.

Typical of post-war Jeep-type utility vehicles, with steel doors, folding two-piece windscreen and hinged rear tailgate, the prototype resembled the British Land Rover. However, the four-cylinder twin-cam dry-sump engine was considerably more advanced than anything used by Land Rover. Independent front suspension was standard using torsion bars. The production vehicle used the same components of the prototype. Production ended in 1955 after some 2,200 had been built, 50 of which were sold to civilians.

LEFT: **The 1900M retained a post-war Jeep-like styling.**

Alfa-Romeo 1900M *Matta*, AR51, AR52

Type: Truck, ¼-ton, utility, 4x4
Manufacturer: Alfa-Romeo (Societa Anonima Lombarda Fabbrica Automobili); Milano
Production: 1951 to 1955
Powerplant: Alfa-Romeo AR1307; four cylinders in-line; petrol; water-cooled; 1,884cc; overhead valves; power output, 65bhp at 4,500rpm
Transmission: 4F1Rx2; 4x2
Suspension: Independent suspension using wishbones and torsion bars at front; live axles on semi-elliptical multi-leaf springs at rear
Brakes: Hydraulic
Electrical system: 12V
Dimensions: Length – 3,520mm/139in
  Width – 1,575mm/62in
  Height – tilt in place, 1,820mm/72in
  Wheelbase – 2,200mm/87in
Weight: Unladen – 1,425kg/3,141lb
  Payload – 470kg/1,036lb
Performance: Maximum speed – 100kph/62mph

Fiat *Tipo* 508C *Militare*

The Italian company Fiat was established in 1899 and started to manufacture trucks in 1903, supplying the Italian Army during

the Italian–Turkish conflict in Libya in 1911 and World War I. The company remained a significant supplier of trucks of up to 6-ton capacity to the Italian forces during World War II. Among the smallest of these was the *Tipo* 508C *Militare*, a light truck which went into production in 1939, using the chassis of the 1937 Fiat Balilla 1100.

The steel bonnet and wings of the original Balilla were combined with

timber half-doors and a timber pick-up body rated for a 350kg/772lb payload. The running gear

ABOVE LEFT AND LEFT:
The 508C *Militare* was based on the Balilla 1100, which was also supplied as a canvas-topped staff car.

was all derived from the Balilla and included a 1,089cc four-cylinder engine and four-speed gearbox. Independent suspension was fitted at the front, combined with a live axle and semi-elliptical springs at the rear.

An extended wheelbase variant was produced under the designation *Tipo* 508 LRM.

Fiat *Tipo* 508C *Militare*

Type: Truck, cargo, 4x2
Manufacturer: Fabbrica Italiana d'Automobili (Fiat); Torino
Production: 1939 to 1945
Powerplant: Fiat 108C; four cylinders in-line; petrol; water-cooled; 1,089cc; overhead valves; power output, 32bhp at 2,800rpm
Transmission: 4F1R; 4x2
Suspension: Independent at front; live axle at rear on semi-elliptical multi-leaf springs
Brakes: Hydraulic
Electrical system: 12V
Dimensions: Length – 4,005mm/158in
  Width – 1,510mm/59in
  Height – 2,150mm/85in
  Wheelbase – 1,920mm/76in
Weight: Unladen – 2,710kg/5,974lb
  Payload – 2,500kg/5,511lb
Performance: Maximum speed – 80kph/50mph

Fiat *Tipo* 665NL, 665NM

Produced by Fiat's truck division – Fiat Veicoli Industriali – which had been established in 1929, the *Tipo* 665 was a heavy road-going military cargo truck rated for a 5-ton payload. It entered service from 1942. Fitted with a forward-control steel cab it was a modern-looking vehicle, and was effectively a militarized version of the civilian *Tipo* 665 announced in 1939.

The truck was also produced with an armoured (*Blindato*) cab.

Like all of the *Tipo* 600 series trucks, power came from a 9,365cc six-cylinder diesel engine, driving the rear wheels through a four-speed main gearbox and two-speed auxiliary gearbox. A reduction gear was fitted between the clutch and gearbox. The suspension was by semi-elliptical multi-leaf springs. In common with other Italian military vehicles, the cab was equipped with a right-hand driving position which was felt to be safer on narrow Alpine passes. The *Tipo* 665NL – the N suffix indicates *Nafta* (diesel fuel) – had steel cab doors with wind-up windows. The *Tipo* 665NM (*Nafta Militare*) had half doors and was fitted with a differential lock to improve performance on rough tracks.

Military production continued until 1944, although it would appear that the truck was built only in small numbers. There were many more examples produced of the militarized long-wheelbase *Tipo* 666, rated at 6 tons. This chassis was developed into the *Tipo* A10000 with a 10-ton payload in 1945.

The series was put back into production after the war for commercial customers and the cab remained standard on Fiat trucks until a new design was introduced in 1952. Fiat Veicoli Industriali merged with the German Klöckner-Humboldt-Deutz in 1974 and although the company continues to produce trucks, they are now badged Iveco. The Fiat name was dropped in 1982.

MIDDLE: **Production of the *Tipo* 665 continued in small numbers until 1944. The vehicle was put back into production after the war for the civilian market. The modern-looking all-steel cab remained a standard on Fiat trucks until a new design was introduced in 1952.**

LEFT: **The *Tipo* 665 was also produced with an armoured (*Blindato*) cab. Firing ports in the rear body suggest that this vehicle has been adapted for use as an armoured personnel carrier.**

Fiat *Tipo* 665NL, 665NM

Type: Truck, heavy, 5-ton, 4x2
Manufacturer: Fiat Veicoli Industriali; Torino
Production: 1942 to 1944
Powerplant: Fiat 365; six cylinders in-line; diesel; water-cooled; 9,365cc; overhead valves; power output, 110bhp at 2,200rpm
Transmission: 4F1Rx2; 4x2; differential lock on Tipo 665NM
Suspension: Live axles on semi-elliptical multi-leaf springs
Brakes: Air-pressure assisted hydraulic
Electrical system: 24V
Dimensions: Length – 7,095mm/279in
    Width – 2,670mm/105in
    Height – tilt in place, 3,210mm/126in
    Wheelbase – 3,760mm/148in
Weight: Unladen – 7,200kg/15,873lb
    Payload – road, 5,140kg/11,332lb;
    cross-country, 4,140kg/9,127lb
Performance: Maximum speed – 55kph/34mph

Fiat AR51, AR55, AR59 *Campagnola*

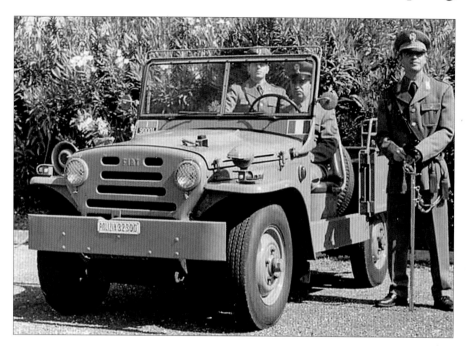

LEFT: Introduced in 1951, the military version of the Fiat *Campagnola* was designated AR51, and was produced especially for the Italian Army and the police service. The vehicle was typical of post-war efforts to improve on the US-built Jeep.

The Fiat *Campagnola* (Country) was a civilian multi-purpose utility vehicle very much in the mould of the World War II Jeep. Launched in 1951, the civilian variant was soon followed by the military AR51 *Autovettura da Ricognizione* (reconnaissance vehicle), which was produced especially for the

BELOW: The Fiat *Campagnola* was originally introduced for civilian usage and was aimed at the market which had been developed by Land Rover and Jeep since the end of the war.

Italian Army. In 1955, the original AR51 was replaced by the improved AR55. The AR59, which was modified to conform with various NATO requirements, including the use of a 24V electrical system, followed in 1959.

Suspension at the front was independent using upper and lower wishbones with coil springs enclosed in an oil-bath housing. At the rear, there was a live axle on conventional multi-leaf semi-elliptical springs. The vehicle was powered by a four cylinder 1,901cc

petrol engine driving both axles through a four-speed gearbox and two-speed transfer box. In 1953, the civilian version was also made available with the option of a diesel engine. The original petrol-engined version was then identified as *Campagnola* A, while the diesel version was designated *Campagnola* B and C.

The body was typical of such vehicles, with a removable canvas cover and folding windscreen. The half-height steel doors could be secured in the open position, folded back against the body sides.

Alongside service with Italian forces, the vehicle was also exported, for example to Mexico, Venezuela and Bolivia, as well as various African countries. A licence-built version, the Zastava AR51, was produced in Yugoslavia.

Fiat AR51, AR55, AR59 *Campagnola*

Type: Truck, ¼-ton, utility, 4x4
Manufacturer: Fabbrica Italiana d'Automobili (Fiat); Torino
Production: 1951 to 1959
Powerplant: Fiat 105B017; four cylinders in-line; petrol; water-cooled; 1,901cc; overhead valves; power output, 56–63bhp at 4,000rpm
Transmission: 4F1Rx2; part-time 4x4
Suspension: Independent front suspension using upper and lower wishbones and fully-enclosed coil springs in oil-bath housing; live axle at rear on semi-elliptical multi-leaf springs
Brakes: Hydraulic
Electrical system: 12V, (AR59) 24V
Dimensions: Length – 3,600mm/142in
 Width – 1,570mm/62in
 Height – tilt in place, 1,800mm/71in; minimum, 1,370mm/54in
 Wheelbase – 2,250mm/89in
Weight: Unladen – 1,430kg/3,153lb
 Payload – 487kg/1,074lb
Performance: Maximum speed – 100kph/62mph

Moto-Guzzi *Mulo Meccanico*

During the inter-war years and into World War II, the Italian Army made widespread use of commercial motor tricycles, typically the front end of a motorcycle attached to a two-wheeled rear sub-frame on which was mounted a cargo box. The narrow width made the machines particularly useful on the restricted roads of the Alpine passes.

In 1959, Moto-Guzzi started the design work for the ultimate purpose-designed military load-carrying tricycle, which was described as the *Mulo Meccanico* (Mechanical Mule).

Although the rider was presented with a steering wheel, which turned the front wheel through a reduction gearbox, rather than a pair of handlebars, the *Mulo Meccanico* was clearly derived from a motorcycle. The vehicle was assembled around a tubular-steel duplex frame and was powered by a 745cc V2 fan-cooled

engine installed transversely beneath the saddle. The front suspension was by coil springs. The rear axle, on which the track was adjustable on the move between 1,300mm/51in and 850mm/33in, was carried on rubber-sprung trailing arms.

All three wheels were driven, through a six-speed gearbox. A torque-dividing locking differential at the centre split the power between the front and rear wheels (80 per cent rear, 20 per cent front). A locking differential on the cross-shaft and bevels translated the power to the separate rear wheels. The front wheel was shaft-driven through a bevelled box at the steering head. Demountable caterpillar tracks, which were tensioned by drop-down idler wheels, were available for the rear wheels.

A single front seat was mounted ahead of bodywork which housed the battery, fuel tank and spare wheel.

Moto-Guzzi *Mulo Meccanico*

Type: Motor tricycle, cargo, 3x3
Manufacturer: Moto-Guzzi; Mandello del Lario
Production: 1961 to 1962
Powerplant: Moto-Guzzi; V2; petrol; forced air cooled; 745cc; overhead valves; power output, 20bhp at 5,500rpm
Transmission: 6F1R; 3x3; lockable differentials, front and rear
Suspension: Coil-sprung friction-damped front forks; trailing arms at rear with rubber suspension
Brakes: Hydraulic
Electrical system: 12V
Dimensions: Length – 3,000mm/117in
 Width – maximum, 1,570mm/62in
 Height – 1,420mm/56in
 Wheelbase – 2,030mm/80in
Weight: Unladen – 1,000kg/2,200lb
 Payload – 500kg/1,102lb
Performance: Maximum speed – 50kph/31mph

At the rear, there was a small load platform with a capacity of 500kg/1,102lb, which also included simple mudguards. Around 500 were built during 1961 and 1962.

ABOVE: **With the rear tracks in place, the Moto Guzzi *Mulo Meccanico* provides wall-climbing performance.**

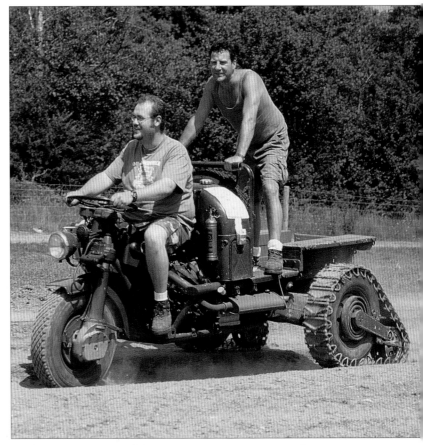

ABOVE: **All three wheels on the machine are driven. The rear track width can be adjusted on the move, between 1,300mm/51in and 850mm/33in.**

IVECO 320-45 WTM

In 1975, Magirus-Deutz and Fiat established the Industrial Vehicle Corporation (IVECO), a joint company headquartered in the Netherlands, to develop and manufacture trucks for the civilian and defence markets in competition with other leading world manufacturers such as Mercedes-Benz. The intention was that the heavy trucks would be produced in the former Fiat plant in Turin, while the medium and lighter vehicles were produced at the Magirus-Deutz plant in Ulm. The 320-45 WTM tractor-truck was prototyped in 1978 to satisfy an Italian Army requirement for a heavy equipment transporter to tow a semi-trailer carrying a Leopard main battle tank. The truck began to enter service in 1981 and, at the time, it was the largest IVECO military vehicle in production.

LEFT: The standard 60-ton semi-trailer was a four-axle design by OTO Melara. Production trailers were manufactured by Bartoletti. Two 20-ton capacity winches on the tractor were used to assist in loading and unloading disabled or damaged tanks.

LEFT: The Iveco 320-45 WTM tractor-truck was put into production in 1981 for use as a heavy equipment transporter to carry a Leopard, the Italian Army's main battle tank. At the time, it was the largest military vehicle built by IVECO.

Powered by a 17,174cc V8 turbocharged diesel engine, the 320-45 WTM was described by the manufacturer as being suitable for transporting tanks up to 60 tons both on-road and across country. The engine was coupled to all six wheels through a torque converter, eight-speed gearbox and single-speed transfer box, the latter including a lockable torque divider. Suspension was by semi-elliptical leaf springs. The truck could be specified with single or twin rear wheels, and the rear axles were fitted with differential locks. Both open- and closed-cab and left- and right-hand drive versions were available. The open cab was fitted with a canvas top and was designed to allow the side windows to be removed and the screen to be folded forward. Two 20-ton winches were fitted behind the cab to assist with loading disabled or damaged tanks. The standard 60-ton four-axle semi-trailer was designed by OTO Melara and produced by Bartoletti. Magirus-Deutz left IVECO in 1980, and in 1986 IVECO merged with the truck division of Ford UK.

IVECO 320-45 WTM

Type: Truck-tractor, heavy equipment, 60-ton, 6x6
Manufacturer: IVECO, Defence Vehicle Division; Bolzano
Production: 1981 to 2001
Powerplant: IVECO 8280.22; eight cylinders in V configuration; turbocharged diesel; water-cooled; 17,174cc; overhead valves; power output, 450bhp at 2,400rpm
Transmission: 8F1R; full-time 6x6; differential locks at rear
Suspension: Live axles on semi-elliptical multi-leaf springs
Brakes: Air-pressure
Electrical system: 24V
Dimensions: Length – 7,520mm/296in
   Width – 2,775mm/109in
   Height – 3,051mm/120in
   Wheelbase – 3,600mm/142in
   Bogie centres – 1,380mm/54in
Weight: Unladen – 15,400kg/33,950lb
   Gross train weight – 93,420kg/205,525lb
Performance: Maximum speed – 65kph/40mph

OM *Tipo* 32, 35, 36, 37

OM *Tipo* 32, 35, 36, 37

Type: Truck, light, 4x4
Manufacturer: Officine Meccaniche (OM);
Brescia, Eritrea
Production: 1932 to 1937
Powerplant: OM; four cylinders in-line; petrol;
air-cooled; 1,616cc; side valves;
power output, 23bhp at 2,400rpm
Transmission: 4F1R, 4F1Rx2; full-time 4x4;
lockable centre differential
Suspension: Independent suspension by parallel
transverse semi-elliptical multi-leaf springs
Brakes: Mechanical
Electrical system: 6V
Dimensions: Length – 3,600mm/142in
Width – 1,360mm/54in
Height – tilt in place, 2,150mm/85in
Wheelbase – 2,000mm/79in
Weight: Unladen – 1,615kg/3,535lb
Payload – 800kg/1,764lb
Performance: Maximum speed – 50kph/31mph

Prototyped by Ansaldo and originally introduced in 1932 as the *Tipo* 32, the OM *Autocarretta da Montagne* (mountain vehicle) was an unusual forward-control short-wheelbase light truck. Although the solid tyres of the original model, combined with the use of an engine of less than 2,000cc, restricted speed on metalled surfaces, the independent suspension, all-wheel drive and four-wheel steering provided excellent performance in the mountains of Italy.

A 1,616cc four-cylinder air-cooled engine was permanently coupled to both axles incorporating a lockable differential through a four-speed gearbox. Independent suspension was fitted on all four wheels using transverse leaf springs. Development

LEFT: **A parade of Autocarretta 32s of the Italian Army in Abyssinia.**

continued through the life of the vehicle with improvements such as pneumatic tyres (*Tipo* 36M), electric lighting and auxiliary gearbox introduced into subsequent models, which were designated by the year of introduction.

Pavesi P4-100

Pavesi P4-100

Type: Tractor, heavy, artillery, 4x4
Manufacturer: Societa Ligure Piemontese
Automobili (Fiat-SPA); Torino
Production: 1936 to 1942
Powerplant: Fiat P4/1; four cylinders in-line; petrol;
water-cooled; 4,724cc; overhead valves; power
output, 55bhp at 2,800rpm
Transmission: 4F1R; 4x4; locking differentials
Suspension: Live axles on semi-elliptical
multi-leaf springs
Brakes: Mechanical
Electrical system: 6V
Dimensions: Length – 4,155mm/164in
Width – 2,045mm/80in
Height – 1,650mm/65in
Wheelbase – 2,425mm/95in
Weight: Unladen – 4,800kg/10,582lb
Payload – Not available
Performance: Maximum speed – 22kph/14mph

Designed by Ugo Pavians, the Pavesi P4 articulated agricultural tractor was first produced in 1914. Exceptional off-road abilities, and particularly a small turning circle assisted by articulated steering, made the vehicle ideal for military usage. The type was adopted by the Italian Army as an artillery tractor. In 1923, the Italian Army began trials for a high-performance artillery tractor. In June 1924, a heavy version of the P4 was ordered, with series production starting in 1926.

Three different models were deployed during World War II, both produced by Fiat-SPA. The TL-31 (L140) *Trattore Leggero* (light tractor), entered service with Italian artillery units in 1931–32. The P4-100 *Trattore Pesante* (heavy tractor) appeared in 1936, followed by the P4-110. At first, the P4-100 ran on dual solid tyres, but these were

LEFT: **The Pavesi P4-100 began life as an agricultural tractor.**

replaced by pneumatics in 1938. The Italian Army continued to experiment with the design, even building an armoured version. The Pavesi was trialled in Britain and was used by Bulgaria, Denmark and Finland.

SPA AS37

SPA AS37

Type: Truck, light, 1- to 2-ton, 4x4
Manufacturer: Societta Ligure Piemontese Automobili (Fiat-SPA); Torino
Production: 1937 to 1948
Powerplant: Fiat 18TL; four cylinders in-line; petrol; water-cooled; 4,053cc; side valves; power output, 57bhp at 2,000rpm
Transmission: 5F1R; part-time 4x4; lockable centre differential
Suspension: Independent front suspension using twin wishbone links and coil springs; live axle at rear on semi-elliptical springs
Brakes: Mechanical
Electrical system: 6V
Dimensions: Length – 4,700mm/185in
    Width – 2,100mm/83in
    Height – 2,120mm/84in
    Wheelbase – 2,500mm/98in
Weight: Unladen – 3,500kg/7,716lb
    Payload – 1,000kg/2,205lb
Performance: Maximum speed – 80kph/50mph

Societta Ligure Piemontese Automobili (SPA) started producing trucks in 1910 and was taken over by Fiat in 1925. In the years immediately following the takeover, Fiat produced lighter vehicles. SPA tended to concentrate on trucks with a payload rating above 5 tons.

Dating from 1937, the AS37 (*Autocarro Sahariano*) was a short-wheelbase, high-mobility truck for use in North Africa. Features included four-

ABOVE: **Production of the AS37 finally ended in 1948 after some 3,000 had been built.**

wheel drive and four-wheel steering together with independent front suspension using wishbones and coil springs. A 4,053cc four-cylinder petrol engine drove the wheels through a five-speed gearbox, with a lockable centre differential and separate drive-shafts to each wheel. The standard variant was

fitted with a 1-ton cargo body, and the chassis was also used as the TL37 – *Trattore Leggero* (artillery tractor), and as a self-propelled gun mount and desert reconnaissance vehicle.

SPA *Dovunque Tipo* 35

The *Autocarro Dovunque* ("go anywhere truck") was prototyped at the beginning of the 1930s and put into production at Fiat's SPA division in 1933 as the *Tipo* 33. Subsequent service proved that the design was underpowered and, in 1935, it was replaced by the improved *Tipo* 35, which remained in production until 1948.

The engine was a 4,053cc four-cylinder petrol unit, driving the rear wheels through a four-speed main gearbox and two-speed auxiliary box. The suspension was by rigid axles on semi-elliptical multi-leaf springs; a single spring was fitted transversely at the front, with inverted longitudinal springs at the rear. Early production used air-pressure brakes, but later models had hydraulic operation. Most were bodied as cargo vehicles, but other variants included an anti-aircraft gun mount and integral signals van.

SPA *Dovunque Tipo* 35

Type: Truck, medium, 2- to 3-ton, 6x4
Manufacturer: Societta Ligure Piemontese Automobili (Fiat-SPA); Torino
Production: 1935 to 1948
Powerplant: Fiat 18D; four cylinders in-line; petrol; air-cooled; 4,053cc; side valves; power output, 60bhp at 2,000rpm
Transmission: 4F1Rx2; 6x4
Suspension: Live axles on transverse semi-elliptical multi-leaf spring at front, longitudinal inverted springs at rear
Brakes: Air-pressure or hydraulic
Electrical system: 6V
Dimensions: Length – 5,030mm/198in
    Width – 2,070mm/81in
    Height – tilt in place, 2,905mm/114in
    Wheelbase – 3,200mm/126in
    Bogie centres – 1,000mm/39in
Weight: Unladen – 4,490kg/9,899lb
    Payload – 2,670kg/5,886lb
Performance: Maximum speed – 50kph/31mph

LEFT AND FAR LEFT: **The SPA *Tipo* 35 was the Italian Army's all-terrain vehicle – *Dovunque*.**

SPA *Dovunque Tipo* 41

The development of the SPA *Autocarro Dovunque Tipo* 41 started in 1941, with production taking place between 1942 and 1948. Rated for a 5- to 6-ton payload, the vehicle was described as a "medium" 6x6 truck, and was assembled using a large number of Fiat components.

The engine was a 9,365cc six-cylinder diesel unit, which gave the vehicle a top speed of 80kph/50mph on metalled

BELOW: The *Tipo* 41 was also fitted with an open-topped artillery tractor body. This provided accommodation for the gun crew and space for stores, equipment and ammunition.

surfaces. The engine was coupled to all six wheels through a five-speed gearbox and two-speed transfer box, with a reduction gear interposed between the clutch and the main gearbox. Lockable centre and axle differentials were also fitted to assist in cross-country performance. Front suspension was by a single transverse multi-leaf semi-elliptical spring; inverted longitudinal springs were used at the rear. In common with other *Dovunque* trucks, two free-running spare wheels were fitted to either side of the chassis, immediately behind the cab, to prevent the vehicle from grounding during ditch crossings.

Standard variants included a general-service load carrier and an open-topped artillery tractor. Both variants were fitted with a 6-ton capacity under-chassis winch. The standard cargo truck shared the same all-steel forward-control cab with other Fiat trucks built since 1939, although the radiator panel was different. In 1950, the *Dovunque Tipo* 41 was replaced by the uprated *Tipo* 50.

SPA *Dovunque* Tipo 41

Type: Truck, medium, 5- to 6-ton, 6x6
Manufacturer: Societta Ligure Piemontese Automobili (Fiat-SPA); Torino
Production: 1942 to 1948
Powerplant: Fiat 366; six cylinders in-line; diesel; water-cooled; 9,365cc; overhead valves; power output, 110bhp at 2,000rpm
Transmission: 5F1Rx2; part-time 6x6; lockable centre and axle differentials
Suspension: Live axle on transverse semi-elliptical multi-leaf spring at front, longitudinal inverted springs at rears
Brakes: Air-pressure assisted hydraulic
Electrical system: 6V
Dimensions: Length – 7,040mm/277in
  Width – 2,350mm/93in
  Height – tilt in place, 3,150mm/124in; minimum, 2,800mm/110in
  Wheelbase – 3,900mm/154in
  Bogie centres – 1,360mm/54in
Weight: Unladen – 9,210kg/20,304lb
  Payload – 5,270kg/11,618lb
Performance: Maximum speed – 80kph/50mph

Isuzu Type 94A (TU10)

The name Isuzu was first used on the Type 94 military truck produced by Ishikawajima Dockyard & Engineering – the number indicates the year of its introduction (1934, or 2594 in the Japanese system). Ishikawajima had started building cars in 1918, and had been assembling Wolseley trucks for military use under licence since 1922. In 1933, Ishikawajima merged with the truck division of Dat Auto Manufacturing and, in 1937, merged with Tokyo Gas & Electric to form the Tokyo Jidosha Kogyo Group (TJKG). A new factory for manufacturing heavy trucks was constructed at Kawasaki in 1938, and the name Isuzu was subsequently applied to all of the vehicles produced by the TJKG.

Based heavily on European 6x4 truck designs of the mid-1930s, the Type 94 was developed to support the Japanese invasion of China. The truck was

produced in perhaps as many as 40 variants, including cargo truck, prime mover, refueller, aircraft-starting unit, searchlight truck and armoured car. The standard design used an open cab with a canvas top and steel half-doors, but there were also closed-cab variants, as well as short-wheelbase and forward-control designs. A 4x2 chassis was also produced which simply lacked the rear bogie.

Power for the Type 94A was provided by a 4,390cc six-cylinder side-valve engine, connected to the worm-drive rear axle(s) through a four-speed gearbox. Smaller numbers of the Type 94B were produced, equipped with a 4,800cc four-cylinder diesel engine. For both models, live axles were suspended on semi-elliptical springs, inverted at the rear.

The truck was also manufactured under other names, and subsequently

ABOVE: **A captured Isuzu Type 94A in storage at the Aberdeen Proving Grounds in Maryland, USA.**

supplied under a "subsidy" scheme to civilian users as the TU10, when it was rated for a 3-ton load.

Isuzu Type 94A (TU10)

Type: Truck, 1½-ton, cargo, 6x4
Manufacturer: Tokyo Jidosha Kogyo; Tokyo
Production: 1934 to 1945
Powerplant: Isuzu XA; six cylinders in-line; petrol; water-cooled; 4,390cc; side valves; power output, 70bhp at 2,800rpm
Transmission: 4F1R; 6x4
Suspension: Live axles on semi-elliptical multi-leaf springs, inverted at rear
Brakes: Mechanical
Electrical system: 12V
Dimensions: Length – 5,430mm/214in
  Width – 2,500mm/77in
  Height – 2,680mm/106in
  Wheelbase – 3,550mm/140in
  Bogie centres – 1,100mm/43in
Weight: Unladen – 3,400kg/7,496lb
  Payload – 1,900kg/4,189lb
Performance: Maximum speed – 60kph/37mph

Nihon Nainenki Kurogane

Nihon Nainenki Kurogane

Type: Car, light, 4x4
Manufacturer: Nihon Nainenki; Tokyo
Production: 1935 to 1944
Powerplant: Nihon Nainenki; two cylinders in V-formation; petrol; air-cooled; 1,399cc; overhead valves; power output, 33bhp at 3,300rpm
Transmission: 3F1R; part-time 4x4
Suspension: Independent front suspension, using wishbones and coil springs; live axle at rear using semi-elliptical multi-leaf springs
Brakes: Mechanical, rear wheels only
Electrical system: 12V
Dimensions: Length – 3,550mm/140in
Width – 1,250mm/49in
Height – 1,500mm/59in
Wheelbase – 2,000mm/79in
Weight: Unladen – 1,060kg/2,337lb
Payload – 190kg/419lb
Performance: Maximum speed – 80kph/50mph

The smallest of the Imperial Army's staff cars during World War II, and the only entirely Japanese product, the small Type 95 Kurogane was designed by Tetsushi Makita. A lightweight 4x4 open-bodied reconnaissance vehicle, it was the first all-wheel-drive vehicle produced in Japan. As with all Japanese military vehicles, the

ABOVE: **The Kurogane was the most widely used vehicle of its type in the Japanese Imperial Army. The total produced was some 4,800. There were several body types, including a small truck.**

designation "Type 95" indicated the year of development, in this case 1935 (2595 in the Japanese system).

Power came from a V-twin magneto-ignition air-cooled petrol engine, with a three-speed gearbox and single-speed transfer box. The suspension was independent at the front by double wishbones and coil springs, with a live axle at the rear on semi-elliptical springs.

Mitsubishi Type 73 Kogata

Mitsubishi Type 73 Kogata

Type: Truck, cargo, 1¹/₂-ton, 4x4
Manufacturer: Mitsubishi Motors; Tokyo
Production: 1996 to date
Powerplant: Mitsubishi 4M40; four cylinders in-line; turbocharged diesel; water-cooled; 2,835cc; overhead valves; power output, 125bhp at 4,000rpm
Transmission: 4F1Rx2 automatic; part-time 4x4; lockable centre differential
Suspension: Live axles on coil springs; double-acting telescopic shock absorbers
Brakes: Hydraulic with vacuum-servo assistance
Electrical system: 24V
Dimensions: Length – 4,140mm/163in
Width – 1,765mm/69in
Height – tilt in place, 1,970mm/78in
Wheelbase – 2,420mm/95in
Weight: Unladen – 1,940kg/4,277lb
Payload – 1,500kg/3,307lb
Performance: Maximum speed – 105kph/65mph

Mitsubishi Shipbuilding & Engineering Company had started to build trucks during the 1920s. During World War II, the company built tanks, ships and armaments. In 1950, under US control, the company was split into three – Mitsubishi Shipbuilding & Engineering Company, Mitsubishi Heavy Industries (Reorganized), and Mitsubishi Nippon Heavy Industries, the latter continuing to build Mitsubishi Fuso trucks. Mitsubishi Motors was formed in 1970 from the automotive division of Mitsubishi Heavy Industries.

Originally introduced in 1973, the first Type 73s, known as Kyus in Japanese, were based on the Jeep CJ3B that Mitsubishi had been producing under licence since 1953. The current Kogata variant was introduced in 1996 and is derived from the Mitsubishi Pajero. It is powered by a 2,835cc four-cylinder diesel engine, driving all four wheels through a four-speed automatic transmission

LEFT: **The Type 73 is used by the Japanese Self Defense Force. Earlier versions were supplied to the Philippines, Burma and South Vietnam.**

and two-speed transfer box, with a lockable centre differential. Suspension is by coil springs and dampers.

Nissan 4W73 Carrier

The Nissan Motor Company can trace its origins back to 1912 when Masujiro Hashimoto established the Kwaishinsha Motor Works and built the Dat light car. In 1925, Kwaishinsha changed its name to the Dat Motor Company and, following more than one subsequent change of ownership, was finally renamed Nissan in 1933. The company's first trucks were manufactured in 1937.

In 1958, Nissan developed the 4W72, a ³/₄-ton 4x4 short-wheelbase truck intended for the Japanese Self Defense Force. It was initially based on the Dodge WC52 weapons carrier. The more-powerful 4W73 followed in 1959, taking its body cues from the post-war Dodge M37. Where the 4W72 had been powered by a 3,670cc four-cylinder side-valve engine of the contemporary Nissan Patrol, in the 4W73, this was replaced by a 3,956cc overhead-valve engine with power output subsequently increased from 125bhp to 140bhp. There was also a diesel-engined version designated 4W73(U). The engine was coupled to a four-speed gearbox and single-speed transfer box. The live axles were suspended on semi-elliptical springs with dampers.

As well as the weapons carrier, standard variants included an integral-bodied ambulance and a fire vehicle. Both variants were also available commercially under the name "Carrier". A version of the 4W73 was built under licence in India at the Jabalpur Ordnance Factory. Similar vehicles were also produced by Toyota.

ABOVE: **Clearly based on the design of the Dodge WC series of World War II, also the post-war Dodge M37 and "Power Wagon". The 4W73 was produced as a weapons carrier, integral-bodied ambulance and a fire tender. An optional front-mounted winch was available.** RIGHT: **The 4W73 was introduced in 1959, and was available on the civilian market as the "Carrier". A version was built under licence in India.**

DAF YA328

DAF had already started work on a range of innovative-design military vehicles in 1949–50. One of the first vehicles to appear was the 3-ton YA318 6x6, approved for production in 1952. Some 300 examples were built before it was decided that it was underpowered. It was superseded by the improved YA328 in 1952, with the vehicles coming off the production line in 1953.

Although manufactured at DAF's Eindhoven factory, the vehicle was partly the product of the post-war Marshall Plan that had sought to re-establish the

BELOW: **The artillery tractor (above) was the first variant to be produced. Other types included a 3-ton cargo truck, fire/crash tender (below), also an aviation oil-service truck for the Air Force.**

shattered European economies. For this reason, it was powered by a Hercules six-cylinder engine. A JXC unit, with a four-speed gearbox was used in the original YA318, and the more-powerful JXLD, together with a five-speed gear box, in the YA328.

Unusually for a soft-skin vehicle, the drive-line was laid out in an H pattern, with a centrally mounted transfer box and differential from which individual drive-shafts transferred the power to worm-gear casings at the wheels. Suspension was independent on all six wheels, using trailing arms and torsion bars at the front, with a walking beam and leaf springs at the rear.

The artillery tractor was the first to enter production, but the most common variant

LEFT: **Post-war DAF military vehicles were part funded by US aid and, for this reason, were powered by US-built Hercules engines. Unusual features included World War II type free-running spare wheels and independent torsion-bar front suspension.**

was the 3-ton cargo truck. There was also a fire/crash tender (YC328), and an aircraft oil-service truck (YF318). Modifications to the cargo vehicle included anti-aircraft gun mount, workshop, mobile store, crane truck, communications vehicles and field canteens among others.

Production continued until 1958–59, by which time DAF had delivered around 4,825 vehicles. Three hundred were the YA318, (210 artillery tractors and 90 others). A total of 4,525 of the YA328 variant were built.

The vehicles remained in service until the mid-1970s, when disposals began. Nevertheless, many were used for a further two decades by which time vehicle performance was becoming outdated. It was planned that 600 would be upgraded by replacing the JXLD with a White G-3000 overhead-valve petrol engine, with a 15 per cent power increase. For some reason, the modification was not a success and was abandoned after only a few vehicles had been converted in 1976.

DAF YA328

Type: Truck, 3-ton, cargo, 6x6
Manufacturer: Van Doorne's Automobielfabriek (DAF); Eindhoven
Production: 1953 to 1959
Powerplant: Hercules JXLD; six cylinders in-line; 5,556cc; petrol; water-cooled; side valves; power output, 131bhp at 3,200rpm
Transmission: 5F1Rx2; part-time 6x6
Suspension: Independent front suspension using parallel trailing arms and transverse torsion bars; walking-beam rear suspension using parallel arms and semi-elliptical multi-leaf springs; telescopic hydraulic shock absorbers
Brakes: Vacuum hydraulic
Electrical system: 24V
Dimensions: Length – 6,130mm/241in
　　　　Width – 2,400mm/95in
　　　　Height – 2,650mm/104in
　　　　Wheelbase – 3,400mm/134in
　　　　Bogie centres – 1,300mm/52in
Weight: Unladen – 6,140kg/13,536lb
　　　　Payload – 3,000kg/6,614lb
Performance: Maximum speed – 80kph/50mph

DAF YA126

Dating from 1952, the DAF YA126 was a 1-ton 4x4 cargo vehicle designed to replace the Dodge WC Series, many of which had been supplied to the Dutch Army. Like the larger YA328, it was powered by a US-built Hercules six-cylinder engine and production was partly funded with US money from the Marshall Plan.

Suspension was independent on all four wheels, using trailing arms and torsion bars. The driveline was laid out in an H pattern, using a centrally mounted transfer box and differential with longitudinal drive-shafts running to worm-gear casings at the wheel stations. Some examples were fitted with a 2½-ton horizontal-spindle winch mounted between the chassis rails at the rear and driven by a power take-off from the gearbox.

DAF YA126

Type: Truck, 1-ton, cargo, 4x4
Manufacturer: Van Doorne's Automobielfabriek (DAF); Eindhoven
Production: 1952 to 1960
Powerplant: Hercules JXC; six cylinders in-line; 4,620cc; petrol; water-cooled; overhead inlet valves, side exhaust; power output, 102bhp at 3,200rpm
Transmission: 4F1Rx2; part-time 4x4
Suspension: Independent at all four wheels by means of trailing arms suspended on lateral torsion bars; hydraulic double-acting shock absorbers
Brakes: Vacuum hydraulic
Electrical system: 24V
Dimensions: Length – 4,550mm/179in
Width – 2,100mm/83in
Height – 2,180mm/86in
Wheelbase – 2,830mm/111in
Weight: Unladen – 3,400kg/7,496lb
Payload – 1,000kg/2,205lb
Performance: Maximum speed – 84kph/52mph

Production continued until 1960, and most of the 7,200 produced were bodied for the cargo (weapons carrier) role.

LEFT: **The DAF YA126 only saw service with the Dutch Army.**

DAF YT514

Introduced in 1961, the 5-ton DAF YT514 was a militarized version of the standard civilian-type DS256 road tractor. With the flat-panelled soft-top cab and folding windscreen, it was clearly a product of the same thinking

BELOW: **A DAF YT514 with a standardized Dutch Army military-pattern semi-trailer.**

which had produced other post-war DAF military trucks. The cab was the same as fitted to the YA314 and YA324.

The YT514 was a multi-terrain truck designed for use with the DAF YF101 and YAF1014 fuel tankers, together with a range of other standardized military semi-trailers. Power came from a DAF six-cylinder supercharged diesel engine

DAF YT514

Type: Truck, 5-ton, tractor, 4x4
Manufacturer: Van Doorne's Automobielfabriek (DAF); Eindhoven
Production: 1961 to 1966
Powerplant: DAF DS575; six cylinders in-line; 5,750cc; supercharged diesel; water-cooled; overhead valves; power output, 165bhp at 2,400rpm
Transmission: 5F1Rx2; part-time 4x4
Suspension: Live axles on semi-elliptical multi-leaf springs
Brakes: Air pressure
Electrical system: 24V
Dimensions: Length – 6,130mm/241in
Width – 2,350mm/92in
Height – tilt in place, 2,620mm/103in; minimum, 2,090mm/82in
Wheelbase – 3,580mm/141in
Weight: Unladen – 5,200kg/11,464lb
Gross train weight – 36,650kg/80,798lb
Performance: Maximum speed – 80kph/50mph

driving both axles through a five-speed gearbox and two-speed transfer box. Suspension was by semi-elliptical springs at the front and rear.

LEFT: **Although very similar to the US-built CJ5 and military M38A1, the NEKAF can be identified by its smaller headlamps and by the small reflectors mounted on the front wing panels.**

NEKAF M38A1 (MD)

Between 1951 and 1953, the Dutch Army had purchased around 600 Willys CJ3A Jeeps. However, the Army also had more than 3,000 war-surplus Jeeps. To replace these, they had tested the DAF YA054, Willys CJ3B, Land Rover, French Delahaye VLR-D and Fiat AR59 *Campagnola*. A prototype of the US-built M422 "Mighty Mite" was also trialled. The DAF was the obvious choice, but production could not be approved because US funding was not available. The CJ3B was selected as second choice and an order for 2,000 issued in 1953. A year later, this order was cancelled when the US State Department agreed to approve assembly of the Willys M38A1 (or MD) Jeep in the Netherlands.

The M38A1 had been introduced as a replacement for the MC (M38) in 1952, with the almost identical civilian CJ5 and the military equivalent, the CJ5M, following in 1954. Although the CJ5M was available to qualifying nations under the Marshall Aid Plan, the Dutch Army preferred the original military M38A1 and it was agreed that production would be undertaken by Rotterdam-based Nederlandse Kaiser-Frazer Fabrieken (NEKAF). The company had been building Kaiser cars in the Netherlands since 1947, as well as the CJ3B, some of which had already been supplied to the Dutch Air Force.

A contract for 4,000 vehicles was awarded to NEKAF in January 1955, with the first M38A1 to be delivered in May of that year. All of the major components were supplied from the USA. Dutch content was restricted to tyres, electrical equipment and upholstery, which comprised 25 per cent.

The NEKAF version was little more than the US-built M38A1 with changes made to comply with Dutch traffic regulations; for example, white reflectors were attached to the front wing panels, and flashing indicator signals were mounted to the body sides. Blackout lights were fitted to the grille. Like the original, the vehicle was powered by a Willys Hurricane four-cylinder engine, driving live axles through a three-speed gearbox and two-speed transfer box. Suspension was by semi-elliptical leaf springs.

The total number manufactured by NEKAF was 5,674, under three contracts. After the NEKAF contracts were complete, a further 2,237 were constructed, during 1959–63, by Kemper & Van Twist of Dordrecht. The vehicles remained in service with the Dutch Army from 1955 into the late 1990s.

LEFT: **In 1955, production of the NEKAF M38A1 started in Rotterdam. A total of 7,911 were built over a nine-year period. By the time production came to an end in 1963, 25 per cent of the vehicle was assembled from Dutch components.**

NEKAF M38A1 (MD)

Type: Truck, 1/4-ton, utility, 4x4
Manufacturer: Nederlandse Kaiser-Frazer Fabrieken (NEKAF); Rotterdam. Kemper & Van Twist; Dordrecht
Production: 1955 to 1963
Powerplant: Willys Hurricane; four cylinders in-line; 5,556cc; petrol; water-cooled; side inlet valves, overhead exhaust; power output, 72bhp at 4,000rpm
Transmission: 3F1Rx2; part-time 4x4
Suspension: Live axles on semi-elliptical multi-leaf springs; telescopic hydraulic shock absorbers
Brakes: Hydraulic
Electrical system: 24V
Dimensions: Length – 3,510mm/138in
  Width – 1,550mm/61in
  Height – 1,900mm/75in
  Wheelbase – 2,060mm/81in
Weight: Unladen – 1,225kg/2,700lb
  Payload – road, 544kg/1,199lb;
  cross-country, 363kg/800lb
Performance: Maximum speed – 90kph/56mph

FSC Lublin L-51

In 1950, FSC was established in the Polish town of Lublin to produce Soviet trucks under licence for the Polish Army. The company's first product was the 2¹/₂-ton L-51, the first of which was completed on November 7, 1951.

The L-51 was based on the GAZ-51, the design of which dated back to 1938, although it did not enter production in the Soviet Union until 1946. It was widely used in most Soviet Bloc countries, both for military and civilian use. The L-51 was identical in almost every respect, and used the same 3,485cc six-cylinder engine as the Soviet original, driving the twinned rear wheels through a four-speed gearbox. Suspension was by means of conventional semi-elliptical leaf springs. As well as a fabricated-timber cargo body, a six-stretcher ambulance was also produced.

FSC Lublin L-51	
Type: Truck, 2¹/₂-ton, cargo, 4x2	
Manufacturer: Fabryka Samochodów Ciężarowych (FSC); Lublin	
Production: 1951 to 1959	
Powerplant: FSC; six cylinders in-line; petrol; water-cooled; 3,485cc; side valves; power output, 70bhp at 2,800rpm	
Transmission: 4F1Rx2; 4x2	
Suspension: Live axles on semi-elliptical multi-leaf springs	
Brakes: Hydraulic	
Electrical system: 12V	
Dimensions: Length – 5,550mm/219in	
Width – 2,200mm/87in	
Height – 2,150mm/85in	
Wheelbase – 3,300mm/130in	
Weight: Unladen – 2,710kg/5,974lb	
Payload – 2,500kg/5,511lb	
Performance: Maximum speed – 73kph/45mph	

LEFT: **An FSC Lublin L-51 fitted with the standard timber-type cargo body.**

Polski-Fiat 508/518 Mazur

Polski-Fiat was established in Warsaw in 1932 following an agreement between the Polish and Italian governments. The company's first product was a version of the Fiat Balilla, slightly re-engineered by Zygmunt Okolow, and assembled from knocked-down kits.

BELOW: **A 518 with canvas covers erected. Note the side-mounted anti-grounding revolving spare wheel.**

In 1935, a licence was granted for the new Fiat 508, with practically the complete vehicle produced in Poland.

The 508/518 Mazur was a specialized military vehicle using components of both the Ballila 508 and the *Ardita* 518. The original engine was a 1,758cc unit but, in 1937, was replaced by the more powerful 1,994cc of the Fiat *Ardita* (Daring). Drive was through a four-speed gearbox with optional auxiliary gear. Rotating spare

wheels were fitted to help prevent bellying on ditch crossings. The rear axle was fitted with a differential lock.

Some 400 were produced between 1935 and 1939, with variants including a field car, radio van, telephone line layer, pick up and an artillery tractor for anti-tank guns.

Polski-Fiat 508/518 Mazur	
Type: Truck, light, 4x2	
Manufacturer: Polski-Fiat (PZInz); Warsaw	
Production: 1935 to 1939	
Powerplant: Fiat/PZInz 118A or 157; four cylinders in-line; petrol; water-cooled; 1,758cc or 1,944cc; side valves; power output, 36–45bhp at 3,600rpm	
Transmission: 4F1R plus auxiliary gear; 4x2	
Suspension: Live axles on semi-elliptical multi-leaf springs	
Brakes: Hydraulic	
Electrical system: 12V	
Dimensions: Length – 3,695mm/145in	
Width – 1,580mm/62in	
Height – 1,870mm/74in	
Wheelbase – 2,300mm/100in	
Weight: Unladen – 1,500kg/3,307lb	
Payload – 400kg/882lb	
Performance: Maximum speed – 100kph/62mph	

GAZ-64, 67, 67B

Work on designing the GAZ-64 started in February 1941. The vehicle was based on the four-wheel drive chassis of the GAZ-61 and powered by a licence-built version of the Ford Model A four-cylinder engine, identical to that used in the GAZ-AA truck. The vehicle was little more than a pre-production prototype, designed over a very short timescale by Vitaliy Grachev. Nevertheless, the GAZ-64 was the Soviet Union's first attempt at building an off-road vehicle in the style of the Jeep, thousands of which had been supplied to the Red Army under the Lend-Lease arrangements.

The open bodywork, of decidedly crude appearance, was clearly derived from the Jeep. However, the resemblance ended there because, although part-time four-wheel drive was included in the design, there were no low-ratio gears. Out-of-date features such as the mechanical brakes and front quarter-elliptical springs must have seriously restricted performance when compared to the original. Live axles were fitted at front and rear, the latter suspended on more conventional semi-elliptical springs. Special 6.50-16 tyres were developed for the vehicle, but shortages often led to road tyres being used. This further reduced the off-road performance.

The first vehicle was assembled in just 51 days before being turned over to the Red Army for trials. Production started in August 1941, with just 646 having been built by the summer of 1942 when it was superseded by the improved GAZ-67. This was followed, soon after, by the wider-tracked and more-powerful GAZ-67B.

There were no variants, but the GAZ BA-64 armoured car was built on the chassis of the original GAZ-64, while the chassis of the GAZ-67B was used for the BA-64B armoured car.

The design remained in production until 1953, by which time a total of 63,489 had been built of all three types. The vehicle was used by the Soviet Union and by a number of Soviet satellite states.

GAZ-64, 67, 67B

Type: Car, 4 seat, 4x4
Manufacturer: Gorkiy Auto Zavod; Gorkiy
Production: 1941 to 1953
Powerplant: GAZ-M1; four cylinders in-line; petrol; water-cooled; 3,285cc; side valves; power output, 50bhp at 2,800rpm (54bhp for GAZ-67B)
Transmission: 4F1R; part-time 4x4
Suspension: Live axles on quarter-elliptical multi-leaf springs at front, semi-elliptical at rear; single- or double-acting hydraulic shock absorbers
Brakes: Mechanical
Electrical system: 6V
Dimensions: Length – 3,350mm/132in
Width – 1,685mm/66in
Height – tilt in place, 1,700mm/67in; minimum, 1,300mm/51in
Wheelbase – 2,100mm/83in
Weight: Unladen – 1,200kg/2,645lb
Payload – 400kg/882lb
Performance: Maximum speed – 75kph/47mph

ABOVE: **In 1934, an improved version of the the GAZ-AA 6x4 entered service, designated GAZ-AAA. At the same time, ZIS produced an almost identical ZIS-6. The vehicles are carrying multiple machine-gun anti-aircraft mounts.** LEFT: **The GAZ-AA was a licence-built version of a US 1930 Ford Model AA. The Ford Motor Company assisted GAZ with the design of the factory and production line. The GAZ-AA remained in production until 1938.**

GAZ-AA, AAA

Type: Truck, 1½-ton, cargo, 4x4; truck, 2-ton, cargo, 6x4
Manufacturer: Gorkiy Auto Zavod; Gorkiy
Production: 1932 to 1943
Powerplant: GAZ-A or GAZ-M1; four cylinders in-line; 3,285cc; petrol; water-cooled; side valves; power output, 40–50bhp at 2,800rpm
Transmission: 4F1Rx2; 4x2 or 6x4
Suspension: Live axles on semi-elliptical multi-leaf springs, cantilevered at the rear
Brakes: Mechanical
Electrical system: 6V
Dimensions: Length – 5,335mm/210in
   Width – 2,040mm/80in
   Height – 1,970mm/121in
   Wheelbase – GAZ-AA, 3,340mm/131in; GAZ-AAA, 3,200mm/118in
   Bogie centres – GAZ-AAA, 940mm/37in
Weight: Unladen – GAZ-AA, 1,810kg/3,990lb; GAZ-AAA, 2,475kg/5,456lb
   Payload – GAZ-AA, 1,700kg/3,748lb; GAZ-AAA, 2,200kg/4,850lb
Performance: Maximum speed – 70kph/44mph

GAZ-AA, AAA

The GAZ-AA was a 1½-ton 4x2 road-going cargo truck which went into production at the Soviet Gorkiy Auto Zavod motor plant in 1932. It was effectively a licence-built copy of the 1930 Ford Model AA. The Ford company had provided assistance with designing the factory and the production line. In 1934, the GAZ-AA was joined by an upgraded 6x4 variant, GAZ-AAA – also known as GAZ-3A or GAZ-Timken – which was fitted with a Timken-designed tandem-drive rear bogie. This allowed the payload to be increased to 2,032kg/4,480lb. Prototypes for the latter, which had no US equivalent, were assembled by the Soviet NAMI (National Automobile Research Institute) and in the workshops of the Soviet Army.

In both trucks, the engine was a Soviet-built version of the 3,285cc Ford four-cylinder side-valve unit, upgraded in 1936 to give an additional 10bhp. Drive to the rear wheels was through a four-speed gearbox, with a two-speed auxiliary box on the 6x4 variant. The rear axles were of the worm-drive type, and all axles were suspended on semi-elliptical springs. The rear wheels were twinned. The brakes on the vehicle were mechanically operated.

Alongside the basic drop-side cargo truck, standard variants included communications vehicle, searchlight mount, recovery vehicle, anti-aircraft gun mount, bus and command vehicle.

The GAZ-AA remained in production until 1938. The GAZ-AAA survived until 1943 by which time the factory had produced 37,373. A low-cost utility variant of the AAA was produced between 1941 and 1943 which had a simplified front, no front bumper, one headlamp, no front brakes and single rear wheels.

LEFT: **The GAZ-69 replaced the GAZ-67B in 1952. In 1956, the production line was moved to Ulyanovsk, when the vehicle became known as the UAZ-69. The vehicle is powered by a 2,438cc four-cylinder water-cooled petrol engine.**

GAZ-69, UAZ-69

In 1952, the GAZ-69 field car was introduced to replace the wartime GAZ-67B. At first production took place at the Molotov plant of Gorkiy Auto Zavod but, in December 1954, Ulyanovsk Auto Zavod also began to assemble the vehicle, using parts supplied by GAZ. In the summer of 1956, the entire production line was moved to Ulyanovsk, at which time the designation officially became UAZ-69.

Standard variants included a four-door field car, identified as GAZ-69A or UAZ-69A, and a two-door cargo vehicle, designated simply GAZ-69 or UAZ-69. There was also a modification allowing it to be used as a launch vehicle for the Soviet *Schmel* wire-guided anti-tank missile.

The open-topped cargo or five-seat bodywork was typical of a field car or utility vehicle of the period. It was a robust and simple vehicle, powered by a 2,112cc four-cylinder side-valve engine, driving both axles through a three-speed gearbox and two-speed transfer box. The primitive quarter-elliptical springs of the earlier GAZ-67 were replaced by semi-elliptics. In 1957, a more powerful 2,438cc engine producing an additional 10bhp was fitted. The designation was amended by the use of an "M" suffix, for example GAZ-69AM.

By 1959, the vehicle was being exported to more than 22 countries across the world and was widely used by the Red Army and other nations within the Soviet Bloc. Production continued into the early 1970s, when it was replaced by the improved UAZ-469. A four-speed variant designated M461 was produced by MICM-UMM in Romania.

LEFT: **By 1959, the GAZ/UAZ-69 had been exported to more than 22 countries across the world and was widely used by the Red Army and by other Warsaw Pact nations. This example has been equipped as a communications vehicle for the East German Army.**

GAZ-69, UAZ-69

Type: Truck, cargo, 4x2
Manufacturer: Gorkiy Auto Zavod; Gorkiy. Ulyanovsk Auto Zavod; Ulyanovsk
Production: 1952 to 1971
Powerplant: GAZ-69B/UAZ-69B; four cylinders in-line; petrol; water-cooled; 2,112cc (GAZ-69A/UAZ-69A), 2,438cc (UAZ-69AM); side valves; power output, 55–68bhp at 3,800rpm
Transmission: 3F1Rx2; part-time 4x4
Suspension: Live axles on semi-elliptical multi-leaf springs
Brakes: Mechanical
Electrical system: 12V
Dimensions: Length – 3,850mm/152in
Width – 1,750mm/69in
Height – tilt in place, 1,950mm/112in
Wheelbase – 2,300mm/91in
Weight: Unladen – 1,535kg/3,384lb
Payload – 425kg/937lb
Performance: Maximum speed – 95kph/59mph

GAZ-46

GAZ-46

Type: Car, 5-seat, amphibious, 4x4
Manufacturer: Gorkiy Auto Zavod; Gorkiy
Production: 1952 to 1956
Powerplant: GAZ-69B; four cylinders in-line; petrol; water-cooled; 2,112cc; side valves; power output, 55bhp at 2,800rpm
Transmission: 3F1Rx2; part-time 4x4; selectable propeller drive
Suspension: Live axles on semi-elliptical multi-leaf springs
Brakes: Hydraulic
Electrical system: 24V
Dimensions: Length – 4,930mm/194in
Width – 1,735mm/68in
Height – tilt in place, 1,790mm/70in
Wheelbase – 2,300mm/91in
Weight: Unladen – 1,850kg/4,078lb
Payload – 400kg/822lb
Performance: Maximum speed – on land, 83kph/52mph; in water, 10kph/6mph

ABOVE: **The GAZ-46 was an almost identical copy of the US-built Ford GPA.**

The Soviet Army used large numbers of Ford GPA amphibians during World War II. Between 1944 and 1945, after US production had ceased, GAZ produced a licence-built version designated GAZ-011, which used the engine, transmission and components of the GAZ-67B.

After the war, the GAZ-46, a larger version of the GAZ-011, was developed using the engine and transmission of the GAZ/UAZ-69. Like the GPA, the vehicle had a welded-steel hull with a steeply raked bow and sloped rear to aid entry and exit from rivers. A folding windscreen was fitted across the foredeck and a canvas roof could be erected over the crew compartment. The hull provided seating for five. Power was provided by a four-cylinder engine installed immediately above the front axle, driving either the wheels, or a small three-blade propeller, via a three-speed gearbox and two-speed transfer box. Suspension was by semi-elliptical springs. Production started in 1952 and was terminated around 1956.

GAZ-39371 Vodnik

GAZ-39371 Vodnik

Type: Truck, cargo/personnel, amphibious, 1½- to 2½-ton, 4x4
Manufacturer: Gorkiy Auto Zavod; Gorkiy
Production: 1999 on
Powerplant: GAZ-562; six cylinders in-line; turbocharged diesel; water-cooled; 6,230cc; side valves; power output, 55bhp at 2,800rpm
Transmission: 5F1Rx2; full-time 4x4
Suspension: Independent suspension using upper and lower wishbones and torsion bars
Brakes: Vacuum servo-assisted hydraulic
Electrical system: 24V
Dimensions: Length – 5,380mm/212in
Width – 2,600mm/102in
Height – 2,150–2,570mm/85–101in
Wheelbase – 3,000mm/118in
Weight: Unladen – 6,600–7,500kg/14,550–16,534lb
Payload – 1,500–2,500kg/3,307–5,511lb
Performance: Maximum speed – on land, 112kph/76mph; in water, 4–5kph/2.5–3mph

Nicknamed Vodnik, the GAZ-39371 is an amphibious four-wheel drive high-mobility multi-purpose vehicle developed from the GAZ-2975 Tigr. The hull is of welded construction and is made up of separate front and rear modules. The front contains the power unit and driving position. The rear, which is interchangeable, allows the vehicle to be used for different roles, for example as a passenger-carrying vehicle with seats for up to ten personnel, or as a cargo vehicle.

Power comes from a mid-mounted GAZ six-cylinder diesel engine driving through a five-speed gearbox. Other engine options include Caterpillar 3114, JaMZ-460 or HINO JO7C diesels. Suspension is independent on all four wheels by the use of upper and lower wishbones and torsion bars.

LEFT: **A civilian version of the Vodnik is available under the designation GAZ-3937.**

Entering service in 1999, the GAZ-39371 is in use with the Russian Army, and is available for export; Uruguay ordered 48 vehicles in 2006.

YaAZ-214, KrAZ-214

Type: Truck, cargo, 7-ton, 6x6
Manufacturer: Yaroslav'l Auto Zavod; Yaroslav'l. Kremenchug Auto Zavod; Kremenchug
Production: 1956 to 1967
Powerplant: YaAZ M206B; six cylinders in-line; two-stroke diesel; 6,972cc; power output, 205bhp at 2,000rpm
Transmission: 5F1Rx2; part-time 6x6
Suspension: Live axles on semi-elliptical multi-leaf springs
Brakes: Air-pressure
Electrical system: 12V (early production), 24V
Dimensions: (cargo vehicles)
    Length – 8,530mm/336in
    Width – 2,700mm/106in
    Height – tilt in place, 3,170mm/125in; minimum, 2,880mm/113in
    Wheelbase – 5,300mm/209in
    Bogie centres – 1,400mm/55in
Weight: Unladen – 12,300kg/27,060lb
    Payload – 7,000kg/15,400lb
Performance: Maximum speed – 55kph/34mph

YaAZ-214, KrAZ-214

The YaAz-214 – or JAAZ-214 – was a heavy-duty 7-ton 6x6 truck first produced at the Yaroslav'l Auto Plant in 1956. In 1959, production was moved to the Kremenchug plant in Ukraine and the designation changed to KrAZ-214.

Power was provided by a 6,972cc six-cylinder two-stroke diesel engine driving all six wheels through a five-speed

ABOVE: **In 1967 the YaAZ-214 model was replaced by the similar, but improved KrAZ-255.**

gearbox (with overdrive on top gear) and a two-speed transfer box. An inter-axle differential was fitted. Suspension was provided by basic multi-leaf semi-elliptical springs, inverted at the rear. The standard variant was a steel-bodied cargo vehicle

and was probably the most numerous vehicle of the class in the Soviet Army. Other variants included a tractor for a semi-trailer, bridge-layer, multiple rocket launcher, crane carrier and shovel. The chassis was fitted with a 12-ton winch and many vehicles were also equipped with a "Central Tyre Inflation System" (CTIS).

LuAZ 967M

LuAZ 967M

Type: Truck, cargo, amphibious, 4x4
Manufacturer: Lutskiy Auto Zavod; Lutskiy
Production: 1961 to 1975
Powerplant: MeMZ-967A; four cylinders in V configuration; petrol; air-cooled; 887cc; overhead valves; power output, 37bhp at 2,250rpm
Transmission: 4F1Rx2; part-time 4x4
Suspension: Independent suspension all round using semi-trailing arms and coil springs
Brakes: Hydraulic
Electrical system: 12V
Dimensions: Length – 3,682mm/145in
    Width – 1,712mm/67in
    Height – maximum, 1,580mm/62in
    Wheelbase – 1,800mm/71in
Weight: Unladen – 950kg/2,094lb
    Payload – 450kg/992lb
Performance: Maximum speed – 75kph/47mph

The LuAZ 967M was an airborne amphibious vehicle intended for ferrying supplies to the front line across difficult terrain. It could also be adapted for casualty evacuation, with stretchers carried on either side of the driver.

The first prototype was developed at the Moskvitch (MeMZ) factory in 1958, and constructed around a steel chassis

with permanent all-wheel drive and independent torsion-bar suspension using semi-trailing arms. Power came from a MD-65 motorcycle engine and the open body was of composite glass-fibre construction. The second prototype used front-wheel drive with selectable rear axle drive. The engine was a MeMZ air-cooled V4 as used in the ZAZ motor car.

The body was now of steel construction, with a central driving position which allowed the driver to also operate the vehicle from a prone position. The torsion bars were replaced by coil springs. In 1961, the vehicle went into production at the Ukranian Lutskiy factory.

LEFT: **The LuAZ 967 also provided the basis for the civilian LuAZ 969A, a small four-wheel-drive vehicle intended for agricultural use.**

MAZ-535, 537

Design work for the MAZ-535 and 537 began at the end of the 1950s. The intention was to produce a heavy load carrier and civilian construction vehicle that could be used in even the most remote and inhospitable terrain. Prototypes date from 1958, with the truck entering production around 1960. It was first seen by Western military observers at the 1964 May Day parade in Moscow.

There were three variants. Firstly, the original MAZ-535 cargo vehicle. The later, more-powerful, MAZ-537 was built both as a cargo/prime mover vehicle for heavy artillery, and as a fifth-wheel tractor (MAZ-537A) for use as a heavy equipment transporter. The latter was typically seen towing a Soviet ChMZAP-5247 or ChMZAP-5247G semi-trailer carrying an armoured fighting vehicle, or a missile, such as the SS-5 (Skean), SS-8 (Sasin), SS-N-6 (Sawfly), SS-X-10 (Scrag), or the ABM-1 (Galosh) – all are

NATO reporting names. Finally, there was the MAZ-537D, a 75-ton tractor-truck with a power generator mounted behind the engine compartment.

Both variants were built on the same chassis and were powered by effectively the same V12 diesel engine. For the MAZ-535, the engine was down-rated to 375bhp, while that used in the MAZ-537 produced 525bhp and was used in Soviet tanks of the period. The engine was mounted at high level behind the cab, and drove all eight wheels through a torque converter and three-speed planetary gearbox, the latter incorporating a smooth-start device on both first and reverse gears. A manual two-speed transfer box and an auxiliary

BELOW: **Typical of the Russian approach to military-vehicle design, the MAZ-535/537 is massive, powerful and unsophisticated. Power comes from an 18,300cc V12 water-cooled diesel engine.**

reduction gear incorporating an inter-axle self-locking differential were fitted.

Suspension on the first two axles – and on the rear axles of the MAZ-535 – was independent using torsion bars. The two rear axles of the MAZ-537 had no conventional springing but incorporated what was described as a "suspension equalizer". There was hydraulic power steering on axles one and two, together with air-hydraulic brakes all round. The first series of the MAZ-537 was produced at the Minsk Automobile Plant in Byelorussia until 1964. Production was subsequently moved to the KAVZ factory at Kurgan in the Urals.

MAZ-535, 537

Type: Truck, tractor, heavy equipment transporter, 8x8

Manufacturer: Minsk Auto Zavod; Minsk. Kurgan Auto Zavod; Kurgan

Production: 1960 to 1968

Powerplant: D-12-A-525; 12 cylinders in V formation; diesel; water-cooled; 18,300cc; overhead valves; power output, 375–525bhp at 2,100rpm

Transmission: 3F1Rx3; 8x8

Suspension: Independent suspension by torsion bars on forward two axles; no suspension on rear axles; hydraulic double-acting shock absorbers

Brakes: Air-assisted hydraulic

Electrical system: 24V

Dimensions: Length – 8,960mm/353in
Width – 2,885mm/113in
Height – 2,885mm/113in
Wheelbase – 1,800+2,650mm/71+104in

Weight: Unladen – 21,600kg/47,619lb
Gross train weight (MAZ-537A) – 112,500kg/248,016lb

Performance: Maximum speed – 60kph/37mph

263 UXR

LEFT: Introduced in 1958 to replace the earlier ZiL-151 range, the ZiL-157 was a versatile 6x6 truck adapted for a wide range of military roles. Like many Soviet trucks of the period, it was equipped with a "Central Tyre Inflation System" (CTIS). BELOW: Although superseded by the ZiL-157 from 1962, the ZiL-151 remained in production until 1966. The vehicle was also available to civilian users. Many were later fitted with the ZiL-157KD diesel engine.

ZiL-151, 157

Unashamedly based on the US Army 6x6 trucks of World War II, thousands of which had been supplied to the Soviet Union under the Lend-Lease arrangements, the ZiL-151 – originally described as the ZIS-151 – was a multi-terrain military load carrier which was the "workhorse" of the early post-war Red Army.

Introduced in 1948, it was to remain in production at the Likhachev Automobile Plant, Moscow, until 1958. It was then superseded by the broadly similar, ZiL-157, which was fitted with a more-powerful engine and larger-section single rear tyres in place of the original twins.

The engine was a 6,550cc six-cylinder side-valve petrol unit producing 92 or 104bhp, according to variant. Transmission was by five-speed gearbox (overdrive top gear) and a two-speed transfer box. The suspension arrangements were thoroughly conventional, with live axles on semi-elliptical leaf springs.

Both trucks were rated at a nominal 2$\frac{1}{2}$ tons, although the chassis was perfectly capable of carrying 4$\frac{1}{2}$ tons on surfaced roads. As well as a standard fixed-side wooden cargo body, there were crane, fuel-tanker, fuel service, water and oil service, multiple rocket launcher and tractor variants. It could also be equipped with various types of shop van-type bodies to cover the workshop, signals and stores roles. The ZiL-157 was equipped with a "Central Tyre Inflation System" (CTIS) which could be operated with the truck on the move. Both vehicles could be fitted with a front-mounted drum winch.

Production ended in 1966 with the introduction of the ZiL-131.

ZiL-151, 157

Type: Truck, 2$\frac{1}{2}$-ton, cargo, 6x6

Manufacturer: Likhachev Auto Zavod; Moscow. Ulyanovsk Auto Zavod; Ulyanovsk

Production: 1948 to 1966

Powerplant: ZiL-121; six cylinders in-line; petrol; water-cooled; 6,550cc; side valves; power output, 92bhp (ZiL-151) or 104bhp (ZiL-157) at 2,600rpm

Transmission: 5F1R; part-time 6x6

Suspension: Live axles on semi-elliptical multi-leaf springs; double-acting hydraulic shock absorbers on front axle

Brakes: Air-pressure

Electrical system: 12V

Dimensions: Length – 6,930mm/273in
Width – 2,320mm/91in
Height – tilt in place, 2,740mm/108in; minimum, 2,320mm/91in
Wheelbase – 4,225mm/166in
Bogie centres – 1,120mm/44in

Weight: Unladen – 5,540kg/12,213lb
Payload – road, 4,500kg/9,920lb; cross-country, 2,500kg/5,511lb

Performance: Maximum speed – 65kph/40mph

ZiL-135L4

In the early 1960s, the Likhachev factory in Moscow started the development work on what became the ZiL-135L4 – the vehicle is also sometimes described as the BAZ-135 to reflect the Bryansk factory where it was produced.

Although the truck was also supplied for heavy civilian usage, there were three major military variants. The 9P113 "Transporter-Erector-Launcher" (TEL) for the 9K52 Luna-M missile system (NATO name: "Frog 7") carried a single surface-to-surface artillery rocket on a hydraulically raised launch rail; a crane was fitted to the right-side of the vehicle to assist with reloading. The 9T290 was a resupply vehicle carrying three Luna-M missiles. There was also a 10-ton cargo/prime mover variant with a fixed-side cargo body and drop tailgate. With a different cab, the same chassis was also used to produce a transporter-launcher for the S-35, SSC-1a (Shaddock) surface-to-surface missile.

The truck was powered by two 7,000cc V8 petrol engines mounted

ABOVE: Powered by two V8 diesel engines, each driving the wheels on one side of the truck, the ZiL-135L4 was produced both as a 10-ton cargo vehicle, and as a missile loading vehicle (shown). The vehicle was also used as a missile "Transporter-Erector-Launcher" (TEL) unit.

behind the cab. Each engine drove the wheels on one side of the vehicle through a hydro-mechanical transmission system. There was torsion-bar suspension on the first and fourth axles; both provided steering. The centre axles were mounted as a fixed bogie unit without suspension. For military use, the truck was equipped with a "Central Tyre Inflation System" (CTIS).

This massive forward-control truck, with eight huge wheels, was fitted with a wide two-door glass-fibre composite cab providing seating for a crew of four or five. It could easily be recognized by the triple windscreen, which could be shuttered to protect against blast as the rocket was fired. The truck began to enter service in 1964 and was used by the Soviet Army and other Warsaw Pact countries as well as by other nations friendly to the Soviet Union. A number were captured from Iraqi forces during the First Gulf War.

ABOVE: A ZiL-135L4 missile "Transporter-Erector-Launcher" (TEL) with a Luna-M (NATO name: "Frog 7") missile in the ready-to-launch position. A number of TEL vehicles were captured from Iraqi forces.

ZiL-135L4

Type: Truck, missile "Transporter-Erector-Launcher" (TEL), 10-ton, 8x8

Manufacturer: Bryansk Auto Zavod; Bryansk

Production: 1964 on

Powerplant: 2x ZiL-375; each of eight cylinders in V configuration; petrol; water-cooled; 7,000cc; overhead valves; power output, 150bhp at 1,800rpm

Transmission: Hydro-mechanical; full-time 8x8

Suspension: Independent suspension by upper and lower wishbones and torsion bars on first and fourth axles; no suspension on centre axles

Brakes: Air-pressure

Electrical system: 24V

Dimensions: Length – 9,270mm/365in
Width – 2,800mm/110in
Height – to top of cab, 2,530mm/100in; missile in place, 3,375mm/133in
Wheelbase – 6,300mm/248in
Bogie centres – 2,415+1,500+2,415mm/ 95+59+95in

Weight: Unladen – 9,000kg/19,8041lb
Payload – 10,000kg/22,046lb

Performance: Maximum speed – 65kph/40mph

ABOVE AND LEFT: **The ZiL-167E was effectively a high-mobility 6x6 version of the ZiL-135. It was originally intended as a civil engineering vehicle, but the Soviet authorities believed it could be easily adapted into an all-terrain heavy artillery tractor or prime mover.**

ZiL-167E

Dating from the mid-1960s, the ZiL-167E was an experimental version of the 8x8 BAZ-135/ZiL-135. Although not specifically designed for military usage, since it was eminently suitable for use as a heavy tractor for civil engineering, it was believed that the truck could be developed into a high-mobility artillery tractor or prime mover that would be capable of providing exceptional performance in extremely difficult terrain.

Like the BAZ-135/ZiL-135, it was powered by two ZiL 7,000cc V8 petrol engines, although for this vehicle the engines were mounted at the extreme rear. Each engine was arranged to drive the wheels on one side of the vehicle through a hydro-mechanical transmission system located between the first and second axles. The axles were not selectable and the truck had full-time six-wheel drive. Torsion-bar suspension was fitted on the first and third axles, both of which provided steering. The centre axle was not fitted with suspension.

BELOW: **It is thought that a single example was produced and that there was no series production.**

At least for early prototypes, the truck shared the same two-door glass-fibre composite cab of the BAZ-135/ZiL-135. A covered crew accommodation area was located between the driving and the engine compartments.

It is not known whether there was any series production, but there is some evidence to believe that the same chassis was used on a 6x6 "Transporter-Erector-Launcher" (TEL) for the Soviet SA-8A (NATO name: "Gecko") surface-to-air missile.

ZiL-167E

Type: Truck-tractor, high mobility, 5-ton, 6x6
Manufacturer: Likhachev Auto Zavod; Moscow
Production: 1967
Powerplant: 2x ZiL-375; each of eight cylinders in V configuration; petrol; water-cooled; 7,000cc; overhead valves; power output, 180bhp at 1,800rpm
Transmission: Hydro-mechanical; full-time 6x6
Suspension: Independent suspension by upper and lower wishbones and torsion bars on first and third axles; no suspension on centre axle
Brakes: Air-pressure assisted hydraulic
Electrical system: 24V
Dimensions: Length – 9,260mm/365in
    Width – 3,130mm/123in
    Height – to top of cab, 3,060mm/120in
    Wheelbase – 3,150+3,150mm/248+248in
Weight: Unladen – 7,000kg/15,432lb
    Payload – 5,000kg/11,023lb
Performance: Maximum speed – 65kph/40mph

Pegaso model 3055

In 1946, the Spanish state-owned Empresa Nacional de Autocamiones (ENASA) acquired the Barcelona-based truck-building operation of Hispano-Suiza and relaunched the products under the name Pegaso. The Hispano-based models were discontinued in 1958 and a range of entirely new vehicles was launched. In 1960, Leyland acquired an interest in ENASA which led to the widespread adoption of Leyland engines and running gear. In 1981, International-Harvester acquired a 35 per cent stake, but withdrew a year or so later. At this time, ENASA acquired Seddon-Atkinson, which had also been previously owned by International-Harvester.

DAF had also been under International-Harvester control for a while and, in the late 1960s, had designed trucks for Pegaso. ENASA maintained design links with DAF following the withdrawal of International. The model 3055, dating from 1982, is a good example of this shared development process. It was effectively a 6x6 development of the Pegaso 3046 which, in turn, had been based on the DAF-designed 3045. There was considerable commonality of components between the types.

Rated at a nominal 10 tons, the 3055 was powered by a six-cylinder turbocharged diesel engine driving through a six-speed gearbox and two-speed, pneumatically operated, transfer box. Suspension was by semi-elliptical multi-leaf springs.

The truck shared a canvas-topped cab with the 3046. A hard-top cab variant was also available. Standard variants included a cargo/personnel carrier, artillery tractor, multiple rocket launcher, fuel tanker, water tanker, heavy crane carrier, tipper, fire tender, workshop and refrigerated van. There was also a tractor for semi-trailers which could be used as a tank transporter. In 1987, the model 3055 was replaced by the longer-wheelbase model 7323.

Pegaso model 3055

Type: Truck, cargo, 6- to 10-ton, 6x6
Manufacturer: Empresa Nacional de Autocamiones (ENASA); Madrid
Production: 1982 to 1987
Powerplant: Pegaso 9220/10; six cylinders in-line; turbocharged diesel; water-cooled; 10,581cc; overhead valves; power output, 200–220bhp at 2,000rpm
Transmission: 6F1Rx2; part-time 6x6
Suspension: Live axles on semi-elliptical springs; double-acting hydraulic shock absorbers at front
Brakes: Air-pressure
Electrical system: 24V
Dimensions: Length – chassis-cab, 6,956mm/274in
Width – 2,400mm/94in
Height – top of cab, 2,710mm/107in
Wheelbase – 3,245mm/128in
Bogie centres – 1,484mm/58in
Weight: Unladen – 9,000kg/19,841lb
Payload – road, 10,000kg/22,046lb;
cross-country, 6,000kg/13,228lb
Performance: Maximum speed – 80kph/50mph

Santana S-2000

In 1956, the Santana company began building Land Rovers in Spain, and by 1981 was producing 18,000 vehicles a year. Early production matched the Solihull product but, once the Spanish Army became a customer, Santana vehicles started to develop along different lines to those produced in the UK.

Dating from 1978, and intended for both military and civilian users, albeit rated at 2 tons. The vehicle was powered by a six-cylinder petrol engine, although a diesel option was also available, driving through a four-speed gearbox and two-speed transfer box. Suspension was by live axles on semi-elliptical multi-leaf springs.

The distinctive flat-panelled cab shared little with the Solihull product. Standard variants included a drop-side truck, personnel carrier, workshop, command/communications vehicle and shelter carrier. The Spanish Army also used the vehicle as a mount for a 20mm Oerlikon anti-aircraft cannon. The company name was changed to Land Rover Santana in 1981, although the relationship with Land Rover ended in 1983.

LEFT: The S-2000 could be considered a Spanish version of the British-built Land Rover 101 forward-control model.

Santana S-2000

Type: Truck, cargo, 2-ton, 4x4
Manufacturer: Metalúrgica de Santa Ana; Madrid
Production: 1978 on
Powerplant: Six cylinders in-line; petrol; water-cooled; 3,429cc; overhead valves; power output, 100bhp at 4,000rpm
Transmission: 4F1Rx2; part-time 4x4
Suspension: Live axles on semi-elliptical springs
Brakes: Hydraulic
Electrical system: 24V
Dimensions: Length – 4,918mm/194in
Width – 1,925mm/76in
Height – 2,235mm/88in
Wheelbase – 2,565mm/101in
Weight: Unladen – 2,360kg/5,203lb
Payload – 2,000kg/4,409lb
Performance: Maximum speed – 90kph/56mph

Volvo TP21 P2104

Nicknamed *Sugga* (Sow) in recognition of its snout-shaped front, the Volvo TP21 was a field command car very much in the mould of the World War II ³/₄-ton Dodge WC series. The vehicle was introduced in 1953 and was built on the chassis of the Volvo TL11 four-wheel drive truck on to which the bodyshell of the PV830 taxi had been mounted. The military bonnet and front wings were similar to those used on TL11 trucks of the same period. The TP21 was designed to replace the wartime TPV command car and was produced in two variants – a five-seat radio car and a seven-seat command car. The same chassis was also used to mount a station wagon body.

The engine was a six-cylinder side-valve unit, coupled to a four-speed gearbox and two-speed transfer box. Live axles were suspended on semi-elliptical springs.

Vacuum-operated differential locks were fitted to both axles. Total production was 720 vehicles over six years.

LEFT: The vehicle used a light truck chassis and a taxi body.

Volvo TP21 P2104

Type: Car, 5/7 seat, command/radio, 4x4
Manufacturer: Volvo; Göteborg
Production: 1953 to 1958
Powerplant: Volvo ED/90; six cylinders in-line; petrol; water-cooled; 3,650cc; side valves; power output, 90bhp at 3,600rpm
Transmission: 4F1Rx2; part-time 4x4
Suspension: Live axles on semi-elliptical multi-leaf springs
Brakes: Hydraulic
Electrical system: 12V
Dimensions: Length – 4,500mm/177in
Width – 1,900mm/75in
Height – 1,950mm/77in
Wheelbase – 2,680mm/106in
Weight: Unladen – 2,600kg/5,732lb
Payload – 600kg/1,323lb
Performance: Maximum speed – 105kph/65mph

Volvo TL31

Volvo TL31

Type: Truck, cargo, 3-ton, 6x6
Manufacturer: Volvo; Göteborg
Production: 1956 to 1962
Powerplant: Volvo D96As, TD96AS; six cylinders in-line; diesel (TD96AS, turbocharged); water-cooled; 9,586cc; overhead valves; power output, 150bhp at 2,200rpm (185bhp for TD96AS)
Transmission: 5F1Rx2; part-time 6x6
Suspension: Live axles semi-elliptical multi-leaf springs
Brakes: Air-pressure assisted hydraulic
Electrical system: 24V
Dimensions: (cargo vehicles)
Length – 7,150mm/281in
Width – 2,150mm/85in
Height – tilt in place, 2,950mm/116in
Wheelbase – 3,920mm/154in
Bogie centres – 1,250mm/49in
Weight: Unladen – 7,320kg/16,138lb
Payload – 3,000kg/6,614lb
Performance: Maximum speed – 73kph/45mph

ABOVE: **The Volvo TL31 was developed from the company's L395 truck of the early 1950s.**

Volvo's TL31 6x6 was developed from the company's L395 Titan truck in the early 1950s and entered production in 1956. Designed specifically for the military, the original cab of the Titan was replaced by a strictly functional all-steel type fabricated by Nyström of Umea. Standard variants included cargo/prime mover (L3154), recovery (L3164), and fire-crash-rescue (L3154S).

The cargo and recovery variants were powered by a six-cylinder diesel engine, while the variants produced for the Swedish Air Force used a turbocharged version of the same power unit with an additional 35bhp. The engine was coupled to double-reduction axles via a five-speed gearbox (overdrive top) and a two-speed transfer box. Suspension was by live axles on semi-elliptical leaf springs, inverted at the rear. An 8-ton capacity winch was fitted under the chassis. A total of 921 had been built when production ended in 1962.

Volvo Laplander L3314

Nicknamed *Valp* (Pup or Cub), the Laplander was a small utility vehicle based largely on the Amazon motor car and designed to replace the Swedish Army's ageing Willys Jeeps.

Following a run of 91 of the pre-production L2304 version during 1959 and 1960, building of the definitive L3314 began in 1961.

Where the L2304 had been powered by Volvo's B16 four-cylinder engine, this was replaced by the iconic B18 and then the B20 for the L3314. The engine drove both axles through a four-speed gearbox and two-speed transfer box. Suspension was by live axles on semi-elliptical leaf springs. The combination of a forward-control driving position, differential locks, flexible suspension and large low-pressure tyres, provided excellent off-road performance.

Standard variants included personnel/cargo carrier, missile carrier, radio vehicle, ambulance and fire tender.

LEFT: **Over a ten-year period 7,737 of the Laplander L3314 and 1,116 of the L3315 were built.**

Volvo Laplander L3314

Type: Truck, personnel/cargo, 4x4
Manufacturer: Volvo; Göteborg
Production: 1961 to 1970
Powerplant: Volvo B18A, B20A; four cylinders in-line; petrol; water-cooled; 1,778cc, 1,978cc; overhead valves; power output, 65–82bhp at 4,500rpm
Transmission: 4F1Rx2; part-time 4x4; differential locks, front and rear
Suspension: Live axles on semi-elliptical multi-leaf springs
Brakes: Vacuum servo-assisted hydraulic
Electrical system: 12V, 24V
Dimensions: Length – 4,050mm/159in
Width – 1,660mm/65in
Height – tilt in place, 2,100mm/83in
Wheelbase – 2,100mm/83in
Weight: Unladen – 1,600kg/3,527lb
Payload – 850kg/1,874lb
Performance: Maximum speed – 90kph/56mph

There was also a fully enclosed variant designated L3315. Total production, over a ten-year period, amounted to 7,737 examples of the L3314, plus 1,116 of the L3315.

Volvo Laplander L4140, L4141

In 1966, Volvo started the development work on a replacement for the L3314 Laplander. Early prototypes were powered by the B20A four-cylinder engine as used in the earlier vehicle but by 1974, when the truck went into production, this had been replaced by the B30A six-cylinder unit. Designated L4140 in open form and L4141 when fitted with an enclosed body, the new Laplander all-terrain vehicle had been designed under the direction of Mans Hartelius. It was manufactured at the company's "A Plant" at Lundby, which had previously been used for the P1800 and Duett motor cars. The chassis was identified as the C300 series, and there were long- (C304) and short-wheelbase (C303) versions.

Like the earlier L3314, the truck was fitted with a forward-control driving position, which ensured excellent visibility. The use of reduction-gear portal-type axles improved the ground clearance, and vacuum-operated differential locks made it unlikely that the truck would become immobilized in even the roughest terrain. The engine was a down-rated version of the company's B30 six-cylinder twin-carburettor unit, driving both axles through a four-speed gearbox and two-speed transfer box. Suspension was by live axles on semi-elliptical multi-leaf springs with hollow rubber assisters.

The vehicle was intended for use by the Swedish and Norwegian defence forces and also for public utilities and fire services. Standard variants included a hard-topped personnel cargo carrier (Swedish Army TGB 111A MT), the C404 open-topped mount for an anti-tank gun (PVP JTGB 1111A) and a hard-topped radio communications vehicle (RATGB 1112A MT). There was also a three-axle 6x6 variant designated L4143 (C306). An 8x8 was prototyped, but not put into production. Total production, over an 11-year period, amounted to 8,718 of all variants.

A civilian version was launched in 1976, and production of the old L3314 was transferred to Hungary where it was designated as the C202.

ABOVE: **In the mid-1960s, Volvo's chief designer of off-road vehicles, Nils Magnus 'Måns' Hartelius, began work on a replacement for the Volvo L3314 Laplander. Early prototypes were fitted with the Volvo B20A four-cylinder engine as used in the L3314. On production vehicles this was replaced by the B30A six-cylinder engine. Variants included the L4140 (open-topped) and the L4141 (enclosed cab).**

Volvo Laplander L4140, L4141

Type: Truck, personnel/cargo, 1-ton, 4x4
Manufacturer: Volvo; Göteborg
Production: 1974 to 1984
Powerplant: Volvo B30A; six cylinders in-line; petrol; water-cooled; 2,980cc; overhead valves; power output, 117bhp at 4,000rpm
Transmission: 4F1Rx2; part-time 4x4; differential locks front and rear
Suspension: Live portal axles on semi-elliptical multi-leaf springs; double-acting telescopic shock absorbers
Brakes: Vacuum servo-assisted hydraulic
Electrical system: 24V
Dimensions: Length – 4,350mm/171in
Width – 1,900mm/75in
Height – tilt in place, 2,170mm/86in
Wheelbase – 2,300mm/91in, 2,530mm/100in
Weight: Unladen – 2,400kg/5,291lb
Payload – 1,250kg/2,756lb
Performance: Maximum speed – 120kph/75mph

MOWAG GW4500

In 1950, MOWAG Motorwagenfabriek was established in Kreuzlingen, Switzerland. The company's first product was the GW4500, a purpose-designed ³/₄-ton 4x4 cross-country military truck.

Despite the use of a forward-control driving position, and the company's proud boast of employing a "patented framework chassis", the vehicle was very much the same type as the

T214-engined WC Dodge trucks of World War II, even to the extent of being powered by a similar engine and transmission.

The engine was a Dodge T137 six-cylinder, driving both axles through a four-speed crash gearbox, with synchromesh being introduced during the production run. The vehicle was subsequently upgraded to 1 ton and then 1¹/₂ tons, using a 103bhp version of the engine giving a useful increase in top speed. Final drive was via a two-speed transfer box. The live axles were suspended on conventional semi-elliptical leaf springs.

Standard variants included an open-cabbed weapons/personnel carrier, for which there was also a bolt-on hardtop, box-bodied five-stretcher ambulance, radio command vehicle, civil-defence vehicle, fire-tender and police vehicle. The chassis was also used as the basis for a tank-training vehicle. Like all Swiss military vehicles, it had a right-hand steering position.

A total of 1,688 were built, with production taking place between 1950 and 1956. Production restarted with the upgraded version in 1962.

MOWAG remains in defence manufacturing and is now part of the General Dynamics Group.

ABOVE: **A steel-bodied ambulance variant of the GW4500 with the canvas cab roof rolled back.**

LEFT: **Other variants of the GW4500 included an open-bodied weapons carrier. The vehicle was also built with a fully enclosed body which could be used as a radio command, civil-defence or police vehicle. A crew cab fire-tender body was available for the Swiss Air Force.**

MOWAG GW4500

Type: Truck, ³/₄- to 1¹/₂-ton, cargo, 4x4
Manufacturer: MOWAG Motorwagenfabriek; Kreuzlingen
Production: 1950 to 1956, 1962
Powerplant: Dodge T137; six cylinders in-line; water-cooled; petrol; 3,770cc; side valves; power output, 91–103bhp at 3,600rpm
Transmission: 4F1Rx2; part-time 4x4
Suspension: Live axles on semi-elliptical multi-leaf springs
Brakes: Hydraulic
Electrical system: 6V, 12V
Dimensions: Length – 4,740mm/187in
  Width – 1,830mm/72in
  Height – soft-top variants, 2,215mm/87in; hard-top variants, 2,480mm/98in
  Wheelbase – 2,600mm/102in
Weight: Unladen – 3,200kg/7,055lb
  Payload – 750-1,500kg/1,653-3,307lb
Performance: Maximum speed – 90kph/55mph

MOWAG DURO

The high-mobility multi-role DURO (*Dauerhaft*, *Unabhängig*, *Robust*, *Oekonomisch* – durable, self-reliant, robust, economical) was developed in the late 1980s to replace the Swiss Army's ageing logistics fleet. After a period of extensive trials, an initial order for 2,000 vehicles was placed in 1993 with deliveries commencing in 1994. Initially manufactured by a consortium of Swiss engineering companies led by Bucher-Guyer, from 2003 the truck has been marketed under General Dynamics MOWAG, with recent upgrades designated DURO II and DURO III.

The DURO is available as a standard- and long-wheelbase 4x4, and as a 6x6, with a high degree of component commonality across the configurations. Early examples were powered by a VM six-cylinder diesel engine, but this was subsequently replaced by a Cummins six-cylinder unit, driving all axles through a four- or five-speed automatic gearbox, and two-speed transfer box. All axles are fitted with self-locking differentials to provide enhanced mobility and an inter-axle differential lock. The torsion-free underslung chassis is of tubular design and incorporates swing-arm independent suspension with an integral roll-stabilizing system.

All soft-skin variants use the same forward-control tilt-cab of aluminium/composite construction. Variants include cargo, personnel, shelter carrier, ambulance, communications, command, fire tender and police command. An armoured variant (DURO 4x4SP, 6x6SP) is available for cargo, personnel and ambulance roles. There is also an armoured variant based on the standard 4x4 and 6x6 chassis.

The DURO is in widespread service, including the Swiss, German, Danish, and Irish armies. Also the British Army and RAF.

ABOVE: **The DURO was initially manufactured by a consortium of Swiss engineering companies led by Bucher-Guyer. From 2003 the vehicle has been marketed under General Dynamics MOWAG. Both 4x4 and 6x6 versions have been produced.**

LEFT: **The armoured DURO 4x4SP, and the similar 6x6SP, are intended for the cargo, personnel and ambulance roles. The type is in widespread service, including with the armed forces of Venezuela and Malaysia. The German Army also uses the DURO IIIP 6x6 ballistic and mine-protected version.**

MOWAG DURO

Type: Truck, 2-ton, cargo, 4x4
Manufacturer: MOWAG Motorwagenfabriek; Kreuzlingen
Production: 1993 on
Powerplant: VM-642 LM; six cylinders in-line; direct-injection turbocharged diesel; water-cooled; 4,171cc; overhead valves; power output, 160bhp at 3,000rpm Cummins ISBe 185; six cylinders in-line; direct-injection turbocharged diesel; water-cooled; 5,883cc; overhead valves; power output, 185bhp at 2,500rpm
Transmission: 4F1Rx2 or 5F1Rx2; automatic; full-time 4x4
Suspension: Independent suspension using leading and trailing arms with coil springs, twinned at the rear
Brakes: Hydraulic
Electrical system: 24V
Dimensions: Length – 5,200mm/205in, 6,350mm/250in
Width – 1,990mm/78in
Height – to top of cab, 2,600mm/102in
Wheelbase – 3,230mm/127in, 3,880mm/153in
Weight: Unladen – 3,800kg/8,377lb
Payload – 2,970–3,100kg/6,548–6,834lb
Performance: Maximum speed – 110kph/68mph

AEC Y Type

ABOVE: **By 1918, AEC had built 8,821 Y Types. The truck was also used by US forces in France.**

The Associated Equipment Company Limited (AEC) was originally founded at Walthamstow in June 1912 to manufacture and repair buses for the London General Omnibus Company (LGOC). By 1913, AEC employed more than 1,200 workers, and by the outbreak of World War I, the company had also turned its hand to manufacturing motor lorries for the War Office. A sales agreement signed in 1912 meant that, at first, these were marketed by Daimler, as had been the early buses, and were also identified with that company's brand.

The Y Type dated from March 1915 and was actually little more than a lower-geared version of the earlier X Type, which, had been a development of the W Type with heavy-duty rear hubs. At the end of June 1916, the AEC factory was placed under direct Government control and from that date the trucks were identified as AEC, although the distinctive Daimler radiator remained. A moving production line was installed in 1917 when the factory was extended and this helped to raise output to 130 chassis per week.

The original Y Type was powered by a 5,700cc four-cylinder 40bhp Daimler sleeve-valve engine, driving the rear wheels, which were shod with solid rubber tyres, through a four-speed gearbox to a worm-drive rear axle. By 1917, the Daimler engine had been replaced by a 7,700cc Tylor four-cylinder unit, with the model designation becoming YA to signify the change. The YB was similar but used a pressed-steel frame and the YC used a David Brown worm-gear final drive.

Mounting a fixed-side timber body combined with a canvas-covered open cab, the Y Type was the typical military cargo vehicle of the period and was used by the British and US armies during World War I.

By the time of the armistice in 1918, AEC had built 8,821, of which 5,200 were fitted with the Tylor engine. The War Office purchased a further 822 Y Types during 1919, and the vehicle remained in production for commercial customers into the early 1920s.

After the war, many Y Types passed to civilian operators, where the standard military body was often removed to convert the vehicle to an omnibus.

LEFT: **The 3-ton timber cargo body was typical of those fitted to vehicles of the period.**

AEC Y Type

Type: Truck, 3-ton, cargo, 4x2
Manufacturer: Associated Equipment Company; Walthamstow
Production: 1915 to 1922
Powerplant: Y Type – Daimler; four cylinders in-line; petrol; water-cooled; 5,700cc; sleeve valves; power output, 40bhp at 1,300rpm. YA, YB, YC Type – Tylor JB4; four cylinders in-line; water-cooled; petrol; 7,700cc; side valves; power output, 49bhp at 1,300rpm
Transmission: 4F1R; 4x2
Suspension: Live axles on semi-elliptical multi-leaf springs
Brakes: Mechanical, rear wheels only
Electrical system: Magneto only
Dimensions: Length – 7,163mm/282in
Width – 2,108mm/83in
Height – tilt in place, 3,099mm/122in
Wheelbase – 4,343mm/171in
Weight: Unladen – 4,277kg/9,492lb
Payload – 3,048kg/6,720lb
Performance: Maximum speed – 19kph/12mph

LEFT: **The Matador was widely considered to be the best British-built truck of World War II. Many remained in military service into the 1960s.**

AEC Model O853 Matador

Design work on what became the Matador medium artillery tractor was carried out by Charles Cleaver of the Four Wheel Drive Motor Company (FWD), in conjunction with Hardy Motors who were working on a 4-ton 4x4 chassis for the War Department. AEC purchased FWD of Southall, Middlesex, and Cleaver completed the work. The first prototype, which was petrol-engined and designated Model 853, was trialled in 1938. Following the successful conclusion of the trials, AEC received a Ministry of Supply contract for 200 vehicles. By the time World War II was over, almost 10,500 Matadors had been

supplied, the majority of which were diesel-engined, designated Model O853, with the "O" indicating the "oil" engine.

Powered by AEC's own 7,580cc A173 six-cylinder diesel engine, the forward-control layout placed the engine between the driver and passenger seat. The engine was coupled to a four-speed unitary gearbox and a remote two-speed transfer box, driving both axles.

The most numerous variant was the artillery tractor, which was fitted with a

BELOW: **An early production Matador; note that the vehicle does not have the distinctive double-skin domed roof on the cab.**

composite wood and steel body, with seating for a gun crew of nine or ten. Shell carriers attached to rails in the floor were intended to make it easy to offload the ammunition. Most vehicles were fitted with a 5- or 7-ton underfloor winch. Alongside the artillery tractor, there was also a cargo variant used by the RAF, as well as a range of specialized bodies including an armoured command post. Matador mechanical components were also used to develop the AEC heavy armoured car.

The Matador was the first all-wheel-drive truck to be produced in Britain in quantity. It served all through the war, and right into the 1950s and 1960s. Indeed, in 1953, with problems being encountered in the development of a post-war replacement, a further 1,800 Matadors were purchased, with an uprated A187 engine.

Rugged and powerful, the Matador was used over all types of terrain. This reputation for reliability also made the vehicle a popular choice with fairground operators, and round-timber and heavy-haulage contractors.

AEC Model O853 Matador

Type: Tractor, medium artillery, 4x4
Manufacturer: AEC Motors; Southall
Production: 1938 to 1953
Powerplant: AEC A173 or A187; six cylinders in-line; direct-injection diesel; water-cooled; 7,580cc; overhead valves; power output, 95bhp (105bhp for A187) at 1,800rpm
Transmission: 4F1Rx2; part-time 4x4
Suspension: Live axles on semi-elliptical multi-leaf springs
Brakes: Air-assisted hydraulic or air-pressure
Electrical system: 12V
Dimensions: Length – 6,325mm/249in
    Width – 2,426mm/95in
    Height – tilt in place, 3,099mm/122in; minimum, 2,946mm/116in
    Wheelbase – 3,848mm/151in
Weight: Unladen – 7,190kg/15,850lb
    Payload – 3,833kg/8,450lb
Performance: Maximum speed – 61kph/38mph

Although it had originally been designed as a cargo truck and most of those produced were bodied for this role, a total of 349 artillery tractors were built between 1954 and 1964. The artillery tractor was intended to be used as a prime mover for artillery pieces weighing up to 16 tons, for example the 5.5 or 7.2in howitzer. It was a replacement for the similar Matador and Mack vehicles from World War II. A fixed-side wood and steel composite body was fitted, produced by Crossley Motors. This could accommodate a crew of nine together with stowage space for 4,491kg/9,900lb of stores and ammunition. A 5- or 7-ton Turner chain-driven winch was mounted behind the auxiliary gearbox.

A multi-fuel engined Mk 2 version was produced in 1962 and, although, this did not enter series production, it provided a useful test-bed for further development work. The original Militant was eventually superseded in the cargo role by the much updated Mk 3.

AEC Militant Mk 1

Development work on the AEC Militant started in 1951, with the vehicle entering production the following year. Rated at 10 tons, the chassis was derived from the 6x6 Model O854 which the company had produced for the RAF during World War II. The Militant was produced in both 6x6 (Model O860) and 6x4 (Model O859) configurations, also in two wheelbase lengths. It was offered both as a military and commercial vehicle and was widely exported, with a total of 3,200 examples produced during

13 years in production. British Army variants included a medium/heavy artillery tractor, cargo vehicle, three-way tipper and a crane carrier.

The standard engine was an 11,310cc AEC A223 six-cylinder direct-injection diesel unit driving the rear, or front and rear, axles through a five-speed gearbox and separately mounted two-speed auxiliary gearbox which also contained the front axle selector for 6x6 vehicles. Suspension was entirely conventional, using semi-elliptical leaf springs, inverted at the rear.

LEFT: **The cargo variant was fitted with a fabricated steel drop-side body. The side panels were removable to provide a flat bed for containers. The truck was also available to civilian customers and was popular in foreign markets. A total of 3,200 were produced.**

AEC Militant Mk 1

Type: Tractor, medium/heavy artillery, 10-ton, 6x4, 6x6; FV11001, FV11002
Manufacturer: AEC Motors; Southall
Production: 1952 to 1964
Powerplant: AEC A223; six cylinders in-line; diesel; water-cooled; 11,310cc; overhead valves; power output, 150bhp at 1,800rpm
Transmission: 5F1Rx2; 6x4 or part-time 6x6
Suspension: Live axles on semi-elliptical multi-leaf springs, inverted at the rear
Brakes: Air-pressure
Electrical system: 24V
Dimensions: Length – 7,353mm/289in
Width – 2,438mm/96in
Height – tilt in place, 2,946mm/116in; minimum, 2,807mm/111in
Wheelbase – 3,924mm/154in, and (cargo variants only) 4,880mm/192in
Bogie centres – 1,372mm/54in
Weight: Unladen – 10,304–10,558kg/ 22,715–23,276lb
Payload – 5,100kg/11,220lb
Performance: Maximum speed – 40kph/25mph

Albion CX22S

ABOVE: **Only 532 Albion CX22S vehicles were built between November 1943 and June 1945.**

Albion CX22S

Type: Tractor, heavy artillery, 6x4
Manufacturer: Albion Motors; Scotstoun
Production: 1943 to 1945
Powerplant: Albion EN244; six cylinders in-line; diesel; water-cooled; 9,060cc; overhead valves; power output, 100bhp at 1,750rpm
Transmission: 4F1Rx2; 6x4
Suspension: Live axles on semi-elliptical multi-leaf springs
Brakes: Air-assisted mechanical, rear wheels only
Electrical system: Hybrid 12V/24V
Dimensions: Length – 7,777mm/306in
  Width – 2,669mm/105in
  Height – 3,162mm/124in
  Wheelbase – 4,474mm/176in
  Bogie centres – 1,372mm/54in
Weight: Unladen – 10,605kg/23,379lb
  Payload – 5,216kg/11,500lb
Performance: Maximum speed – 45kph/28mph

Albion Motors was founded in Glasgow in 1899 and began building trucks in 1910. The company produced 6,000 trucks for the British Army during World War I and remained an important supplier of military vehicles throughout the 1930s and into World War II.

Dating from late 1943 and designed to supplement the Scammell R100 Pioneer (which was never available in large enough numbers) the Albion CX22S was a heavy artillery tractor for towing the 7.2 or 6in howitzers. Developed from the company's CX23N 10-ton truck, it was powered by a six-cylinder diesel engine driving the rear wheels through a four-speed gearbox and two-speed auxiliary gearbox.

The cab provided bench seating for two/three, while the rear body had a bench seat for four, together with folding seats for another two. There was also stowage for ammunition, tools and equipment. An 8-ton capacity Scammell vertical-spindle winch was fitted under the rear body.

Albion WD66N

Albion WD66N

Type: Truck, 5-ton, cargo, 6x6; FV14000 series
Manufacturer: Albion Motors; Scotstoun
Production: 1955 to 1956
Powerplant: Rolls-Royce B80 Mk 1D; eight cylinders in-line; petrol; water-cooled; 5,675cc; overhead inlet valves, side exhaust; power output, 165bhp at 3,750rpm
Transmission: 5F1Rx2; part-time 6x6
Suspension: Live axles on semi-elliptical multi-leaf springs
Brakes: Air-assisted hydraulic
Electrical system: 24V
Dimensions: Length – 7,163mm/282in
  Width – 2,438mm/96in
  Height – 3,277mm/129in
  Wheelbase – 3,180mm/125in
  Bogie centres – 1,372mm/54in
Weight: Unladen – 7,069kg/15,584lb
  Payload – 5,480kg/12,078lb
Performance: Maximum speed – 56kph/35mph

In 1951, Albion Motors took over the contract for the FV1300, a 3-ton 6x6 chassis originally developed by Vauxhall and, in June of that year, received an order for 6,000 vehicles. In May 1953,

BELOW: **The WD66N was a promising vehicle, but was cancelled after only nine chassis had been completed.**

before any had been built, the contract was cancelled but, in 1955, Albion was asked to produce a prototype for a 5-ton 6x6 semi-forward control vehicle which would take its place.

Aside from the Rolls-Royce eight-cylinder engine, the vehicle was based on an existing Albion chassis, and was fitted with a five-speed gearbox and two-speed transfer box. The rear axles were of the worm-drive type, while that at the front was fitted with spiral bevel gears. Hub reduction gears were fitted at front and rear. Suspension was by semi-elliptical springs. Just nine chassis were built, some of which were fitted with a steel drop-side cargo body (FV14001).

LEFT: **The prototype for the Alvis Stalwart was based on the company's Salamander, a rear-engined fire tender.**

Alvis Stalwart

The amphibious Stalwart was the last of four vehicles to use the Rolls-Royce-powered Alvis 6x6 chassis; this had already been used for the Salamander airfield fire tender, the Saladin heavy armoured car and the Saracen armoured personnel carrier. Although it was said to have been developed from the front-engined Salamander, initially as a private venture, on the Stalwart the engine was mounted in the centre of the vehicle. A prototype was proposed to the War Office as a possible contender for the cargo-carrying tracked vehicle role for which the FV431 was being considered. Following a series of trials, it was concluded that the Stalwart offered comparable performance at lower cost and further development work was undertaken.

With permanent six-wheel drive, independent suspension on all six wheels, and "Hydrojet" propulsion for the amphibious role, the Stalwart was an impressive vehicle which offered performance equal to tracked vehicles, but without the maintenance requirements. The Corten steel hull was a monocoque fitted with a cab and drop-side cargo bay, which was fitted with a waterproof cover. The driver sat centrally in the cab, for which there were no doors; the crew was required to enter through roof hatches. A typical load comprised 5,080kg/ 5 tons of cargo or 38 fully equipped troops. The engine and transmission were installed beneath the cargo bay floor.

The vehicle was powered by a Rolls-Royce B81 eight-cylinder petrol engine with a five-speed gearbox driving six

BELOW: **In production form, the Stalwart was mid-engined, with the 6,516cc Rolls-Royce power unit installed beneath the cargo bay. The deep corner windows identify this as a Stalwart Mk 2.**

large, equally spaced wheels. There was a single-speed unitary transfer box, which allowed the use of all five gears in forward or reverse and also incorporated a limited-slip differential. Final drive to the wheels was transmitted by bevel-geared boxes and epicyclic reduction gears. This subsequently proved to be something of a weakness, and if the vehicle was driven on hard surfaces for too long, the fact that there was just one differential could lead to transmission stresses causing failure of the bevel-geared boxes and drive shafts. A power take-off on the transfer box was linked to the two Dowty "Hydrojet" units which provided propulsion and directional control when afloat.

Suspension was independent on all six wheels using twin wishbones and longitudinal torsion bars; there were two double-acting hydraulic shock absorbers at each wheel station. Steering was through the front and centre axles.

The first prototypes were submitted for trials in 1960. Two years later, in August 1962, Alvis received contracts for 250 Mk 1 Stalwarts, designated FV620. In 1966, the Mk 1 was replaced by the Mk 2 which offered increased power and mobility, particularly in the water. It also required less maintenance. Alongside the basic cargo vehicle, now designated FV622, there were the FV623 artillery tractor and the FV624 REME fitters' vehicle, both of the latter with an Atlas 3-ton hydraulic crane mounted behind the cab. Field modifications saw the Stalwart fitted with the EMI Ranger anti-personnel mine-laying system, and with "Unit Bulk Replenishment Refuelling Equipment" (UBRE).

The production total for the Mk 2 was 1,322, of which 117 were the FV623 variant and 120 were the FV624. The vehicle saw service with British Army units in West Germany

ABOVE: **A Mk 1 Stalwart, designated FV620. Propulsion in the water was by Dowty "Hydrojet" units at the rear of the vehicle.**

and was sold to the armies of Austria, Sweden and Switzerland. A scheme to allow the vehicle to be built under licence by Berliet in France, under the name Auroch, never progressed beyond the prototype stage.

Changing attitudes towards amphibious vehicles within NATO led to the "Hydrojet" units being removed in 1985, but the Stalwart remained in service until the early 1990s.

Alvis Stalwart

Type: Truck, 5-ton, high-mobility load carrier, 6x6; FV620, FV622, FV623, FV624
Manufacturer: Alvis; Coventry
Production: 1962 to 1971
Powerplant: Rolls-Royce B81 Mk 8B; eight cylinders in-line; petrol; water-cooled; 6,516cc; overhead inlet valves, side exhaust; power output, 195bhp at 3,750rpm
Transmission: 5F5R; full-time 6x6; "Hydrojet" propulsion when afloat
Suspension: Independent at all six wheels by double wishbones and torsion bars; double-acting hydraulic shock absorbers
Brakes: Air-assisted hydraulic
Electrical system: 24V
Dimensions: Length – 6,400mm/252in
 Width – 2,600mm/102in
 Height – tilt in place – 2,640mm/104in; minimum, 2,400mm/94in
 Wheelbase – 1,524+1,524mm/60+60in
Weight: Unladen – 8,408-9,932kg/18,575-21,863lb
 Payload – 5,239kg/11,550lb
Performance: Maximum speed – on land, 48-64kph/30-40mph; in water, 6.4-9.7kph/4-6mph

ABOVE: **The FV623 artillery tractor and the FV624 REME vehicle were both equipped with an Atlas hydraulic arm-type crane mounted behind the cab bulkhead.**

Austin K2

Although it is probably best known in K2/Y ambulance form, a total of 27,800 of the 2-ton Austin K2 were built during World War II, of which approximately half (13,102) were bodied as an ambulance. In this form it was the most widely used ambulance in World War II, and as well as being used by the British Army, it was supplied to France, Norway, Russia and the USA.

Described as a "heavy ambulance", the standardized body of the K2/Y variant was produced by Mann Egerton coachbuilders and was designed to accommodate four stretchers or ten seated casualties, together with a medical attendant. The body was of lightweight construction, by way of painted leathercloth fabric stretched over a timber frame; insulation was incorporated in the body and a heater was fitted. A connecting door gave access from the rear body to the cab. Other roles for what was essentially the same vehicle included mobile office and loudspeaker van. The same body, designated No 2 Mk I/L, was also fitted to the Bedford ML chassis.

The K2 dates from 1940 and was derived from the company's K30, a 30cwt open-cabbed military truck.

ABOVE: **Austin K2/Y ambulance ready for shipment to the Soviet Union, a charitable gift from the people of Scarborough, North Yorkshire.**

In turn, this had been based on the civilian vehicle with which the company had re-entered the commercial vehicle market in 1939. The truck was powered by a 3,462cc six-cylinder petrol engine driving the rear axle through a four-speed gearbox. There were live axles fitted at front and rear, carried on semi-elliptical leaf springs.

Other roles for this chassis included a general-service cargo vehicle, as well as a workshop and power equipment vehicle. In 1944, the K2/A variant was produced for the RAF and equipped as a fire tender.

Austin K2

Type: Truck, 2-ton, ambulance, 4x2
Manufacturer: Austin Motor Company; Longbridge
Production: 1940 to 1945
Powerplant: Austin; six cylinders in-line; petrol; water-cooled; 3,462cc; overhead valves; power output, 60bhp at 3,000rpm
Transmission: 4F1R; 4x2
Suspension: Live axles on semi-elliptical multi-leaf springs; hydraulic shock absorbers
Brakes: Hydraulic
Electrical system: 6V
Dimensions: Length – 5,486mm/216in
Width – 2,210mm/87in
Height – 2,743mm/108in
Wheelbase – 3,404mm/134in
Weight: Unladen – 8,426–9,917kg/18,575–21,863lb
Payload – 1,016kg/2,240lb
Performance: Maximum speed – 88kph/55mph

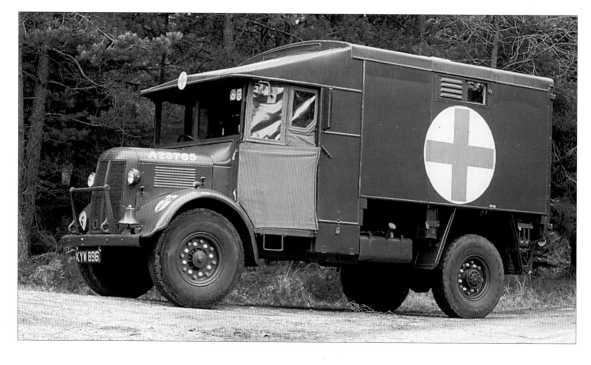

RIGHT: **The four-stretcher, insulated and heated rear body, manufactured by Mann Egerton, was of lightweight construction. A connecting door allowed access from the rear body to the cab. Side doors were not fitted, only canvas sidescreens.**

Austin WN1 "Champ"

Towards the closing years of World War II, the Austin Motor Company had been asked by the War Office to investigate the possibility of producing an all-British replacement for the Jeep. Nothing is known of Austin's reply in this respect but, in 1946, Nuffield Mechanizations produced a number of prototypes for a Jowett-powered vehicle identified as the "Gutty". It is said that Alec Issigonis was involved. In 1949, this was superseded by the FV1801 Wolseley "Mudlark". Retaining very little of the "Gutty" beyond the suspension, the "Mudlark" was powered by a Rolls-Royce B Series four-cylinder engine as used in a range of new British combat vehicles.

Following an almost three-year trials period, the production contract for this vehicle, described as FV1801A, was awarded to Austin. Between 1952 and 1955, some 13,500 were produced in two types – a standard cargo vehicle and a "Fitted For Wireless" (FFW) version intended for the communications role.

It was an advanced vehicle for the time, with a licence-built Rolls-Royce four-cylinder engine, five forward and reverse gears and independent torsion-bar suspension, and of unitary (chassis-less) construction. Screened and waterproofed 24V electrical equipment was fitted. Unfortunately, the WN1 was also expensive and unreliable and was quickly superseded by the cheaper Land Rover.

There were also field ambulance, cable layer and recoilless-rifle mount versions produced as well as a special forces version in the style of the Land Rover "Pink Panther". Few of these special vehicles were produced, and even fewer appear to have been used in action. The FV1801A was used only by the armies of Britain and Australia.

The name "Champ" was actually only officially assigned to the Austin A90-engined civilian version (chassis designation WN3), but was adopted by the National Servicemen who had a love-hate relationship with this advanced but unreliable vehicle. There was also an A90-engined military variant designated WN2.

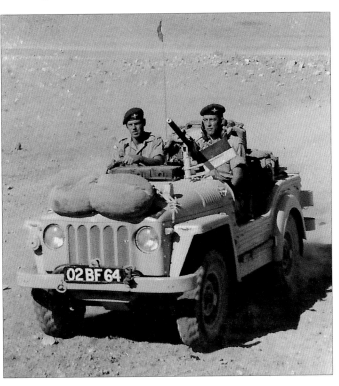

ABOVE: **The Rolls-Royce engined FV1801 Austin "Champ" was intended as a replacement for the Jeep, but in service it was too expensive, complex and unreliable. The Land Rover proved to be an adequate and cheaper alternative.**

LEFT: **The "Champ" began to enter service in 1952 and was used during the Suez Crisis. By 1966, all had been disposed of with some being used by the Territorial Army.**

Austin WN1 "Champ"

Type: Truck, ¼-ton, cargo (or FFW), 4x4; FV1801A

Manufacturer: Austin Motor Company; Longbridge

Production: 1952 to 1955

Powerplant: Licence-built Rolls-Royce B40 Mk 2A or Mk 5A; four cylinders in-line; petrol; water-cooled; 2,880cc; overhead inlet valves, side exhaust; power output, 52bhp at 3,600rpm

Transmission: 5F5R; part-time 4x4

Suspension: Independent suspension using wishbones and torsion bars; telescopic shock absorbers

Brakes: Hydraulic

Electrical system: 24V

Dimensions: Length – 3,670mm/144in
Width – 1,559mm/61in
Height – tilt in place, 1,880mm/74in; minimum, 1,372mm/54in
Wheelbase – 2,134mm/84in

Weight: Unladen – 1,660kg/3,660lb
Payload – 363kg/800lb

Performance: Maximum speed – 97kph/60mph

Bedford MW

During 1935, the British Army issued a specification for a 15cwt 4x2 "General Service" (GS) military truck inviting manufacturers to supply vehicles to take part in the annual comparative trials in north Wales. The trials were repeated, for various classes of vehicle, in 1936 and 1937.

In May 1937, one of Bedford's contributions to the trials was a short, square-fronted vehicle identified as WD-1 and assembled mainly from off-the-shelf components. It performed well in the trials, and did even better the following year by which time it was designated MW and fitted with a more powerful 3,519cc six-cylinder engine producing 72bhp. Although lacking four-wheel drive and thus not suitable for off-road use, the powerful engine, combined with a short wheelbase, low centre of gravity and relatively light weight, gave the vehicle excellent acceleration and almost sportscar-like handling.

Between 1939 and 1945 the company supplied more than 66,000 vehicles equipped for many different roles. The earliest examples were equipped with aero-type screens and canvas doors, but on later models there was a full windscreen, together with

steel doors, which resulted in a 150mm/6in increase in height. The vehicle was always open-cabbed, and the unusually wide bonnet was necessitated by the need for a special WD-type air cleaner. This was never actually fitted to production vehicles.

Alongside the standard cargo bodied vehicle (MWD), anti-aircraft gun tractor (MWT), machinery truck, water tanker (MWC), "Fitted For Wireless" (FFW) communications

ABOVE: **Although never fitted with four-wheel drive, the 15cwt Bedford MW was one of the best British trucks of World War II. It remained in production until 1945, by which time some 66,000 had been produced.**

truck (MWR) and radio van (MWV), there were even armoured versions. During production, the MW was supplied to all three British services as well as other Government departments and overseas customers.

ABOVE: **A Bedford MW being refuelled from a drum using a hand pump. Like all early MWs, the vehicle is fitted with folding aero-type screens.**

Bedford MW

Type: Truck, 15cwt, cargo, 4x2
Manufacturer: Vauxhall Motors; Luton
Production: 1939 to 1945
Powerplant: Bedford; six cylinders in-line; petrol; water-cooled; 3,519cc; overhead valves; power output, 72bhp at 3,000rpm
Transmission: 4F1R; 4x2
Suspension: Live axles on semi-elliptical multi-leaf springs
Brakes: Hydraulic
Electrical system: 12V
Dimensions: Length – 4,369mm/172in
　　Width – 1,981mm/78in
　　Height – tilt in place, 2,286mm/90in; minimum, 1,600mm/63in
　　Wheelbase – 2,515mm/99in
Weight: Unladen – 2,146kg/4,730lb
　　Payload – 1,361kg/3,000lb
Performance: Maximum speed – 64kph/40mph

ABOVE: Dating from 1941, and remaining in production until the end of the war, the QL was Bedford's first 4x4 truck. A total of more than 52,000 were produced.

ABOVE: A QLR signals office van at the headquarters of Field Marshal Montgomery, Commander-in-Chief of 21st Army Group, spring 1945.

Bedford QL

While Bedford's MW and OY trucks had basically been militarized versions of civilian types, the forward-control QL was a purpose-built military vehicle. Discussions about the design of such a vehicle had begun in 1938, with the War Department indicating that it might be interested in a four-wheel drive Bedford in early 1939. Development work started in September of that year and by November was considered to be of the utmost importance. The first prototype, QL-1, was available for trials in February 1940 and further prototypes followed as teething troubles were

BELOW: A Bedford QLC 4x4 truck/tractor with a 6-ton semi-trailer.

eliminated. There were particular problems with cracks appearing in the chassis. Full-scale production finally started in February 1941.

The engine was the same 3,519cc six-cylinder unit as used in the smaller MW, driving all four wheels through a four-speed gearbox and two-speed transfer box, with front axle disconnect. The front and rear axles were similar in design, incorporating spiral bevel gears. The sound of the intermediate gears, particularly when the low ratios were engaged, earned the QL the nickname "Screamer". The suspension was by conventional semi-elliptical leaf springs.

By the end of World War II, Bedford had produced 52,247 QLs, most of which

were fitted with the GS cargo body (chassis version QLD). Other standard variants included a radio/communications van (QLR and QLC), troop carrier (QLT), kitchen (QLD), battery storage (QLD), machinery (QLD), petrol tanker (QLC), fire-fighter (QLC), a tractor for the Bofors light anti-aircraft gun (QLB), winch-equipped air-portable tipper (QLW) and tractor for semi-trailer (QLC).

The QL was a reliable vehicle and was supplied to all three British services, remaining in use well into the post-war years. It was finally succeeded by the Bedford RL.

Bedford QL

Type: Truck, 3-ton, cargo, 4x4
Manufacturer: Vauxhall Motors; Luton
Production: 1941 to 1945
Powerplant: Bedford; six cylinders in-line; petrol; water-cooled; 3,519cc; overhead valves; power output, 72bhp at 3,000rpm
Transmission: 4F1Rx2; part-time 4x4
Suspension: Live axles on semi-elliptical multi-leaf springs
Brakes: Hydraulic with vacuum servo-assistance
Electrical system: 12V
Dimensions: Length – 5,994mm/236in
Width – 2,261mm/89in
Height – tilt in place, 3,048mm/120in; minimum, 2,591mm/102in
Wheelbase – 3,632mm/143in
Weight: Unladen – 3,277kg/7,225lb
Payload – 3,708kg/,8,175lb
Performance: Maximum speed – 60kph/38mph

Bedford RL

In 1950, Bedford introduced the S-Type, or so-called "Big Bedford", a range of new forward-control trucks taking the marque into the 7-ton class. The design and development of a military variant to replace the QL started in December the same year, and the first prototype was delivered to the Fighting Vehicles Research & Development Establishment (FVRDE) in May 1951.

Designated RL and assigned the classification FV13100 series, the vehicle was powered by the new 4,927cc six-cylinder engine first used in the S-Type, driving through a four-speed gearbox and two-speed transfer box. By April 1952, it had been approved for production and over the next 17 years, some 73,135 examples were built in a very wide range of body types.

Although not strictly a military vehicle, the best-known RL variant is probably the RLHZ "Green Goddess" Civil Defence emergency fire pump.

The four-wheel-drive RL was offered to civilians from October 1953. It was also built under licence in Denmark.

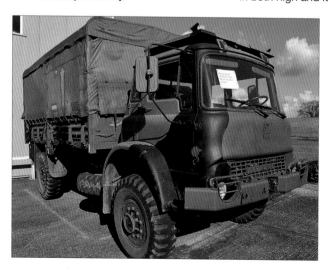

LEFT: **A Bedford RL equipped as a missile launcher.**

Bedford RL

Type: Truck, 3-ton (later 4-ton), cargo, 4x4; FV13100 series
Manufacturer: Vauxhall Motors; Luton
Production: 1952 to 1969
Powerplant: Bedford 300; six cylinders in-line; petrol; water-cooled; 4,927cc; overhead valves; power output, 110–130bhp at 3,200rpm
Transmission: 4F1Rx2; part-time 4x4
Suspension: Live axles on semi-elliptical multi-leaf springs
Brakes: Hydraulic with air-pressure or vacuum-servo-assistance
Electrical system: 24V
Dimensions: Length – 6,350mm/250in
  Width – 2,390mm/94in
  Height – tilt in place, 2,995mm/118in; minimum, 2,591mm/102in
  Wheelbase – 3,353mm/132in or 3,962mm/156in
Weight: Unladen – 4,001kg/8,820lb
  Payload – 3,493kg/7,700lb; subsequently uprated to 3,992kg/8,800lb
Performance: Maximum speed – 64kph/40mph

Bedford MK, MJ

Introduced in 1971, the Bedford M-Type has been the workhorse of the British Army for more than three decades. Design of the truck was derived from Bedford's TK series and started in the early 1960s, with the first example, designated RL Mk 2, demonstrated in 1962. It was powered by a new 5,408cc normally aspirated multi-fuel diesel engine. There was also a new transfer case, giving four-wheel drive in both high and low gears, and a new braking system. Although most were fitted with a steel 4- to 5-ton cargo body like the earlier RL, the MK and MJ were equipped for a very wide range of roles.

In 1981, after 24,000 had been built, the original engine was superseded by a turbocharged unit, and was designated MJ.

Total production was around 50,000, and the truck has been exported widely, notably to Ireland and the Netherlands.

BELOW: **The Bedford MJ remains in service with the British Army to this day.**

Bedford MK, MJ

Type: Truck, 3-ton (later 4-ton), cargo, 4x4; FV 13800 series
Manufacturer: Vauxhall Motors; Luton
Production: 1971 to 1985
Powerplant: Bedford 330D; six cylinders in-line; multi-fuel diesel (MJ, turbocharged); water cooled; 5,408cc; overhead valves; power output, 98–108bhp at 2,600rpm
Transmission: 4F1Rx2; part-time 4x4
Suspension: Live axles on semi-elliptical multi-leaf springs; direct-acting hydraulic shock absorbers
Brakes: Hydraulic with air-pressure servo-assistance
Electrical system: 24V
Dimensions: Length – 6,570mm/259in
  Width – 2,490mm/98in
  Height – tilt in place, 3,403mm/134in
  Wheelbase – 3,353mm/132in or 3,962mm/156in
Weight: Unladen – 5,118kg/11,284lb
  Payload – 3,493kg/7,700lb; subsequently uprated to 3,992kg/8,800lb
Performance: Maximum speed – 80kph/50mph

Commer Q4

During the 1950s, the British Army replaced most of its wartime 3-ton 4x4 trucks with the new Bedford RL. Whether Bedford could not manage to produce the trucks fast enough or for some other reason, similarly rated types were also purchased from Commer, Ford and Thornycroft.

Commer's contribution was the Q4 FV13200 series, and several thousand were built from 1952. The vehicle was effectively a militarized version of the company's civilian "Superpoise" range, with extended wheel arches being used to cover the wider-track axles. Power was by a Commer 4,752cc six-cylinder petrol engine, driving through a four-speed gearbox and two-speed transfer box. Alongside the standard "General Service" (GS) cargo vehicle, there were signals, tipper,

LEFT: **Two Commer Q4s fitted with the signals-type body.**

photographic processing and workshop variants. The Q4 was also used by the Home Office as a pump carrier and hose layer with Civil Defence mobile columns of the 1950s.

Commer Q4

Type: Truck, 3-ton, 4x4; FV13200 series
Manufacturer: Rootes Group, Commer-Karrier Division; Dunstable
Production: 1952 to 1956
Powerplant: Commer; six cylinders in-line; petrol; water-cooled; 4,752cc; overhead valves; power output, 95bhp at 3,000rpm
Transmission: 4F1Rx2; part-time 4x4
Suspension: Live axles on semi-elliptical multi-leaf springs
Brakes: Hydraulic with vacuum servo-assistance
Electrical system: 12V
Dimensions: Length – 6,985mm/275in
    Width – 2,440mm/96in
    Height – tilt in place, 3,175mm/125in
    Wheelbase – 4,242mm/167in
Weight: Unladen – 4,725kg/10,416lb
    Payload – 2,876kg/6,340lb
Performance: Maximum speed – 68kph/42mph

Crossley Q-Type

Crossley Motors were established in the late 19th century, producing Otto engines under licence and from 1904 building motor cars. Armoured cars were produced during the inter-war period, and the company started to manufacture trucks in 1932, eventually abandoning car production in 1937. Crossley trucks were supplied to the British Army and the RAF throughout the 1930s.

During World War II, the company produced some 11,000 of the Q-Type, the majority of which were supplied to the RAF. The standard body was a 3-ton cargo type. Other variants included a ballast-bodied tractor for semi-trailers, used by the RAF for towing the "Queen Mary" low-loader trailer, as well as a mobile workshop. The truck was powered by a Crossley 5,266cc four-cylinder petrol engine driving through a four-speed gearbox and two-speed transfer box.

Crossley never resumed truck manufacture after the war and was absorbed into the AEC-controlled

Associated Commercial Vehicles (ACV) group in 1948. The name was retained by ACV for some export markets.

LEFT: **A Crossley Q-Type 4x4 fire tender fitted with foam-making equipment.**

Crossley Q-Type

Type: Truck, 3-ton, 4x4
Manufacturer: Crossley Motors; Manchester
Production: 1940 to 1945
Powerplant: Crossley 30/100; four cylinders in-line; petrol; water-cooled; 5,266cc; side valves; power output, 90bhp at 2,500rpm
Transmission: 4F1Rx2; part-time 4x4
Suspension: Live axles on semi-elliptical multi-leaf springs
Brakes: Hydraulic with air servo-assistance; vacuum brakes for trailer
Electrical system: 12V
Dimensions: Length – 6,172mm/243in
    Width – 2,286mm/90in
    Height – tilt in place, 3,353mm/132in; minimum, 2,743mm/108in
    Wheelbase – 3,505mm/138in; 2,591mm/102in for tractor
Weight: Unladen – 4,750kg/10,472lb
    Payload – 3,048kg/6,720lb
Performance: Maximum speed – 45kph/28mph

Fordson WOT2

In 1939, the Ford Motor Company started to produce a series of "War Office Trucks", designated WOT1 to WOT6. The smallest of these was the 15cwt WOT2. This was almost certainly derived from the Fordson 7V, a 2- to 3-ton forward-control commercial vehicle available in a choice of wheelbase lengths. Two basic variants were produced – a GS truck and a closed van. The first production vehicles were designated as WOT2A and

this progressed through seven variants to WOT2H each incorporating various changes. There was no WOT2G.

Power was by a Ford V8 side-valve petrol engine, driving the rear axle through a four-speed gearbox. Following Ford's standard practice, the propeller shaft was enclosed in a rigid torque tube that provided location for the rear axle. The suspension was by conventional semi-elliptical springs. At the front, the axle was

supported on a single transverse-leaf spring carried on two radius rods which, in turn, were attached to a ball joint on a chassis cross-member.

Initially, the vehicle was fitted with an open cab with roll-up canvas doors and aero-type screens. A semi-enclosed cab was fitted from the WOT2E onwards, with a full-height windscreen, hinged metal doors and side-screens.

The GS truck was fitted with a steel-framed, fixed-sided timber body with a drop-down tailgate. Later examples were provided with a canvas tilt supported on tubular hoops; on the WOT2F variant the rear body was steel-panelled. The van variant (WOT2B, WOT2D) was not dissimilar in appearance, but the body was enclosed at the rear with a fixed canvas cover stretched across wooden panels. There were also house-bodied variants equipped as office, radio communications and fire service vehicles, the latter used by the National Fire Service and the Home Office. Some were converted to light "Anti-Aircraft" (AA) trucks mounting a 20mm Polsten or Hispano cannon, while others included provision for mounting an anti-aircraft Bren gun above the passenger roof.

Almost 60,000 were produced under 36 or more contracts over a six-year period, and the vehicle remained in service into the 1950s.

ABOVE: **Ford's smallest truck of World War II was the WOT2, which was produced in two basic variants – a GS truck and a closed van.** BELOW: **While the earliest examples were fitted with an open cab that had roll-up canvas doors and aero-type screens, an enclosed cab was fitted from the WOT2E type onwards.**

Fordson WOT2

Type: Truck, 15cwt, cargo, 4x2
Manufacturer: Ford Motor Company; Dagenham
Production: 1939 to 1945
Powerplant: Ford; eight cylinders in V configuration; petrol; water-cooled; 3,621cc; side valves; power output, 60bhp at 2,840rpm
Transmission: 4F1R; 4x2
Suspension: Live axles on semi-elliptical multi-leaf springs; hydraulic shock absorbers
Brakes: Mechanical
Electrical system: 6V, 12V
Dimensions: Length – 4,500mm/177in
　　Width – 2,000mm/79in
　　Height – 2,295mm/90in;
　　minimum, 1,803mm/71in
　　Wheelbase – 2,692mm/106in
Weight: Unladen – 2,050kg/4,520lb
　　Payload – 748kg/1,650lb
Performance: Maximum speed – 80kph/50ph

Fordson WOT1

Type: Truck, 3-ton, cargo, 6x4
Manufacturer: Ford Motor Company; Dagenham
Production: 1940 to 1945
Powerplant: Ford; eight cylinders in V
   configuration; petrol; water-cooled; 3,621cc;
   side valves; power output, 85bhp at 3,800rpm
Transmission: 4F1R, 4F1Rx2; 6x4
Suspension: Live axles on semi-elliptical
   multi-leaf springs
Brakes: Hydraulic (WOT1A/1 with vacuum
   servo-assistance)
Electrical system: 6V
Dimensions: Length – 7,087mm/279in
   Width – 2,134mm/84in
   Height – 3,099mm/122in
   Wheelbase – 4,470mm/176mm; 4,191mm/165in
   Bogie centres – 1,090mm/43in
Weight: Unladen – 3,352kg/7,390lb
   Payload – 3,361kg/7,410lb
Performance: Maximum speed – 72kph/45mph

Fordson WOT1

Rated at 3 tons, and with a Sussex conversion to allow a 6x4 drive line, the Fordson WOT1 was the largest of Ford's "War Office Trucks". It was introduced in 1940, with the majority being supplied to the RAF. The standard variant was a GS truck, but there were also special bodies produced, including parachute drying, power and charging equipment, dental surgery, searchlight carrier, crew coach, and

ABOVE: **A restored WOT1 equipped as an RAF fire/crash tender, painted in desert camouflage.**

office variants. An airfield crash tender equipped with pumping equipment was supplied to the RAF.

The engine was the Ford V8 side-valve, driving the middle axle through a four-speed gearbox; a second crown-wheel and pinion set in this axle conveyed the drive to the rear axle.

Suspension was by semi-elliptical springs, inverted at the rear.

A total of 9,154 Fordson WOT1 vehicles were built, with two chassis variants – the WOT1A had a longer wheelbase, while the WOT1A/1 was equipped with vacuum servo-assisted brakes.

Fordson WOA2

Introduced in May 1941, the Fordson WOA2 was a six-seat heavy utility vehicle derived from the company's WOA1 staff car, a militarized version of the Ford Model 62 sedan. There was a folding map table behind the front seats, and the rear seats could be folded down to provide a load-carrying area. A number were converted to open cars in the field, by cutting through the door pillars at window level.

Power was by a Ford V8 engine driving the rear wheels through a three-speed gearbox. Suspension was by live axles at front and rear, each suspended on a single transverse semi-elliptical spring. The rear axle was located on a torque tube. The WOA2 model was fitted with 9.00x13 tyres, while the WOA2/A used narrow-section 6.50x16 tyres.

LEFT: **A WOA2/A with narrow-section tyres.**

Fordson WOA2

Type: Car, heavy utility, 4x2
Manufacturer: Ford Motor Company; Dagenham
Production: 1941 to 1944
Powerplant: Ford; eight cylinders in V
   configuration; petrol; water-cooled; 3,621cc;
   side valves; power output, 85bhp at 3,600rpm
Transmission: 3F1R; 4x2
Suspension: Live axles on transverse semi-elliptical
   multi-leaf springs; hydraulic shock absorbers
Brakes: Mechanical
Electrical system: 6V, 12V
Dimensions: Length – 4,395mm/173in
   Width – 1,905mm/75in
   Height – 1,778mm/70in
   Wheelbase – 2,742mm/108in
Weight: Unladen – 1,613kg/3,555lb
   Payload – 565kg/1,245lb
Performance: Maximum speed – 80kph/50ph

The vehicle remained in production until 1944, and around 5,000 examples were built. It was widely used by all three of the British services as a staff and command car.

FWD R6T (AEC Model 850)

In 1928, Guy, Leyland, Scammell and FWD were requested by the War Office to submit six-wheel drive tractors as a possible replacement for the Thornycroft "Hathi". This tractor had been developed by Thornycroft and the Royal Army Service Corps, but was proving not powerful enough to tow heavy anti-aircraft guns on wheeled trailer mounts. The War Office required that the new tractors be capable of producing a drawbar pull of 5,443–6,804kg/12,000–15,000lb.

FWD's contribution to this project was the R6T, which had been introduced in 1927 by the company's predecessors. Four Wheel Drive Motors – generally known as FWD – had been formed in 1929, in Slough, as the successor to the British Four Wheel Drive Tractor-Lorry Company and the Four Wheel Drive Tractor-Lorry Engineering Company Limited. The R6T was the company's first six-wheel drive chassis and was powered by a Dorman JUP six-cylinder side-valve engine, driving all wheels through a four-speed gearbox, two-speed transfer box and spur-gear axles with reduction hubs. Front suspension was by a novel centre-pivoted beam with steel sliders at the spring ends to ensure axle location.

A military prototype was supplied to the War Office for trials in 1929 and was judged to be satisfactory. The prototype was returned to FWD and fitted with a new body. At the end of the year, a contract was issued for a further nine vehicles. This batch of vehicles were modified in various respects, with the most significant change being the replacement of the original Dorman engine and gearbox with an 6,126cc AEC A136 overhead-valve engine driving through an AEC gearbox. Changes were also made to both the cab and the body, notably by the provision of seating for six in the rear, with two more seats alongside the driver.

In mid-1932, FWD was taken over by AEC and the R6T became the AEC Model 850. A total of 24 R6Ts were built by FWD at Slough, and a further 33 were built by AEC at Southall between 1932 and 1936. This gave a combined production total of 57.

As well as being used as an artillery tractor, a number were equipped for the recovery role and were used by the Royal Army Ordnance Corps. It was not unknown for the vehicle to be used as temporary tank transporter tractor units.

ABOVE: **The FWD R6T was an all-wheel-drive heavy artillery tractor. Following the take-over of FWD by AEC in mid-1932, the vehicle became known as the AEC Model 850. A total of 58 were produced between 1929 and 1936.** LEFT: **An R6T recovery tractor. A total of 57 were built; 24 by FWD at Slough and 33 by AEC at Southall.**

FWD R6T, (AEC Model 850)

Type: Tractor, heavy artillery, 6x6
Manufacturer: FWD Motors; Slough. AEC Motors; Southall
Production: 1929 to 1936
Powerplant: Prototype – Dorman JUL; six cylinders in line; petrol; water-cooled; 6,597cc; side valves; power output, 78bhp
Production vehicles – AEC A136; six cylinders in line; water-cooled; 6,126cc; overhead valves; power output, 95bhp
Transmission: 4F1Rx2; part-time 6x6
Suspension: Live axles on semi-elliptical multi-leaf springs, transverse at front
Brakes: Air-pressure
Electrical system: 6V
Dimensions: Length – prototype, 5,740mm/226in; production vehicles, 5,867mm/231in
Width – 2,286mm/90in
Height – tilt in place, 2,642mm/104in
Wheelbase – 3,048mm/120in
Bogie centres – 1,220mm/48in
Weight: Unladen – 8,687kg/19,152lb
Performance: Maximum speed – 32kph/20mph

Humber FWD

During World War II, Humber produced a range of small military vehicles based on a common 4x4 chassis, fitted with independent front suspension and a six-cylinder side-valve engine. The chassis was developed from that used for the company's "Super Snipe" saloon car and was introduced in 1940, remaining in production throughout World War II. There was a heavy utility vehicle, nicknamed "The Box" because of the vehicle's square appearance, an 8cwt truck, and an ambulance. A version of the same chassis was also used as the basis for an armoured scout car, an armoured reconnaissance vehicle and a light armoured car.

The front suspension used a semi-elliptical transverse multi-leaf spring as the top link, combined with wishbones at the bottom to provide basic independent suspension. All-wheel drive allowed drivers the benefit of excellent off-road performance. The 4,086cc six-cylinder petrol engine was connected to a four-speed gearbox and two-speed transfer box, the latter including the front axle disconnect.

Most examples were fitted with a steel-panelled four-door heavy utility body equipped with six seats. During

1940–41, a small pick-up truck was also produced with a removable body which could be used as a tent by folding down telescopic legs. Finally, there was an enclosed field ambulance with a steel-panelled body built by Thrupp & Maberly. The BBC operated a fleet of these Humbers for use by war correspondents, using both utility- and ambulance-bodied variants, the latter converted into recording vans. There was also a plan to produce

ABOVE: **The Humber FWD was a well-designed and reliable vehicle. The Humber chassis was also bodied as an 8cwt pick-up truck and as a field ambulance.**

a 4x4 staff car on the same chassis, but it does not appear that any were actually produced.

Total production amounted to 5,199 units, of which the majority (3,960) were of the heavy utility type.

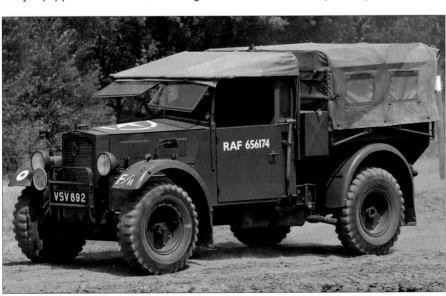

ABOVE: **The Humber FWD 8cwt cargo/personnel truck; the same chassis was also used as the basis for an ambulance, staff car, and wireless vehicle.**

Humber FWD	

Type: Car, heavy utility, 4x4
Manufacturer: Humber; Coventry
Production: 1940 to 1945
Powerplant: Humber; six cylinders in-line; petrol; water-cooled; 4,086cc; side valves; power output, 85bhp at 3,400rpm
Transmission: 4F1Rx2; part-time 4x4
Suspension: Independent front suspension using transverse semi-elliptical multi-leaf spring and wishbone links; live axle at rear on semi-elliptical multi-leaf springs
Brakes: Hydraulic
Electrical system: 12V
Dimensions: (heavy utility variant)
    Length – 4,293mm/169in
    Width – 1,880mm/74in
    Height – 1,956mm/77in
    Wheelbase – 2,845mm/112in
Weight: Unladen – 2,413kg/5,320lb
    Payload – 533kg/1,176lb
Performance: Maximum speed – 80kph/50mph

Humber FV1600

During World War II, the 15cwt truck was the most widely used by the British Army, with vehicles supplied by Ford, Morris-Commercial, Humber and Commer. During the re-equipping of the British Army which followed the end of the war, this class of truck was upgraded to 1-ton capacity. At the same time, current military thinking divided British military vehicles into three broad types. The most sophisticated of these, designated CT or "combat", was a purpose-designed truck incorporating features such as all-wheel drive, built-in waterproofing and radio suppression, independent suspension and common electrical equipment. All CT vehicles were powered by a Rolls-Royce B Series engine, which was produced as a four-, six- or eight-cylinder unit.

The 1-ton CT truck, always known simply by the Fighting Vehicles Development Establishment (FVDE) designation FV1600, was developed by the Rootes Group and was badged Humber. Prototypes were produced during 1951 to an FVDE specification which laid down various performance parameters. Following a series of extensive trials, the FV1600 was assembled at the company's Ryton-on-Dunsmore plant during 1952–53, with a total of 3,700 built.

Humber FV1600

Type: Truck, 1-ton, cargo, 4x4; FV1601
Manufacturer: Rootes Group; Ryton-on-Dunsmore
Production: 1952 to 1953
Powerplant: Rolls-Royce B60 Mk 2A, Mk 5A; six cylinders in-line; petrol; water-cooled; 4,256cc; overhead inlet valves, side exhaust; power output, 109bhp at 3,750rpm
Transmission: 5F1R; part-time 4x4
Suspension: Independent suspension using double wishbones and adjustable torsion bars; double-acting hydraulic shock absorbers
Brakes: Vacuum servo-assisted hydraulic
Electrical system: 24V
Dimensions: (FV1601) Length – 5,054mm/199in
 Width – 2,083mm/82in
 Height – tilt in place, 2,362mm/193in; minimum, 2,114mm/83in
 Wheelbase – 2,743mm/108in
Weight: Unladen – 3,811kg/8,402lb
 Payload – 1,384kg/3,051lb
Performance: Maximum speed – 88kph/55mph

The engine was the six-cylinder B60 unit, driving both axles through a five-speed gearbox and single-speed transfer box. Suspension was independent on all wheels by double wishbones and longitudinal torsion bars. The prototypes had featured an open cab, but production machines had a modern all-steel enclosed cab incorporating drop-down windows and a top-hinged windscreen. The cargo body had fixed sides and a hinged tailgate.

Most of the production total was bodied as the FV1601 cargo vehicle. Other standard variants included the FV1602, a version of the cargo vehicle which was "Fitted For Wireless" (FFW). The FV1604 was fitted with a Marshalls of Cambridge "radio house" body. Around 1960, a small number designated FV1621 and FV1624 were converted as test and support vehicles for trials of Malkara, an anti-tank missile.

Many of those produced were put directly into store, and when demand arose in the mid-1950s for an armoured truck and armoured personnel carrier, the cargo bodies were removed and the chassis were rebodied for the armoured role. In this form, and nicknamed "Pig", the Humber became a common sight on the city streets of Northern Ireland.

ABOVE: **The Humber FV1600 series was powered by a Rolls-Royce six-cylinder engine and fulfilled the 1-ton "combat" role in the post-war inventory of British military vehicles. The steel-bodied cargo variant was designated FV1601, and there was a similar "Fitted For Wireless" (FFW) variant.**
LEFT: **FV1604 with a house-bodied radio truck.**

Hunting-Percival Harrier

In 1957, the Hunting-Percival Aircraft Company built four prototype folding cars for air-drop trials with the British Army. The vehicle was produced to a design which had been patented by J. Dolphin of Marlow in 1953. It was powered by a front-mounted 649cc BSA two-cylinder motorcycle engine, driving the rear wheels via a four-speed transmission and roller chain. For ease of transport, the vehicle could be folded down to a box-shaped unit measuring

3,150x533x914mm/124x21x36in and easily lifted by four men. The vehicle could be made ready for use in around one minute. The Harrier had a conventional steering wheel, and was fitted with four seats. Independent suspension was fitted front and rear, using semi-elliptical springs and

BELOW LEFT AND BELOW: **The Hunting-Percival Harrier was a four-seat lightweight folding vehicle intended for air-dropping.**

Hunting-Percival Harrier

Type: Car, folding, four seat, 4x2
Manufacturer: Hunting-Percival Aircraft; Luton
Production: 1957
Powerplant: BSA A10; two cylinders in-line; petrol; air-cooled; 649cc; overhead valves; power output, 30bhp at 5,500rpm
Transmission: 4F1R; 4x2
Suspension: Independent suspension, front and rear, using lateral semi-elliptical springs and lower wishbone links
Brakes: Hydraulic
Electrical system: Magneto only
Dimensions: Length – 2,667mm/105in
　　Width – 1,220mm/48in
　　Height – 890mm/35in
　　Wheelbase – 2,388mm/94in
Weight: Unladen – 318kg/700lb
　　Payload – 499kg/1,100lb
Performance: Maximum speed – 97kph/60mph

wishbones. The springs were located by coil-sprung struts and formed the upper link on which the stub axles were mounted. There was no series production.

Karrier K6

The Rootes Group started production of the 3-ton Karrier K6 in December 1940. It was bodied as a fixed-side GS cargo vehicle with both fixed and split-waist cabs, the latter intended to be air-portable. Approximately 2,500 of the total

produced were fitted with a 4¹/₂-ton capacity vertical-spindle winch, mounted just forward of the rear axle and driven from a power take-off on the transfer

BELOW: **The Karrier K6 entered service with the British Army in December 1940.**

Karrier K6

Type: Truck, 3-ton, cargo, 4x4
Manufacturer: Karrier Motors; Luton
Production: 1940 to 1945
Powerplant: Humber; six cylinders in-line; petrol; water-cooled; 4,086cc; side valves; power output, 80bhp at 3,200rpm
Transmission: 4F1Rx2; part-time 4x4
Suspension: Live axles on semi-elliptical multi-leaf springs
Brakes: Hydraulic
Electrical system: 12V
Dimensions: Length – 5,791mm/228in
　　Width – 2,210mm/87in
　　Height – tilt in place, 3,150mm/124in
　　Wheelbase – 3,962mm/156in
Weight: Unladen – 4,014kg/8,850lb
　　Payload – 3,504kg/7,726lb
Performance: Maximum speed – 64kph/40mph

box. A short-wheelbase artillery tractor, KT4, was built for the Indian Army.

The engine was the same six-cylinder side-valve unit as installed in the Humber FWD range, fitted with a four-speed gearbox and two-speed transfer box. Unusually for the period, four-wheel drive was available in both the high and low ratios. A total of 4,500 were produced.

RIGHT: **The Wolf Defender can be traced directly to the Series I of 1948. Here members of No. 4001 Armoured Car Flight of the RAF Regiment are on patrol in the Canal Zone, Egypt, in a Series I Land Rover in 1953. The Land Rover is followed by a Humber Mk III airfield-defence armoured car.**

Land Rover Wolf Defender XD

The Land Rover was the brainchild of Maurice Wilks, a director of Rover, who had purchased a military-surplus Jeep in 1946 and found it useful on his farm in Wales. As the vehicle began to wear out, Wilks reasoned that there might be sufficient market for a similar dual-purpose machine to carry the Rover company through the difficult post-war years. The first prototype was based on a Jeep chassis, and used Jeep axles and transfer case. Aluminium was used for the body panels because Rover could not obtain licences to buy sufficient steel. Following the completion of 48 pre-production prototypes, the Series I was launched at the Amsterdam Motor Show in 1948. It was an immediate success.

Although there was no intention for the Land Rover to be used as a military vehicle, it was not long before the British Army realized that the vehicle could provide a low-cost replacement for the inventory of ageing Jeeps. At the same time, it could also be operated alongside the expensive Austin "Champ" which was still in development. The first military purchases came in 1948 and have continued to this day.

BELOW: **A Wolf TUM bogged down in the mud of Iraq. Some vehicles which served in that country carried a small air-conditioning unit installed in the locker ahead of the rear wheel.**

In 1951, the original 1,595cc petrol engine was replaced by a 1,997cc unit. In 1958, the Series I was superseded by the wider and more powerful Series II, which was fitted with a 2,286cc petrol engine. By this time, the original 2,032mm/80in wheelbase had been lengthened to 2,182mm/86in, and then to 2,235mm/88in. A 2,718mm/107in long-wheelbase chassis was introduced in 1954 and lengthened to 2,768mm/109in in 1957. Three years later, the Series IIA was launched and, in 1971, this was replaced by the Series III, still powered by the 2,286cc engine and still fitted with a body that was not dissimilar to that used 20 years earlier. The British Army continued to purchase Land Rovers in their thousands and the vehicle was also widely exported.

At the Geneva Motor Show in March 1983, Land Rover announced the replacement of the Series III by the short-wheelbase "Ninety" and the longer-wheelbase "One-Ten", later to be renamed Defender 90 and Defender 110. For the first time the vehicle featured permanent all-wheel drive and coil-spring suspension, and a V8 petrol engine was offered alongside the standard petrol and diesel options. The body could still be recognized as a Land Rover, but there was a one-piece windscreen and extensions over the wheel arches.

The Defender remains in production at the time of writing, and thousands are in service with the British Army and elsewhere, but it was effectively superseded, at least in British service, by the purpose-designed military Wolf Defender XD.

A specification for a more capable replacement for the Defender was drawn up by the Ministry of Defence in 1988 and Land Rover, IVECO and Pinzgauer all expressed interest in the project which would culminate in a contract for 8,000 vehicles. IVECO and Pinzgauer were eliminated. In late 1991, Land Rover was asked to prepare prototype vehicles in the "light" (short-wheelbase) and "medium" (long-wheelbase) classes. The vehicles which Land Rover produced were based on the then-current Defender but failed to meet the performance parameters.

LEFT: **A Wolf Defender variant with the British Army "Weapons Mount Installation Kit" (WMIK) which allows weapons to be fitted on the roll cage. The photograph shows troopers from the 3rd Battalion, Parachute Regiment, in training with a MILAN anti-tank missile equipped vehicle.**

The trials were called off in 1993. A second prototype, far more radical in its engineering, and now identified as Wolf 2, was more successful. Following the trials, Land Rover was awarded the contract and the Wolf Defender XD – "extra duty" – was first shown to the public in 1995. Production started in late 1996.

The vehicle was powered by a Land Rover 300 Tdi direct-injection turbocharged diesel engine, giving a top speed in the order of 129kph/80mph. The drive-line was by a five-speed gearbox and two-speed transfer box, connected permanently to the four wheels through a lockable centre differential. Suspension was by long-travel coil springs, with the axles located by a Panhard rod at the front and an A frame at the rear.

Two standard variants were produced – the "Truck, Utility, Light" (TUL) on a 2,286mm/90in wheelbase, rated for a payload of 508kg/¹⁄₂ ton, and the "Truck, Utility, Medium" (TUM) on which the wheelbase was extended to 2,794mm/110in and the payload increased to 1,016kg/1 ton. Both hard- and soft-top types were produced and all of the vehicles were fitted with a substantial roll cage. By fitting the "Weapons Mount Installation Kit" (WMIK), any Wolf Defender could be converted to a weapons platform,

typically mounting two 7.62mm general purpose machine-guns or a .50in Browning heavy machine-gun. All of the vehicles were equipped with a 24V electrical system and half of the total produced were "Fitted For Radio" (FFR). There was also a 3,226mm/127in wheelbase variant, which has been used as the basis for a battlefield ambulance.

Production was ended in October 1998 after 7,996 vehicles had been built. Of these, 1,411 were the TUL variant, the remainder being the TUM. Most were supplied to the British Army. The Royal Dutch Marines ordered the TUM and 71 were delivered in 1997.

BELOW: **Soldiers of the Heavy Machine-Gun Platoon of the 1st Battalion Royal Irish Regiment in Iraq during Operation Desert Storm.**

Land Rover Wolf Defender XD

Type: Truck, utility, light, ¹⁄₂-ton, 4x4; truck, utility, medium, 1-ton, 4x4

Manufacturer: Land Rover; Solihull

Production: 1996 to 1998

Powerplant: Land Rover 300 Tdi; four cylinders in-line; direct-injection turbocharged diesel; water-cooled; 2,506cc; overhead valves; power output, 111bhp at 4,000rpm

Transmission: 5F1Rx2; full-time 4x4; lockable centre differential

Suspension: Live axles on coil springs; axle location by Panhard rod at front, A-frame at rear

Brakes: Vacuum servo-assisted hydraulic

Electrical system: 24V

Dimensions: Length – 3,840mm/151in, 4,550mm/179in
Width – 1,800mm/70in
Height – tilt in place, 2,030mm/80in
Wheelbase – 2,286mm/90in, 2,794mm/110in

Weight: Unladen – 1,996kg/4,400lb, 2,595kg/5,720lb
Payload – 599kg/1,320lb, 1,143kg/2,520lb

Performance: Maximum speed – 129kph/80mph

Land Rover 101

The 1-ton forward-control Land Rover – generally described as the 101 – was developed as a heli-portable light artillery tractor which could also carry the gun's crew and a quantity of ammunition.

In 1967, Rover started building five forward-control 1-ton military prototypes, the first of which appeared in 1969. Although it generally resembled the production 101, there was a short bonnet projection, required to house the Rover P5 six-cylinder engine. A General Statement of Requirements (GSR 3463) was issued in June 1968, clarifying the role of the vehicle, stating that it should be capable of towing the new 105mm light gun, or a load of up to 1,814kg/ 4,000lb. Other possible roles included command post, Rapier and MILAN missile launcher, missile test/repair vehicle, signals office, radio repair vehicle, computer exchange unit, dry-air generator, power-supply vehicle, battery-charging truck, line layer, load carrier, and battlefield ambulance. Demountable body panels allowed vehicle weight to be reduced for lifting by a Wessex helicopter. It was also to be air-portable in Andover and Britannia aircraft. The specification also stated that the vehicle be capable of towing a powered-axle trailer via a special coupling and detachable propshaft.

In 1970, Rover produced 10 prototypes for trials, this time using the Buick-designed Rover 3,528cc V8 petrol engine, mated to a Range Rover gearbox with a

permanent four-wheel drive transfer box. There were heavy-duty Salisbury axles incorporating larger half-shafts than normal. An inter-axle differential lock was also fitted. Suspension was by live axles on semi-elliptical tapered multi-leaf springs, with an anti-roll bar at front. Double-acting telescopic shock absorbers were fitted to all four wheels.

Tested in trials against the Volvo-Ailsa 4140 series Laplander, the Land Rover emerged as the clear winner and went into production in 1975 as the FV19000 series. There were four production variants in all – GS, ambulance, and two types of signals body. Both right- and

BELOW: **The 101 was originally intended to be coupled to a powered-axle Scottorn trailer to provide improved mobility. Shown, here, is a Land Rover prototype.**

ABOVE: **The Vampire was a special signals-bodied variant of the 1-ton Land Rover forward-control intended for the re-broadcast or relay role.**

left-hand drive vehicles were produced. The vehicle remained in production until 1978, with 2,669 vehicles manufactured. Of these, 127 went to the RAF and 2,129 went to the British Army. The 101 was also supplied to the armies of Australia, Egypt, Iran and Luxembourg, and evaluated by Canada and others.

Land Rover 101 forward control

Type: Truck, 1-ton, GS, forward control, 4x4; FV19000 series
Manufacturer: Land Rover; Solihull
Production: 1975 to 1978
Powerplant: Rover; eight cylinders in V configuration; water-cooled; petrol; 3,528cc; overhead valves; power output, 128bhp at 5,000rpm
Transmission: 4F1Rx2; full-time 4x4; positive lock on inter-axle differential
Suspension: Live axles on semi-elliptical multi-leaf springs
Brakes: Hydraulic
Electrical system: 12V, 24V
Dimensions: Length – 4,115mm/162in
  Width – 1,830mm/72in
  Height – soft-top variants, 2,133mm/84in; hardtop variants, 2,388mm/94in
  Wheelbase – 2,565mm/101in
Weight: Unladen – 1,920kg/4,233lb
  Payload – 1,179kg/2,600lb
Performance: Maximum speed – 98kph/62mph

Leyland Hippo Mk II

As well as producing tanks and tank engines during World War II, Leyland Motors also supplied trucks, including the 3-ton Retriever, the 3-ton Lynx, and the 10-ton Hippo. The original Hippo Mk I, or WSW17, was essentially a pre-war commercial truck fitted with a military-type open cab and timber GS body, with some 330 examples supplied during 1939–40. The Mk II, introduced in 1944, was an altogether more capable vehicle.

During the planning for D-Day, it became obvious that 10-ton vehicles offered a considerable logistic advantage compared to smaller vehicles and, although Leyland had little spare capacity for producing new trucks, design work on the 10-ton Hippo Mk II started in 1943. Series production began in late 1944, which means that these vehicles were not used in the early days following the invasion. However, some 1,000 examples were in service by VE Day and the vehicle remained in use by both the Army and the RAF well into the 1950s.

The new vehicle used few components from the Mk I. It was powered by a Leyland 7,399cc

RIGHT: **The Leyland Hippo Mk II was a 10-ton 6x4 cargo vehicle intended for transporting supplies in Europe after D-Day. Production began in 1944 and around 1,000 had been shipped to Europe by the end of the war.** BELOW: **The Hippo was fitted with a fabricated-steel body as standard. For the signals/command role a house-type body was fitted. The Mk IIB had dual rear wheels and smaller-section tyres at the front.**

six-cylinder diesel engine driving the rear wheels through a five-speed gearbox and two-speed auxiliary box. The rear axles were of the full-floating worm-drive type. Suspension was by semi-elliptical springs, inverted at the rear. Large bar-grip tyres were fitted, with singles at the rear, although the Mk 2B reverted to twin rears.

The two-man steel-panelled cab was an all-new, enclosed design with

pull-down windows. The cab could be split to reduce shipping height. A circular observation hatch was provided in the roof above the passenger seat to allow the use of an anti-aircraft machine-gun on a pintle mount. The steel-framed timber GS body was of the well type, incorporating wheel arches to provide a reduced loading height. Various van bodies were fitted during the post-war years.

Leyland Hippo Mk II

Type: Truck, 10-ton, cargo, 6x4
Manufacturer: Leyland Motors; Leyland
Production: 1944 to 1945
Powerplant: Leyland L6; six cylinders in-line; diesel; water-cooled; 7,399cc; overhead valves; power output, 100bhp at 1,800rpm
Transmission: 5F1Rx2; 6x4
Suspension: Live axles on semi-elliptical multi-leaf springs, inverted at rear
Brakes: Hydraulic with vacuum servo-assistance
Electrical system: Hybrid 12V/14V
Dimensions: Length – 8,306mm/327in
   Width – 2,464mm/97in
   Height – tilt in place, 3,327mm/131in; minimum, 2,921mm/115in
   Wheelbase – 4,674mm/184in
   Bogie centres – 1,397mm/55in
Weight: Unladen – 8,433kg/18,592lb
   Payload – 11,583kg/25,536lb
Performance: Maximum speed – 48kph/30mph

Leyland Martian

Produced in long- and short-wheelbase cargo, artillery tractor and recovery-tractor variants, the FV1100 series Leyland Martian was one of the purpose-designed Rolls-Royce-engined "CT" (combat) rated British military vehicles of the 1950s. Nominally rated at 10 tons, with six-wheel drive, it was the largest production vehicle in the "CT" series.

Development work began in 1950, with the first entering series production around 1953. This was the crew-cabbed FV1103 medium artillery tractor, intended to replace the AEC Matador as a towing vehicle for the 5.5, 7.5 and 8in howitzer and for the 40mm anti-aircraft gun. This was followed by the FV1110 cargo truck using a longer wheelbase, and later by the FV1119 recovery vehicle, which was fitted with Royal Ordnance/Thornycroft recovery equipment. A short-wheelbase cargo vehicle was also subsequently produced, based on the chassis of the artillery tractor.

The first 25 production vehicles used a Rolls-Royce B80 eight-cylinder petrol engine, but this was changed later for the more-powerful B81. In all cases, the transmission was by a four-speed gearbox and three-speed transfer box; the lowest of the transfer box gears could only be engaged when all-wheel drive was selected. Drive from the rear axle was conveyed to the wheels via a walking-beam gearcase, while at the front, the kingpins were used to drive the wheels through bevel gears as used on Mack trucks of World War II. The front suspension was similar to that used by Scammell with a single transverse leaf spring, allowing the live axle to pivot across the frame from a perch bar mounted further back on the chassis. At the rear, the bogie was suspended on semi-elliptical multi-leaf springs. The recovery vehicle was fitted with additional "helper" springs and the suspension could be locked out during lifting operations. Production continued over an almost 10-year period, finally ending in 1964. Total production was 1,380, of which 60 were bodied as artillery tractors and 280 as recovery vehicles; the remainder were the cargo type. The vehicle was also offered to civilian users and exhibited at the Commercial Motor Show in 1954, but was far too expensive to market.

BELOW: **The Martian was built as an artillery tractor, and also as long- and short-wheelbase cargo vehicles. The heavy recovery vehicle was fitted with Royal Ordnance/Thornycroft recovery equipment.**

Leyland Martian

Type: Truck, 10-ton, medium artillery tractor; FV1103
Manufacturer: Leyland Motors; Leyland
Production: 1953 to 1964
Powerplant: Rolls-Royce B80 Mk 2H (first 25 vehicles), or B81 Mk 2H, 5H or 5K; eight cylinders in-line; petrol; water-cooled; 5,675cc (B80), 6,516cc (B81); overhead inlet valves, side exhaust; power output, 165bhp (B80) or 220bhp (B81) at 3,750rpm; civilian version offered with Leyland 0.600 diesel engine
Transmission: 4F1Rx3; part-time 6x6
Suspension: Front suspension by transverse semi-elliptical multi-leaf spring and centre-pivoted axle; walking-beam gearcase at rear, suspended on semi-elliptical multi-leaf springs
Brakes: Air-pressure
Electrical system: 24V
Dimensions: Length – 8,185mm/322in
Width – 2,591mm/102in
Height – 3,073mm/121in
Wheelbase – 4,420mm/174in; FV1110 cargo vehicle, 5,140mm/202in
Bogie centres – 1,397mm/55in
Weight: Unladen – 14,301kg/31,528lb
Payload – 8,464kg/18,660lb
Performance: Maximum speed – 42kph/26mph

Morris-Commercial CD Series

In 1924, William Morris established Morris-Commercial at Soho, Birmingham, initially to build light trucks which were based on the company's heavier motor car chassis. In 1930, the company moved to the former Wolseley factory at Adderley Park and, by 1933, had added heavier vehicles to the range. The War Office was soon listed among the company's customers and the military CD 6x4 was introduced in 1933. This replaced the civilian D Type of 1927 in military service.

Utilizing a standard War Department rear bogie, the CD was powered by a 3,519cc Morris EB four-cylinder side-valve engine, driving overhead worm axles at the rear through a five-speed gearbox. Suspension was by semi-elliptical multi-leaf springs, inverted at the rear. The hydraulic brakes were modern for the period, albeit only acting on the front and centre axles.

Standard variants included the CD six-seat open-topped command car, of which 80 were built, also a 30cwt truck and field ambulance. The CDF, and the winch-equipped CDFW variants, were of the semi-forward control pattern and fitted with GS cargo, office and breakdown bodies. All of the truck variants were fitted with a canvas-covered cab; the CDF and CDFW models lacked a windscreen.

ABOVE: **The last variant to be built on the Morris-Commercial CD 30cwt chassis was the CDSW breakdown/recovery vehicle.**

Production of the CD ceased in 1939, but the CDF and CDFW continued to be produced into 1940. In 1935, the range was extended by the addition of the CDSW which shared a military-pattern cab with the smaller military Morris-Commercials of the period.

LEFT: **Produced from 1939, the second version of the Morris-Commercial CDSW was intended as a tractor for the Bofors light anti-aircraft gun. The rear body provided covered accommodation for the gun crew, as well as including stowage lockers for tools, equipment and ammunition.**

Morris-Commercial CD Series

Type: Truck, cargo, 30cwt, 6x4
Manufacturer: Morris-Commercial; Adderley Park, Birmingham
Production: 1933 to 1940
Powerplant: Morris EB; four cylinders in-line; petrol; water-cooled; 3,519cc; side valves; power output, 55bhp at 2,750rpm
Transmission: 5F1R; 6x4
Suspension: Live axles on semi-elliptical multi-leaf springs, inverted at the rear
Brakes: Hydraulic
Electrical system: 6V
Dimensions: (CDF variant) Length – 5,232mm/206in
    Width – 1,880mm/74in
    Height – tilt in place, 2,642mm/104in
    Wheelbase – 3,251mm/128in
    Bogie centres – 1,016mm/40in
Weight: Unladen – 2,743kg/6,048lb
    Payload – 1,930kg/4,256lb
Performance: Maximum speed – 60kph/37mph

Morris-Commercial CS8

The Morris-Commercial CS8 went into production in 1934 and became the most numerous ¾-ton 4x2 truck in British service during the years leading up to World War II. The engine was a six-cylinder side-valve unit driving the rear

BELOW: **Many CS8s were abandoned at Dunkirk only to be used by the *Wehrmacht*. Some were even fitted with German military-pattern bodies.**

axle through a four-speed gearbox. Suspension was by live axles mounted on semi-elliptical leaf springs. Mechanical brakes were used throughout the production run.

Early production featured an open cab with aero screens and roll-up doors. This was eventually replaced by a full windscreen and half-doors. Most were bodied for the GS cargo

Morris-Commercial CS8	

Type: Truck, cargo, ¾-ton, 4x2
Manufacturer: Morris-Commercial Cars; Adderley Park, Birmingham
Production: 1934 to 1941
Powerplant: Morris OH; six cylinders in-line; petrol; water-cooled; 3,485cc; sided valves; power output, 60bhp at 2,800rpm
Transmission: 4F1R; 4x2
Suspension: Live axles on multi-leaf semi-elliptical springs
Brakes: Mechanical
Electrical system: 12V
Dimensions: Length – 4,216mm/166in
   Width – 1,981mm/78in
   Height – tilt in place, 2,261mm/89in; minimum, 1,676mm/66in
   Wheelbase – 2,489mm/98in
Weight: Unladen – 2,041kg/4,500lb
   Payload – 1,007kg/2,220lb
Performance: Maximum speed – 64kph/40mph

role but there were also water tank, fire tender, wireless truck, fuel tanker, and office variants. There was also a portee for a 2pdr anti-tank gun. Captured examples were used by the *Wehrmacht*, occasionally with their own bodywork fitted. The CS8 remained in production until 1941.

Morris-Commercial MRA/1

The FV16100 series Morris-Commercial MRA/1 was an all-wheel-drive 1-ton military truck based on the company's civilian 3- and 5-ton NVS

chassis. Prototypes were produced in 1950, and the first of a total of 7,238 was delivered in 1952. The all-steel cab was the same as that on the civilian NSV range, and featured pull-up lockable side windows and a rubber glazed two-piece fixed windscreen.

Power came from a 4,966cc overhead-valve petrol engine, driving all four wheels via a four-speed gearbox and two-speed transfer box. Live axles at front and rear were suspended on semi-elliptical multi-leaf springs with double-acting telescopic shock absorbers.

Of the total number built, 5,624 were fitted with a steel cargo/personnel body. The remaining 1,614 were supplied in chassis-cab form to be fitted with a 900-litre/200-gallon steel water tank and ancillary pumping equipment.

Morris-Commercial MRA/1	

Type: Truck, cargo, 1-ton, 4x4; FV16101
Manufacturer: Morris-Commercial Cars; Adderley Park, Birmingham
Production: 1952 to 1954
Powerplant: Morris SEA/5; six cylinders in-line; petrol; water-cooled; 4,196cc; overhead valves; power output, 72bhp at 2,750rpm
Transmission: 4F1Rx2; part-time 4x4
Suspension: Live axles on multi-leaf semi-elliptical springs; hydraulic double-acting shock absorbers
Brakes: Hydraulic
Electrical system: 12V
Dimensions: Length – 5,372mm/212in
   Width – 2,083mm/82in
   Height – tilt in place, 2,654mm/105in; minimum, 2,235mm/88in
   Wheelbase – 3,124mm/123in
Weight: Unladen – 3,239kg/7,140lb
   Payload – 1,293kg/2,850lb
Performance: Maximum speed – 80kph/50mph

LEFT: **The Morris-Commercial MRA/1 was produced for only two years.**

Reynolds-Boughton RB-44

Originally produced as a private venture by the Boughton Group in 1978, when it was designated RB-510, the Renault-cabbed RB-44 was purchased by the British Army as a replacement for the Land Rover forward-control 1-ton truck. It was to be a tractor for the 105mm light gun.

The vehicle featured a bolted chassis in three wheelbase lengths, with the axles suspended on conventional semi-elliptical springs. A 3,000cc Perkins Phaser diesel engine drove all four wheels through a five-speed manual gearbox and two-speed transfer box. Automatic transmission was also offered as an option.

The standard British Army variant was the 2-ton cargo/prime mover. Other possible roles included transporter-launcher for the Swingfire anti-tank or Rapier surface-to-air missiles, and lubrication servicing and electronics communications vehicles. The company has also produced demonstrators for an ambulance, light recovery and command vehicles.

Production finally began in 1992, with the British Army purchasing some 846.

Reynolds-Boughton RB-44

Type: Truck, 2-ton, cargo/prime mover, 4x4
Manufacturer: Reynolds-Boughton; Amersham
Production: 1992 to 1993
Powerplant: Perkins Phaser 110MT; four cylinders in-line; direct-injection diesel; water-cooled; 3,000cc; overhead valves; power output, 109bhp at 2,800rpm
Transmission: 5F1Rx2; full-time 4x4
Suspension: Live axles on semi-elliptical multi-leaf springs with rubber assisters; double-acting hydraulic shock absorbers
Brakes: Servo-assisted hydraulic
Electrical system: 12V, 24V
Dimensions: Length – 5,060mm, 5,650mm, 6,030mm/199in, 222in, 237in
Width – 2,100mm/83in
Height – minimum, 2,348mm/92in
Wheelbase – 3,226mm, 3,680mm, 4,060mm/ 127in, 145in, 160in
Weight: Unladen – 2,994kg/6,600lb
Payload – 2,041kg/4,500lb
Performance: Maximum speed – 109kph/68mph

LEFT: **The RB-44 was beset by reliability problems requiring a lengthy modifications programme.**

Rotinoff Atlantic, Super Atlantic GR7

George A. Rotinoff, a White Russian émigré to Britain, started his post-war career converting Sherman tanks into bulldozers. By 1955, his company was building a heavy tank-transporter tractor. Available with either a ballast body or fifth wheel, the Atlantic GR7 was powered by a Rolls-Royce six-cylinder supercharged (later turbocharged), diesel engine driving through a 12- or 15-speed transmission. In 1957, the Super Atlantic GR7 was launched, with an eight-cylinder turbocharged diesel engine and 15-speed transmission. Automatic transmission and all-wheel drive were optionally available on both trucks.

The British War Office trialled an Atlantic in 1955. The Swiss Army purchased 10 ballast tractors in 1958; 18 went to the Iraqi Army and one to the South African Army. In 1960, the company name changed to Lomount. In 1962, the models were taken over by Atkinson. Total production was approximately 35–50 vehicles.

LEFT: **The Rotinoff Atlantic was used by the Swiss, Iraqi and South African armies.**

Rotinoff Atlantic, Super Atlantic GR7

Type: Truck, 35-ton, tractor, 6x4
Manufacturer: Rotinoff Motors; Colnbrook
Production: 1955 to 1963
Powerplant: Rolls-Royce C6TFL, C6SFL, C8TFL; six or eight cylinders in-line; supercharged or turbocharged diesel; water-cooled; 12,170cc, 16,227cc; overhead valves; power output, 250–366bhp at 2100rpm
Transmission: 4F1Rx3, 5F1Rx3; 6x4
Suspension: Live axles on semi-elliptical multi-leaf springs
Brakes: Air-pressure
Electrical system: 24V
Dimensions: Length – 8,738mm/344in; 8,992mm/354in
Width – 2,972mm/117in
Height – 3,400mm/134in
Wheelbase – 5,258mm/207in
Bogie centres – 1,730mm/68in
Weight: Unladen – 17,600kg/38,800lb; 18,280kg/40,300lb
Gross train weight – 142,249kg/313,600lb; 203,213kg/448,000lb
Performance: Maximum speed – 64kph/40mph

Scammell Pioneer

ABOVE: **Dating from 1935, and used by the British Army well into the 1950s, the Scammell Pioneer R100 was a heavy artillery tractor.**

Design work on the Pioneer began in 1925 with Percy G. Hugh working under the direction of Oliver Danson North at the Scammell factory, Tolpits Lane, Watford. The vehicle was originally developed for use in the oilfields of the Middle East and, although it lacked all-wheel drive, the combination of Oliver North's superb walking-beam gearcase at the rear and a transversely pivoted front axle meant that it was useful over rough terrain. The original engine was a Scammell four-cylinder petrol unit, but this was eventually replaced by a Gardner diesel engine. The Pioneer acquired a reputation for providing a reliable, if somewhat slow, performance on the road. The first vehicles were produced in 1927, and although it was not originally intended for military service, more than 3,500 Pioneers were used by the British Army over three or more decades.

The Pioneer entered service in 1932 when the British War Office purchased a single example, powered by a petrol engine and equipped for use as a tank transporter. Rated at 16–18 tons, it was a six-wheeled tractor unit permanently coupled to an 18-ton semi-trailer. Loading was by removing the rear bogie of the trailer; mechanical screw jacks were provided for raising and lowering the trailer which must have been laborious. The vehicle was quickly assigned to a training unit, and it was not until 1937 that further tank transporters were purchased.

In 1935, a second Pioneer variant was specified and purchased, this time as a heavy artillery tractor. Designated R100, the Scammell engine of the 1932 prototype had been replaced by the Gardner. The vehicle was fitted with a large steel body which provided accommodation for the gun's crew as well as providing space for stowing tools, ammunition and other equipment. A tow hitch at the rear allowed the tractor to be coupled to the heavy guns of the period, typically the 60pdr and the 6 or 7.2in howitzer. A year later, deliveries began of the first production batch of 114 vehicles. By the time the war was over, Scammell had produced 980 of these heavy gun tractors.

The third Pioneer variant, dating from 1936, was a heavy recovery vehicle. There were three versions – the first two, designated SV/1S and SV/1T, were fitted with a collapsible 3-ton jib. After just 43 had been built, a redesigned extending jib was

LEFT: **Introduced in 1936, the Pioneer SV/2S was a heavy recovery vehicle and was fitted with an under-chassis winch and a sliding jib crane.**

fitted and the vehicle designation became SV/2S. Deliveries of the SV/2S began in 1938 and continued throughout the war. By 1945, a total of 1,975 had been produced.

Despite having first been supplied in 1932, series purchases of the tank transporter did not begin until 1937, using what was effectively a longer-wheelbase version of the chassis that had been adopted for the artillery tractor and recovery vehicles. By this time the vehicle had been uprated to 20 tons and was designated TRMU20. The trailer, which still required the bogie to be removed for loading, was designated TRCU20. The trailer was soon redesigned to allow loading by means of rear ramps. However, by the time 115 examples of this version had been built, a new rear-loading version appeared, rated at 30 tons and designated TRMU30/TRCU30. With some small changes, this version remained in production throughout World War II, and the total number manufactured was 459.

With the exception of the original 1932 tank transporter, all of the military Pioneers were powered by a Gardner 6LW six-cylinder direct-injection diesel engine driving the rear wheels through a six-speed constant-mesh gearbox fitted with a power take-off for an under-chassis winch. The winch was fitted to all variants to help with loading, and to provide a means for self-recovery. The single rear axle, which was attached to the chassis by semi-elliptical multi-leaf springs, incorporated walking-beam gearcases which allowed the

ABOVE: **In 1932, the British War Office acquired a Scammell Pioneer for use as a tank transporter. The trailer was raised and lowered at the rear by means of screw jacks.**

wheels on either side of the vehicle to rise and fall independently by as much as 300mm/12in. At the front, the axle was mounted on a single inverted transverse semi-elliptical spring pivoted in a fulcrum bracket. The axle was located by means of an A frame, the apex of which was attached to a perch bar further back on the chassis.

Although the Pioneer was almost certainly obsolete for most of the war years, and was never available in sufficient numbers, it was a reliable vehicle held in much affection by its crews. The tank-transporter variant was effectively superseded by the US-built Diamond T Model 980/981 from 1941 onwards. The artillery tractor and recovery vehicles continued to see service with the British Army through the 1950s into the 1960s. The Pioneer remained in the Scammell catalogue into the 1950s, but the War Office made no further purchases after 1945.

BELOW: **An R100 artillery tractor in typical blue and sand camouflage of the Western Desert. The towed load is a British 5.5in howitzer.**

Scammell Pioneer

Type: Tractor, heavy artillery, 6x4
Manufacturer: Scammell Lorries; Watford
Production: 1936 to 1945
Powerplant: Gardner 6LW; six cylinders in-line; diesel; water-cooled; 8,396cc; overhead valves; power output, 102bhp at 1,700rpm
Transmission: 6F1R; 6x4
Suspension: Pivoting front axle suspended on inverted transverse semi-elliptical multi-leaf spring with axle location by A frame; pivoting walking-beam gearcases at rear suspended on semi-elliptical multi-leaf springs
Brakes: Air-pressure assisted mechanical, rear wheels only
Electrical system: Hybrid 12V/24V
Dimensions: Length – 6,176mm/243in
Width – 2,593mm/102in
Height – top of cab, 2,974mm/117in
Wheelbase – 3,708mm/146in
Bogie centres – 1,302mm/51in
Weight: Unladen – 7,938kg/17,500lb
Payload – 2,994kg/6,600lb
Maximum towed load – road, 19,958kg/44,000lb; 9,979kg/22,000lb
Performance: Maximum speed – 38kph/24mph

Scammell S25 Commander

The Scammell Commander was the fourth-generation tank transporter used by the British Army. The development extended across 16 years and was in danger of cancellation more than once but the Commander finally started replacing the Thornycroft Antar in 1984, serving for 17 years and used during Operation Desert Storm and in Kosovo.

Development started in 1968 when Thornycroft and Scammell, both part of the Leyland Group, were asked to investigate producing a new 55-ton tank transporter tractor which was being described as the Antar Mk 4. It was anticipated that production would begin in 1971. By 1973, nothing had happened except that Scammell and Thornycroft had been merged and had produced a feasibility study. In 1976, a wood and fibreglass mock-up was produced which set down the basic shape of the vehicle. In 1978, this was followed by two engineering prototypes, one powered by

a Cummins engine, the other using a version of the 26,110cc Rolls-Royce CV12 as was fitted in the Challenger tank. The Rolls-Royce engine was selected and by mid-1980, the initial trials had been completed.

In 1982, the contract was cancelled as part of a programme of sweeping defence cuts, but by the end of that year was reinstated. Three new tractors were to be produced, now rated at 62 tons, for trials. Full-scale production was started in 1983, before acceptance trials were complete. The first Commander was delivered in February 1984.

The Commander was effectively an amalgamation of the design thinking which had created the Thornycroft Antar Mk 3 and the Scammell Contractor. It was an ultra-heavy fifth-wheel tractor for tank-transporter duties, what is currently termed a "Heavy Equipment Transporter" (HET), and was powered by a 26,110cc V12 twin turbocharged diesel engine driving the rear wheels through a GM

ABOVE: **It took almost 15 years before the Rolls-Royce-engined Scammell Commander began to replace the Thornycroft Antar Mk 3 in 1984. The Commander was used in the first Gulf War (Operation Desert Storm) and in Kosovo.**

Allison six-speed semi-automatic gearbox. Suspension was by semi-elliptical springs with shock absorbers at the front only.

A total of 122 were manufactured, and three of the trials vehicles were reworked making a total of 125. The Commander was replaced by the Oshkosh M1080E1 from 2001 and the surplus vehicles were sold to a Middle Eastern nation.

Scammell S25 Commander

Type: Tractor, wheeled, semi-trailer, 98-ton, 6x4
Manufacturer: Leyland Specialised Vehicles, Scammell Motors Plant; Watford
Production: 1983 to 1985
Powerplant: Rolls-Royce CV12-TCE; 12 cylinders in V configuration; turbocharged diesel; water-cooled; 26,110cc; overhead valves; power output, 625bhp at 2,100rpm
Transmission: 6F1R; semi-automatic; 6x4
Suspension: Live axles on semi-elliptical multi-leaf springs, inverted at rear; double-acting hydraulic shock absorbers at front
Brakes: Air-pressure
Electrical system: 24V
Dimensions: Length – 9,011mm/355in
Width – 3,150mm/124in
Height – 3,356mm/132in
Wheelbase – 5,029mm/198in
Bogie centres – 1,600mm/63in
Weight: Unladen – 21,755kg/47,960lb
Gross train weight – 101,189kg/223,080lb
Performance: Maximum speed – 64kph/40mph

LEFT: **Both Cummins and Rolls-Royce engines were trialled. The production vehicle had a down-rated version of the Rolls-Royce CV12 power unit as used in the Challenger main battle tank.**

Thornycroft J-Type

In 1895, John I. Thornycroft commenced production of steam wagons in Chiswick and moved to a new site in Basingstoke in 1898. Thornycroft steam wagons were used during the Boer War, but the J-Type truck was the company's first vehicle supplied to the military in significant numbers.

The J-Type was designed to meet a 1911 British War Office specification for a 3-ton "subsidy scheme" cargo truck. Such schemes lowered the price of civilian trucks, but allowed them to be requisitioned by the military should this prove necessary. Thornycroft supplied the War Office with 24 H-, J- and K-Type chassis between August 1912 and May 1913. Further mixed orders followed but, after August 1914, the War Office settled on the J-Type. Approximately 5,000 were

Thornycroft J-Type

Type: Truck, 3-ton, cargo, 4x2
Manufacturer: John I. Thornycroft & Company; Basingstoke
Production: 1911 to 1926
Powerplant: Thornycroft M4; four cylinders in-line; petrol; water-cooled; 6,256cc; side valves; power output, 45bhp at 1,800rpm
Transmission: 4F1R; 4x2
Suspension: Live axles on semi-elliptical multi-leaf springs
Brakes: Mechanical
Electrical system: 6V
Dimensions: Length – 6,756mm/266in
Width – 2,210mm/87in
Height – tilt in place, 3,174mm/125in
Wheelbase – 4,166mm/164in
Weight: Unladen – 4521kg/9,968lb
Payload – 2,994kg/6,600lb
Performance: Maximum speed – 19kph/12mph

delivered over the next four years. Typical of the "subsidy A" trucks of the period, the J-Type was powered by a Thornycroft M4 6,256cc four-cylinder petrol engine driving a worm axle at the rear through a four-speed gearbox.

LEFT: **Ex-military J-Types proved very popular with civilian transport companies after 1918.**

Thornycroft Nubian TF/AC4

A pilot model for the Thornycroft Nubian TF was produced in June 1940, with the vehicle entering production in February 1941. By the time production ended in 1945, the company had built 3,824 vehicles.

Although it was mostly used by the RAF, the forward-control Nubian 3-ton 4x4 was typical of British military cargo vehicles developed during World War II. The engine was the manufacturer's AC4/1, a 3,865cc four-cylinder petrol unit dating from 1934, driving both axles through a four-speed gearbox and two-speed transfer box. The hubs incorporated epicyclic reduction

Thornycroft Nubian TF/AC4

Type: Truck, 3-ton, cargo, 4x4
Manufacturer: John I. Thornycroft & Company; Basingstoke
Production: 1941 to 1945
Powerplant: Thornycroft AC4/1; four cylinders in-line; petrol; water-cooled; 3,865cc; overhead valves; power output, 85bhp at 2,500rpm
Transmission: 4F1Rx2; part-time 4x4
Suspension: Live axles on semi-elliptical multi-leaf springs
Brakes: Hydraulic with vacuum servo-assistance
Electrical system: 6V
Dimensions: Length – 6,098mm/244in
Width – 2,286mm/90in
Height – tilt in place, 3,124mm/123in
Wheelbase – 3,658mm/144in
Weight: Unladen – 4,826kg/10,640lb
Payload – 2,994kg/6,600lb
Performance: Maximum speed – 63kph/39mph

LEFT: **A Nubian at the Thornycroft factory, finished in World War II vehicle camouflage.**

gears. Production resumed between 1950 and 1953, the vehicle being fitted with a Rolls-Royce B80 engine.

Thornycroft Antar

The Thornycroft Antar – it was never "Mighty Antar" in military service – was originally produced for the civil engineering contractor George Wimpey in 1949. Powered by an 18,012cc Rover Meteorite diesel engine, it was intended for hauling steel pipeline sections across the Iraqi deserts, where Wimpey was laying the Homs to Kirkuk pipeline for the Iraq Petrol Company. At around the same time, the War Office had been trying to develop a new prime mover to replace the Diamond T Model 980/981 which had been in service since 1940. It was felt that the Diamond T would not be sufficiently powerful to deal with the

65-ton Conqueror tank which was about to enter service. It was thought that the Antar might represent a low-cost option which would allow time while development of a "more suitable" vehicle continued.

In 1951, the Ministry of Supply agreed to purchase 15 Antars at a price of £8,177 each for use as a tank transporter tractor. A steel ballast box was installed over the rear axle to allow the tractor to be used with a 50-ton drawbar trailer. The Meteorite engine of the civilian vehicle was replaced by a petrol version which offered better torque. The engine was coupled to a four-speed gearbox and three-speed auxiliary box.

LEFT: The first civilian "Mighty Antar" was a diesel-engined fifth-wheel tractor intended for oilfield use. When the vehicle entered military service in 1951, the Mk 1 military Antar was fitted with a petrol engine and equipped with a steel ballast body for use with a draw-bar trailer.

In 1952, Thornycroft started work on the military Mk 2 and Mk 2A variants, the former with a fifth-wheel coupling to allow use with a 60-ton semi-trailer, the latter with a wooden ballast box. The engine and transmission were unchanged. The Mk 2 remained in production until 1957 when it was superseded by the Mk 3 and Mk 3A, with the Rolls-Royce C8SFL diesel engine and a simplified six-speed transmission and overdrive top gear. A new cab was fitted and, again, there were versions for semi-trailer (Mk 3) and drawbar trailer (Mk 3A).

Some 700 Antars were produced, of which 590 were supplied to the British Army and the RAF. The Antar was replaced in British service by the Scammell Commander in 1984. The vehicle was used by the armies of Burma, Kuwait, Pakistan and South Africa.

LEFT: By 1961, the vehicle had evolved into the Mk 3 and Mk 3A, powered by a Rolls-Royce C8SFL diesel-engine. The Mk 3 (shown) was fitted with a fifth wheel. The Mk 3A had a ballast body.

Thornycroft Antar

Type: (Mk 1 variant) Tractor, 30-ton, GS, 6x4; FV12001

Manufacturer: Transport Equipment Thornycroft; Basingstoke

Production: 1951 to 1964

Powerplant: (Mk 1, Mk 2) Rover Meteorite Mk 204; eight cylinders in V configuration; petrol; water-cooled; 18,012cc; overhead valves; power output, 260bhp at 2,300rpm. (Mk 3) Rolls-Royce C8SFL/843; six cylinders in-line; super-charged diesel; water-cooled; 16,200cc; overhead valves; power output, 333bhp at 3,250rpm

Transmission: (Mk 1, Mk 2) 4F1Rx3, (Mk 3) 6F1R; 6x4

Suspension: Live axles on multi-leaf semi-elliptical springs

Brakes: Air-pressure

Electrical system: 24V

Dimensions: (Mk 1 variant)
Length – 8,440mm/332in
Width – 2,820mm/111in
Height – 3,050mm/120in
Wheelbase – 4,720mm/186in
Bogie centres – 1,580mm/62in

Weight: Unladen – 20,058kg/44,220lb
Gross train weight – 142,253kg/313,610lb

Performance: Maximum speed – 45kph/28mph

LEFT: **Surplus "Mighty Mite" vehicles in a Tennessee breakers yard, including both M422 and M422A1 vehicles.**

American Motors "Mighty Mite"

Officially designated M422, but generally known as the "Mighty Mite", this American Motors product is probably the smallest practical Jeep-type military vehicle ever produced. The design was by some of the original team that had been responsible for designing the Bantam BRC40 in 1940. It was produced for the US Marine Corps and light weight was important to allow transportation by helicopter.

Development began in the early 1950s at the Mid-American Research Corporation (MARCO). The first prototype weighed just 680kg/1,503lb and was powered by a Porsche four-cylinder air-cooled engine. Eventually, MARCO handed the final development and production over to American Motors Corporation (AMC) who replaced the engine with a 1,770cc V4 air-cooled engine of their own design. The vehicle was finally accepted for production in April 1958, when it was agreed that AMC would produce seven pre-production vehicles followed by a further 50 production models. If these were satisfactory then a further 243 would be built. By December 1959, AMC had started assembling the first of 1,250 examples of the M422.

In original M422 configuration, the vehicle had a 1,651mm/65in wheelbase, was just 2,718mm/107in long and weighed 679kg/1,496lb. On the later M422A1, the wheelbase was increased to 1,805mm/71in and the length increased to 2,870mm/113in. The weight increased to 771kg/1,700lb. In order to help save weight, only the M422A1 was provided with a canvas top and spare wheel.

The AMC four-cylinder engine was coupled to a four-speed gearbox, and single-speed transfer box. Drive was to all four wheels. The latter included a third differential. Prototype vehicles had utilized a tubular-steel chassis to give the maximum possible strength to weight ratio, but this was subsequently replaced by a conventional channel-section ladder design. However, all of the body parts were of aluminium, and many components were drilled (or "skeletonized") to keep the weight to a minimum. Independent suspension was fitted on all four wheels by means of leading and trailing arms on quarter-elliptical leaf springs. The brakes were inboard. Production continued until early 1963 by which time some 4,000 vehicles had been built, of which 1,250 were the original M422 variant.

American Motors "Mighty Mite"

Type: Truck, utility, lightweight, ¼-ton, 4x4; M422, M422A1

Manufacturer: American Motors Corporation; Detroit, Michigan

Production: 1960 to 1963

Powerplant: AMC AV-108-4; four cylinders in V configuration; petrol; air-cooled; 1,770cc; overhead valves; power output, 55bhp at 3,600rpm

Transmission: 4F1Rx2; part-time 4x4

Suspension: Independent suspension by leading and trailing arms and quarter-elliptical multi-leaf springs

Brakes: Hydraulic

Electrical system: 24V

Dimensions: Length – (M422) 2,718mm/107in; (M422A1) 2,870mm/113in
Width – 1,550mm/61in
Height – tilt in place, 1,473mm/58in; minimum, 1,195mm/47in
Wheelbase – (M422) 1,651mm/65in; (M422A1) 1,805mm/71in

Weight: Unladen – 679–771kg/1,496–1,700lb
Payload – road, 453kg/1,000lb; cross-country, 386kg/850lb

Performance: Maximum speed – 76kph/47mph

ABOVE: **The wheelbase of the M422A1 was lengthened to 1,805mm/71in; subsequently the overall length increased to 2,870mm/113in. Of 4,000 vehicles completed some 2,750 were the M422A1 variant.**

LEFT: The "High Mobility Multi-purpose Wheeled Vehicle" (HMMWV) – known as "Humvee" or "Hummer" in the civilian version – is a considerably larger vehicle than the M151 for which it was a partial replacement. The low centre of gravity and wide track provide excellent off-road performance. The modular construction allows the same basic chassis platform to be used for a range of variants. The vehicle was originally powered by a 6,200cc Detroit-Diesel V8 engine. In 1995, this was replaced with a 6,500cc turbocharged engine.

AM-General M998 Series (HMMWV)

Development of the vehicle that was to replace the M151 began in 1978 when the US Army created a requirement for a go-anywhere "High Mobility Multi-purpose Wheeled Vehicle" (HMMWV) for use as a cargo truck, communications vehicle, weapons platform, personnel carrier and command/reconnaissance vehicle. A detailed specification was published in 1980 and the Chrysler Corporation, Teledyne Continental and AM-General (AMG) submitted vehicles for trials. The AMG vehicle was selected for production and in March 1983, the US Army's Tank, Automotive and Armaments Command (TACOM) awarded AM General a $1.2 billion contract to produce 55,000 vehicles over a five-year period.

The vehicle was officially designated as the M998 Series and was nicknamed both "Humvee" and "Hummer". Subsequent agreements between AM-General and General Motors have attempted to rationalize the use of the two names, assigning one to the military vehicle and one to its civilian counterpart. Production vehicles began to enter service in 1983, and by 1996, more than 100,000 had been built. By the beginning of 2004, more than

160,000 HMMWVs had been delivered to the US Army and to 30 other armies.

The original M998 Series was powered by a 6,200cc Detroit-Diesel V8, driving through a three-speed automatic transmission, incorporated full-time four-wheel drive, and independent coil-spring suspension. Although there were initially five basic models, these were developed into 15 different configurations, allowing the chassis to be used for weapons systems, command and control systems and field ambulance, as well as ammunition, troop and general cargo transport.

In 1992, the M1097 "Heavy Hummer Variant" (HHV) was introduced. The frame and suspension were reinforced to accommodate a payload of 2,000kg/ 4,400lb. Subsequent improvements led to the A1 variants in 1994, and a year later, the A2 series was introduced using a more powerful 6,500cc diesel engine, and electronically controlled four-speed automatic transmission, allowing the payload to be increased to 2,000kg/ 4,400lb. The M1113 "Expanded Capacity Vehicle" (ECV, sometimes ECH) was also introduced in 1995, fitted with a turbocharged version of the engine,

improved differentials, brakes, cooling system and a stronger chassis. This allowed the payload to be increased further to 2,313kg/ 5,100lb. The chassis is also the basis for the O'Gara-Hess & Eisenhardt uparmoured M1114 HMMWV.

As of 2006, the M1113 became the base vehicle for future HMMWV orders.

AM-General M998 Series HMMWV

Type: Truck, weapons carrier, 1-ton, 4x4; M1025, M1026

Manufacturer: AM-General Corporation; South Bend, Indiana

Production: 1983 on

Powerplant: Detroit-Diesel; eight cylinders in V configuration; diesel; water-cooled; 6,200cc; overhead valves; power output, 150bhp at 3,600rpm

Transmission: Automatic 3F1Rx2; full-time 4x4

Suspension: Independent suspension by upper and lower wishbones and coil springs

Brakes: Hydraulic

Electrical system: 24V

Dimensions: Length – 4,570mm/180in
Width – 2,180mm/86in
Height – to top of cab, 1,880mm/74in; minimum, 1,830mm/72in
Wheelbase – 3,300mm/130in

Weight: Unladen – 2,703kg/5,960lb
Payload – 1,016kg/2,240lb

Performance: Maximum speed – 113kph/70mph

American Bantam 40BRC

In mid-1940, Karl Probst, a freelance automotive designer, undertook a project for the ailing American Bantam company which was to change history. Working from little more than a scribbled sketch and a written specification setting out basic parameters, Probst and his team designed and built what was effectively the first Jeep in a matter of days.

Bantam had been one of three companies to respond to a US Quartermaster Corps (US QMC) request for bids for a new lightweight 4x4 reconnaissance vehicle. The timescale dictated that Bantam's prototype was little more than a new chassis and body to which had been bolted an assembly of existing components. The engine was from Continental, the axles and transfer case from Spicer, and the transmission from Warner. By September 1940, the Model 60, as the prototype was called, was driven to Maryland and delivered to the US QMC for trials.

Unable to break the vehicle, US QMC told Bantam to go ahead and build 60 vehicles. This was rapidly followed by a second contract for 1,500 production vehicles, now designated the 40BRC.

LEFT: **A total of 2,675 Bantams were built before production switched to the Willys Jeep.**

American Bantam 40BRC

Type: Truck, 1/4-ton, 4x4, command reconnaissance
Manufacturer: American Bantam; Butler, Pennsylvania
Production: 1940 to 1941
Powerplant: Continental BY-4112; four cylinders in-line; petrol; water-cooled; 1,835cc; side valves; power output, 48bhp at 3,150rpm
Transmission: 3F1Rx2; part-time 4x4
Suspension: Live axles on semi-elliptical multi-leaf springs
Brakes: Hydraulic
Electrical system: 6V
Dimensions: Length – 3,200mm/126in
Width – 1,372mm/54in
Height – tilt in place, 1,816mm/72in; minimum, 1,245mm/49in
Wheelbase – 2,019mm/79.5in
Weight: Unladen – 954kg/2,103lb
Payload – 250kg/551lb
Performance: Maximum speed – 96kph/60mph

Aqua-Cheetah XAC-1, 2, 3

Aqua-Cheetah XAC-1, 2, 3

Type: Truck, 1/2- or 3/4-ton, 4x4, amphibian
Manufacturer: Amphibian Car Corporation; Buffalo, New York
Production: 1941 to 1942
Powerplant: Dodge T214 or T215; six cylinders in-line; petrol; air-cooled; 3,772cc; side valves; power output, 92–99bhp at 3,200rpm
Transmission: 4F1Rx1; part-time 4x4; selectable propeller drive
Suspension: Independent suspension using trailing arm chaincases on coil springs
Brakes: Hydraulic
Electrical system: 12V
Dimensions: Length – 4,978mm/196in
Width – 2,286mm/90in
Height – tilt in place, 1,525mm/64in
Wheelbase – 2,438mm/96in
Weight: Unladen – 2,500kg/5,512lb
Payload – 500–750kg/1,102–1,653lb
Performance: In water – 11kph/6.6mph

The Aqua-Cheetah was designed by Roger W. Hofheins, president of the Amphibian Car Corporation in mid-1941. The XAC-1 was an amphibious 1/2-ton vehicle originally powered by a mid-mounted Ford V8 engine driving a single propeller or all four wheels through trailing-arm chaincases. Independent suspension was fitted on all four wheels. Performance in the water was good, but less so on land.

In May 1942, Hofheins produced the XAC-2, using a rear-mounted Dodge T214 engine, with a mid-mounted gearbox coupled to a chain-driven transfer case. The differential housings were welded to the hull and connected to the chaincases by axles. The prototype was followed by seven pre-production vehicles for evaluation.

By mid-1942, the design had evolved into the XAC-3 using a Dodge T215 engine. Only 12 Aqua-Cheetah amphibians were built before the project was cancelled in late 1942.

BELOW: **The XAC-1 was fitted with a Ford V8 petrol engine. The XAC-2 had a Dodge T214 and the final version, XAC-3, a Dodge T215 petrol engine.**

Autocar U-4144T, U-7144T

The Autocar U-4144T was a 2¹/₂-ton 4x4 tractor, manufactured during 1940 and 1941. In 1941, it was superseded by the 4- to 5-ton U-7144T. Both were derived from a civilian vehicle, and were intended for use with a 6-ton (10-ton gross), or 9,092-litre/2,000-gallon fuel-servicing semi-trailer. The earliest examples were fitted with a civilian-type two-door cab. In 1942, this was replaced by a standard open-cab design with a canvas top and side-screens. A folding windscreen was fitted.

The U-4144T was powered by an Autocar six-cylinder petrol engine, while the U-7144T used a Hercules RXC unit, in combination with a five-speed gearbox and two-speed transfer box. The suspension was by live axles hung on semi-elliptical springs. Total production amounted to 274 of the U-4144T and 13,856 of the U-7144T.

Autocar U-4144T, U-7144T	
Type: Truck, 2¹/₂- or 4- to 5-ton, tractor, 4x4	
Manufacturer: Autocar Company; Ardmore, Pennsylvania. White Motor Company; Cleveland, Ohio	
Production: 1940 to 1945	
Powerplant: U4144-T – Autocar D358; six cylinders in-line; petrol; water-cooled; 5,866cc; side valves; power output, 100bhp at 2,200rpm. U-7144T – Hercules RXC-529; six cylinders in-line; petrol; water-cooled; 8,669cc; side valves; power output, 112bhp at 2,200rpm	
Transmission: 5F1Rx2; part-time 4x4	
Suspension: Live axles on semi-elliptical multi-leaf springs	
Brakes: Air-pressure	
Electrical system: Dual 6V/12V	
Dimensions: (U-7144T) Length – 5,182mm/204in Width – 2,413mm/95in Height – tilt in place, 2,870mm/113in; minimum, 2,337mm/92in Wheelbase – 3,429mm/135in	
Weight: Unladen – 5,264kg/11,606lb Payload – 4,536kg/10,000lb	
Performance: Maximum speed – 64kph/40mph	

LEFT: **An Autocar U-4144T fitted with a civilian-type two-door cab, coupled to a 7,600-litre/2,000-gallon fuel-servicing semi-trailer.**

Autocar U8144, U8144T

The Autocar U8144 was a 5- to 6-ton 4x4 truck produced in two major variants. Of the total of approximately 3,300 manufactured between 1941 and 1945, 2,700 were of the U8144T variant. This was equipped as a fifth-wheel tractor intended for use with bridging equipment semi-trailers.

A large equipment locker for construction tools was fitted behind the cab, and there was a 7¹/₂-ton capacity mechanical winch. The remainder, some 600, were fitted with a large van body built by York-Hoover and were assigned to the US Air Force for the transport of radar and signals equipment.

The engine was an 8,669cc Hercules RXC 8, six-cylinder unit, producing 112bhp, driving either the rear wheels or both axles through a five-speed gear-box with overdrive

LEFT: **An Autocar U8144 tractor unit fitted to the all-metal cab.**

Autocar U8144, U8144T	
Type: Truck, tractor, 5- to 6-ton, 4x4	
Manufacturer: Autocar; Ardmore, Pennsylvania	
Production: 1941 to 1945	
Powerplant: Hercules RXC; six cylinders in-line; petrol; water-cooled; 8,669cc; side valves; power output, 112bhp at 2,200rpm	
Transmission: 5F1Rx2; part-time 4x4	
Suspension: Live axles on semi-elliptical multi-leaf springs, inverted at the rear	
Brakes: Air-pressure	
Electrical system: Hybrid 6V/12V	
Dimensions: (U8144T variant) Length – 6,273mm/247in Width – 2,489mm/98in Height – to top of cab, 2,921mm/115in Wheelbase – 4,166mm/164in	
Weight: Unladen – 7,530kg/16,600lb Payload – 5,321kg/11,730lb	
Performance: Maximum speed – 76kph/47mph	

top gear, and a two-speed transfer box. On late production vehicles, the steel cab was replaced by a standardized open-topped cab with a folding windscreen and canvas cover.

Willys M274 "Mechanical Mule"

LEFT: **Although not road legal, the "Mechanical Mule" is ideal for operating on military bases. The vehicle can be driven in the conventional manner or pedestrian-controlled.**

In 1944–45, Willys built a small motorized platform vehicle which was described as the "jungle burden carrier", and intended for use by airborne infantry. Developed from the chassis of the MB Jeep, it consisted of little more than a flat load-carrying bed on four wheels, with the driver placed at the very front. The engine and transmission were under the floor and both the driver's seat and the steering column could be folded down to provide a completely flat platform which allowed easy stacking. There was no series production, but in the mid-1950s the concept was revisited as the XM274, generally described as the "Mechanical Mule".

The main departure from the earlier version was that the steering column was arranged to tilt forward and the clutch and accelerator were duplicated to allow the operator to either drive the machine in the conventional manner, or to walk along behind using the tilted wheel to steer. The platform was of magnesium-alloy on all variants except the M274A5.

Early versions went into production as the M274, powered by a Willys-Continental AO53 horizontally opposed four-cylinder engine placed at the rear under the floor. In the M274A1 variant, this was replaced by the AO53-1 power unit. Subsequent variants (M274A2, A3, A4 and A5) were fitted with a standard military Continental-Hercules AO42 two-cylinder engine. Permanent four-wheel drive through a three-speed gearbox and two-speed transfer box was fitted, also four-wheel steering (not on A5 variant). No suspension was fitted,

but the over-sized tyres provided some degree of cushioning against road shocks.

Initial production was at Willys' Toledo factory but, from 1965, was moved to Baifield Industries in Texas. From 1970, production was shared between the Brunswick Corporation and Bowen-McLaughlin-York.

Although intended for use as a load carrier, M274s deployed to Vietnam were used as stretcher carriers. It was also equipped with a 106mm anti-tank recoilless rifle or TOW missile system. A similar vehicle was produced in the Netherlands by DAF, described as the YM500 "Pony". In 1965, this was trialled as a possible replacement for the M274.

ABOVE: **The "Mule" also provides a useful weapons platform for a recoilless anti-tank rifle.**

Willys M274 "Mechanical Mule"

Type: Truck, 1/2-ton, platform, utility, 4x4
Manufacturer: Baifield Industries; Carrollton, Texas. Bowen-McLaughlin-York; York, Pennsylvania. Brunswick Corporation; Lake Forest, Illinois. Willys-Overland/Kaiser-Jeep; Toledo, Ohio
Production: 1956 to 1972
Powerplant: (M274, M274A1) Willys-Continental AO53, AO53-1; four cylinders, horizontally opposed; petrol; air-cooled; 877cc; overhead valves; power output, 17bhp at 3,200rpm (M274A2, A3, A4, A5) Continental-Hercules AO42; two cylinders, horizontally opposed; petrol; air-cooled; 688cc; overhead valves; power output, 14bhp at 3,000rpm
Transmission: 3F1Rx2; full-time 4x4
Suspension: Live portal axles, no suspension
Brakes: Mechanical acting on drive shaft
Electrical system: Magneto only
Dimensions: Length – 2,980mm/117in
  Width – 1,780mm/70in
  Height – maximum, 1,193mm/47in;
  minimum, 686mm/27in
  Wheelbase – 1,448mm/57in
Weight: Unladen – 420kg/925lb
  Payload – 500kg/1,102lb
Performance: Maximum speed – 40kph/25mph

Caterpillar M520, M553, M559 "Goer"

During the late 1950s, the US Army started to investigate the possibility of adapting some of the concepts used in the design of all-terrain engineering plant to produce high-mobility military vehicles. Early trials were conducted with commercial vehicles from companies such as Caterpillar, Euclid and International, which were steered by articulation and which used large balloon tyres in place of conventional suspension.

In 1960–61, LeTourneau-Westinghouse, Caterpillar and Clark Equipment were asked to produce prototypes for what was being described as the "Goer" range. Caterpillar developed the 8-ton chassis, LeTourneau's contribution was a 15-ton vehicle and Clark built a 5-ton variant.

In all cases, the vehicles were built of two separate components – a forward-control cab unit which incorporated the engine and transmission, and a separate load-carrying unit, each component carried on its own axle. The two units were coupled together in such a way as to allow them to roll independently. Hydraulic rams between the two units allowed 60 degrees of lateral movement to provide steering; this was sufficient

ABOVE: **Caterpillar "Goer" fitted as a "Transporter-Erector-Launcher" (TEL) for the US Army's Nike Hercules anti-aircraft missile.**

to allow the vehicles to be swung from side to side across soft terrain.

In the 8-ton series, the engine was a Caterpillar six-cylinder turbocharged diesel or multi-fuel diesel unit. On early prototypes the front axle, which incorporated hub-reduction gears, was driven through a five-speed main gearbox and two-speed auxiliary box. Later prototypes used an automatic six-speed gearbox. The standard drive configuration was to use the front axle. The rear wheels were driven by electric motors mounted in the hubs, and could only be used in the two lowest of the gear ratios.

Prototypes were eventually produced for an 8-ton cargo vehicle (XM520E1), wrecker (XM553) and tanker (XM559E1) – all were amphibious. The performance during trials was exceptional and, in 1971, the Army Material Command invited bids from industry for a total

of 1,300 vehicles – 812 cargo trucks (M520 and M877), the latter being fitted with a handling crane, 371 tankers (M559) and 117 10-ton wreckers (M553). The $61.5 million contract was awarded to Caterpillar and production began in 1972.

A 15-ton 6x6 "Goer" prototype was produced in the early 1970s.

Caterpillar M520, M553, M559 "Goer"

Type: Truck, cargo, 8-ton, 4x4; M520
Manufacturer: Caterpillar Tractor Company; Peoria, Illinois
Production: 1972 to 1974
Powerplant: Caterpillar D333 or D333C; six cylinders in-line; multi-fuel diesel (D333C, diesel only); water-cooled; 10,455cc; overhead valves; power output, 192bhp at 2,200rpm
Transmission: Automatic, 6F1Rx2; part-time 4x4; rear-wheel drive by electric motors
Suspension: None, balloon tyres only
Brakes: Air-pressure
Electrical system: 24V
Dimensions: (M520 variant)
　Length – 6,273mm/247in
　Width – 2,743mm/108in
　Height – tilt erected, 2,997mm/118in; minimum, 2,565mm/101in
　Wheelbase – 5,969mm/235in
Weight: Unladen – 10,864kg/23,950lb
　Payload – 7,258kg/16,000lb
Performance: Maximum speed – road, 48kph/30mph; in still water, 13kph/8mph

LEFT: **The articulated two-component assembly helped to ensure that the wheels remained on the ground regardless of the terrain and the steering was by hydraulic rams between the two components. The "Goer" lacked conventional suspension, relying instead on balloon tyres.**

LEFT: **The Chevrolet G4113/G7113 tractor and semi-trailer was used by the US Army on the "Red Ball Express" supply routes after D-Day.**

Chevrolet G4100, G7100 series

First appearing in 1940 and designated as the G4100 series, the normal-control 1¹/₂-ton Chevrolet became the US Army's standard 4x4 vehicle in this weight class throughout World War II. The G4100 was superseded in 1942 by the more militarized G7100.

The truck was derived from a civilian vehicle of the same rating, and incorporated all-wheel drive. The two-man cab was the same as on the GMC CCKW 6x6, but, unlike the GMC, there was no open cab variant. Power was provided by a Chevrolet six-cylinder petrol engine, driving both axles through a four-speed gearbox and two-speed transfer box. The front axle could be disengaged when not required. GM "banjo"-type hypoid axles were fitted, front and rear, suspended on semi-elliptical leaf springs. The brakes were hydraulic, with vacuum servo power assistance. A Warner electric brake hand controller was fitted in the cab to allow the trailer brakes to be operated separately.

Most of the total production was the steel-bodied cargo vehicle. Other standard variants included panel van, airfield crash tender, bomb servicing vehicle, oil servicing vehicle, telephone and maintenance vehicle. There were also tractor variants (G4113 and G7113), of which just 169 were produced, designed for use in conjunction with a range of 6-ton (gross) semi-trailers. Some 168,603 vehicles were built, representing 30 per cent of Chevrolet's total World War II output. The design was widely used by the US Signal Corps and remained in production until 1945.

BELOW: **The Chevrolet G4112 tipper truck was fitted with a hydraulically operated steel-fabricated body produced by Heil or Hercules Steel Products. The designation changed to G7116 from 1942.**

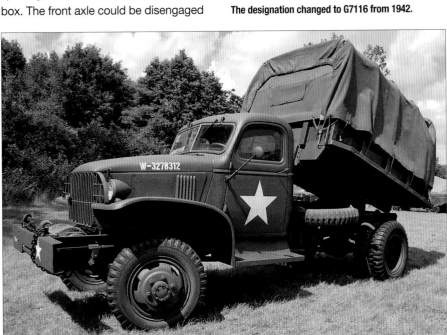

Chevrolet G4100, G7100 series

Type: Truck, 1¹/₂-ton, cargo, 4x4
Manufacturer: Chevrolet Motor Division, General Motors Corporation; Detroit, Michigan
Production: 1940 to 1945
Powerplant: Chevrolet BV1001-UP; six cylinders in-line; water-cooled; 3,859cc; overhead valves; petrol; power output, 84bhp at 3,000rpm
Transmission: 4F1Rx2; part-time 4x4
Suspension: Live axles on semi-elliptical multi-leaf springs
Brakes: Hydraulic with vacuum servo-assistance; electric connection for trailer brakes on tractor variants
Electrical system: 6V
Dimensions: Length – 5,232mm/206in
 Width – 2,185mm/86in
 Height – tilt in place – 2,692mm/106in; minimum, 2,210mm/87in
 Wheelbase – 3,683mm/145in
Weight: Unladen – 3,422kg/7,545lb
 Payload – road, 5,389kg/11,880lb; cross–country, 1,497kg/3,300lb
Performance: Maximum speed – 77kph/48mph

Condec M561, M792 "Gama Goat"

The "Gama Goat" 6x6 was one of the more unusual US military vehicles of the post-war period. The idea for an articulated twin-bodied high-mobility truck, where the two components were able to pitch and roll relative to one another, was based on a hydraulically suspended vehicle produced by the Swiss Meili Company, tested in the USA in 1961. Development work on what was the XM561 was initiated at the Chance-Vought Aircraft Corporation around 1962. Early prototypes were powered by a Chevrolet Corvair air-cooled engine and featured front- and rear-wheel steering, as well as being amphibious.

The name was derived from Roger L. Gamaunt, the designer of the articulating coupling which transmitted power between the two components.

Production was entrusted to the Consolidated Diesel Electric Corporation in 1969. By this time, the Corvair engine had been replaced by a Detroit Diesel 3-53, a three-cylinder supercharged two-stroke engine which was so noisy that the crew were obliged to wear ear defenders. The transmission was a four-speed unit, with a two-speed transfer box. Propulsion and steering in the water was achieved through the wheels alone. The truck was also fitted with

LEFT: The "Gama Goat" was powered by a 2,610cc Detroit-Diesel 3-53 three-cylinder supercharged water-cooled engine mounted behind the cab bulkhead. The proximity and noise from the engine required the crew to wear ear defenders.

outboard brakes using "O" rings in the drums to maintain a water seal.

Suspension was by a centre swing axle suspended on a single transverse leaf spring. Independent coil-spring suspension was fitted on the front and rear axles. In normal road use the centre axle provided drive, but six-wheel drive was also available.

It would be true to say that the "Gama Goat" was not popular with drivers. The curious handling characteristics led to roll-over accidents. The vehicle was also considered difficult to enter and exit. These characteristics were additional to a reputation for poor reliability and high noise levels.

There were two standard variants, M561 cargo vehicle and the M792 field ambulance. A total of 14,000 were built over a five-year period. Some vehicles were fitted with a front-mounted winch which made the vehicle very nose-down in the water.

ABOVE: The M561 was made up of two separate units – the tractor and carrier – both of which were able to roll and pitch relative to one another. The vehicle was also amphibious.

Condec M561, M792 "Gama Goat"

Type: Truck, 1¼-ton, 6x6; M561, M792
Manufacturer: Consolidated Diesel Electric Corporation (Condec); Schenectady, New York
Production: 1969 to 1973
Powerplant: Detroit Diesel 3-53; three cylinders in-line; supercharged two-stroke diesel; water-cooled; 2,610cc; overhead inlet valves; power output, 103bhp at 2,800rpm
Transmission: 4F1Rx2; part-time 6x6; amphibious capability via the road wheels
Suspension: Centre swing axle on transverse leaf spring; independent suspension front and rear using coil springs and wishbones; hydraulic double-acting shock absorbers
Brakes: Hydraulic
Electrical system: 24V
Dimensions: Length – 5,490mm/216in
　　Width – 2,311mm/91in
　　Height – 2,075mm/82in
　　Wheelbase – 2,050+2,154mm/81+85in
Weight: Unladen – 3,308kg/7,293lb
　　Payload – 1,313kg/2,895lb
Performance: Maximum speed – 88kph/55mph

Condec, LeTourneau-Westinghouse LARC-5

The 5-ton "Lighter, Amphibious, Resupply, Cargo, 5" – also described as LARC-5 and LARC-V – dates from the end of the 1950s, and was among the final vehicles directly attributable to the design concept which had originated with the GMC DUKW in 1942. While the rated payload of 5,080kg/11,200lb was twice that of the DUKW, the LARC was intended for ferrying supplies from ship to shore in the same way that the DUKWs had been used during various amphibious landings in World War II.

The vehicle was developed by the Ingersoll-Kalamazoo Division of Borg-Warner during 1958 and 1959 under the direction of the US Transportation Engineering Command (USTEC) at Fort Eustis, Virginia. Early production vehicles used a Ford V8 engine, but most of the production run was installed with a Cummins V8 engine combined with a single-speed transmission, fitted with a lock-up hydraulic retarder. The vehicle lacked conventional suspension, relying on low-pressure sand tyres to absorb road shocks. This led to claims of unacceptable "pitching" on the road when approaching the vehicle's maximum speed of 45kph/28mph.

The hull was fabricated from aluminium sheet, with the engine compartment at the rear, the cargo bay placed centrally and the control position at the front. Propulsion in the water was provided by a combination of propeller and water jet,

both systems operating in a tunnel through the hull.

The first production contract was awarded to the Adams Division of LeTourneau-Westinghouse in June 1961, with a second contract going to Consolidated Diesel Electric Corporation (Condec). A total of 950 vehicles were built between 1962 and 1968. In mid-2004 it was announced that Power Dynamics had been awarded a contract to refurbish 37 LARC-5s, with delivery of the first craft in October 2006.

LARC-5s were used during the Vietnam War, operating across the beach at Cam Ranh Bay, Nha Trang and Phan Rang, Phan Thiet and Vung Ro Bay. Similar vehicles produced around the same time include the 10-ton LARC-XI, the 15-ton LARC-XV, which

ABOVE: **Although probably too large and cumbersome to be used as a road-going truck, the 5-ton LARC-5 was really intended for ferrying supplies from ship to shore. The lack of conventional suspension gave rise to claims of unacceptable "pitching" on the road when approaching maximum speed.**

was fitted with a bow ramp, and the 60-ton LARC-LX. This was also known as the BARC-LX or "Barge, Amphibious, Resupply, Cargo".

LEFT: **In the water, the LARC-5 was probably more useful than the DUKW. The LARC was used in the Vietnam War where it was used to ferry supplies across the beach at Cam Ranh Bay, Nha Trang, Phan Rang and other areas. Despite the LARC-5 being 50 years old, 37 were refurbished for USTEC between 2004 and 2006.**

Condec, LeTourneau-Westinghouse LARC-5

Type: Lighter, amphibious, resupply, cargo, 5-ton, 4x4
Manufacturer: Consolidated Diesel Electric Corporation; Waterbury, Connecticut. LeTourneau-Westinghouse, Adams Division; Peoria, Illinois
Production: 1962 to 1968
Powerplant: Cummins V-903; eight cylinders in V configuration; diesel; water-cooled; 14,798cc; overhead valves; power output, 295bhp at 2,600rpm
Transmission: 1F1R; part-time 4x4
Suspension: None
Brakes: Air-pressure
Electrical system: 24V
Dimensions: Length – 10,675mm/420in
  Width – 3,150mm/124in
  Height – 3,048mm/120in
  Wheelbase – 4,877mm/192in
Weight: Unladen – 4,082kg/9,000lb
  Payload – 4,536kg/10,000lb
Performance: Maximum speed – road, 45kph/28mph; in water, 11kph/7mph

Diamond T Models 980, 981

Considered by many to be the best-looking truck of World War II, at least in original closed-cab form, the Diamond T Models 980 and 981 were developed for the British Army to supplement a shortage of Scammell Pioneer tank transporters. The project began in late 1940, when the British Purchasing Commission approached several US manufacturers of heavy trucks with a specification for a 40-ton diesel-engined tractor. One of the prime considerations was that the chosen vehicle could be put into production immediately.

Diamond T proposed a conventional bonneted 6x4 truck based on their civilian 12-ton Model 512, a design which had already been militarized for the Canadian Diamond T Models 967–975. Under the huge bonnet there was a Hercules DFXE six-cylinder diesel engine – despite running counter to US Army practice at that time, the diesel engine was chosen to provide fuel compatibility with the Gardner-engined Scammell. The transmission was a four-speed unit with a two-speed transfer box. The cab was Diamond T's standard civilian design with a steep 30-degree V-shaped windscreen. At the rear was a steel ballast box designed to allow weight to be placed over the rear axles to provide traction when loaded.

The first production variant was the Model 980, designed for use with either the British 40-ton multi-wheeled trailer, typified by the products of Cranes and British Trailers, or the 45-ton US Army

equivalent produced by Fruehauf, Winter-Weiss and others. The Model 981 followed in 1942–43, the only difference being the provision of winch fairlead rollers in the front bumper to allow the vehicle to be used for tank recovery vehicle. In August 1943, the all-steel closed cab was replaced by a standard open cab designed to save materials and reduce the shipping height.

The Diamond T remained in production until 1945, by which time approximately 6,500 had been built. Of these, 2,255 were used by the British Army. Although it was classified as "substitute standard", the vehicle was also used by the US Army who designated it the M20. The tank-transporter train, including trailer, was the M19.

Large numbers of Diamond Ts remained in British service into the post-war years. It was re-engined in the mid-1950s with a Rolls-Royce C6NFL-143 six-cylinder water-cooled diesel engine.

LEFT: **The Model 981 can be identified by the use of winch fairlead rollers in the front bumper. The vehicle has a ballast body for towing a semi-trailer.**

LEFT: **The Diamond T Models 980, 981 were developed for the British War Office and were used to supplement Scammell Pioneer tank transporters. Although also used by the US Army, the use of a diesel engine meant that it was never considered acceptable. The US Army designated it as "substitute standard".**

Diamond T Models 980, 981

Type: Truck, 12-ton, 6x4; M20
Manufacturer: Diamond T Motor Car Company; Chicago, Illinois
Production: 1941 to 1945
Powerplant: Hercules DFXE; six cylinders in-line; diesel; water-cooled; 14,500cc; overhead valves; power output, 201bhp at 1,800rpm. Rolls-Royce C6NFL-143; six cylinders in-line; diesel; water-cooled; 12,170cc; overhead valves; power output, 175bhp at 2,100rpm
Transmission: 4F1Rx2; 6x4
Suspension: Live axles on multi-leaf semi-elliptical springs
Brakes: Air-pressure
Electrical system: Hybrid 6V/12V/24V
Dimensions: Length – 9,144mm/360in
  Width – 2,896mm/114in
  Height – 1,575mm/62in
  Wheelbase – 4,553mm/179in
  Bogie centres – 1,321mm/52in
Weight: Unladen – 12,117kg/26,712lb
  Gross train weight – 80,777kg/178,079lb
Performance: Maximum speed –
  Hercules engine, 37kph/23mph;
  Rolls-Royce engine – 47kph/29mph

LEFT: **The Diamond T Models 967, 968 chassis was also used for the Model 969 medium wrecker, with Holmes twin-boom recovery gear. The vehicle is being used to recover a captured Panzer III tank.**

Diamond T Models 967, 968

The Diamond T Model 967 was a 4-ton 6x6 cargo truck produced for the US Quartermaster Corps (QMC) in 1940. Approximately 1,000 examples were manufactured. At the same time, the QMC purchased similar 4-ton trucks from Autocar, White and Ward LaFrance, but it was the Diamond T that became standardized in this class in 1941, as the slightly modified Model 968.

For both models, the power unit was an 8,669cc Hercules RXC six-cylinder petrol engine driving through a five-speed gear-box (with overdrive as top gear) connected to all three axles via a two-speed transfer box. Suspension was by semi-elliptical leaf springs, inverted at the rear.

The chassis was built in two wheelbase lengths (4,369mm/172in and 3,835mm/151in), and was generally fitted with a front-mounted 7$\frac{1}{2}$-ton capacity winch driven from a power take-off on the transfer box. The short-wheelbase version was bodied as a cargo vehicle. The long-wheelbase variant was fitted with a cargo/pontoon body for use by the US Corps of Engineers. From around 1943, the manufacturer's attractive closed cab was replaced by a standard military open cab with a canvas cover. One vehicle out of four off the production line was fitted with a machine-gun ring mount.

Special versions of what was essentially the same chassis were also produced for the Canadian Army, designated Models 975 and 975A. Chassis and cab units were available for the fitting of special bodies, for example a crane, photographic-processing or workshop van. The Model 968 chassis was also used to provide a 4-ton dump truck (Model 972), and twin-boom wrecker (Model 969). The latter was occasionally fitted with a canvas cover to make it resemble a cargo vehicle from the air. By the time production came to an end in 1945, almost 31,500 examples of the 4-ton chassis had been produced, of which around 9,000 were bodied as cargo vehicles.

ABOVE: **The Diamond T was the standard US Army 4-ton truck from 1941 and was produced in a number of variants. The Model 975 shown is the longer wheelbase version produced for the Royal Canadian Army.**

Diamond T Models 967, 968

Type: Truck, 4-ton, cargo, 6x6
Manufacturer: Diamond T Motor Car Company; Chicago, Illinois
Production: 1940 to 1945
Powerplant: Hercules RXC; six cylinders in-line; petrol; water-cooled; 8,669cc; side valves; power output, 106bhp at 2,300rpm
Transmission: 5F1Rx2; part-time 6x6
Suspension: Live axles on semi-elliptical multi-leaf springs
Brakes: Air-pressure
Electrical system: Hybrid 6V/12V
Dimensions: Length – 6,832mm/269in, 7,544mm/297in
Width – 2,438mm/96in
Height – tilt in place, 2,997mm/118in; minimum, 2,540mm/100in
Wheelbase – 3,835mm/151in, 4,369mm/172in
Bogie centres – 1,321mm/52in
Weight: Unladen – 7,938kg/17,500lb
Payload – 7,711kg/17,000lb
Performance: Maximum speed – 64kph/40mph

LEFT: **The Dodge WC53 carryall is one of the more unusual variants of the ³/₄-ton WC series. One role for which the WC53 may have been used was as a convoy lead vehicle on any of the supply routes. A total of 8,400 were built between 1942 and 1943.**

Dodge T214 WC series

The T214-engined ³/₄-ton Dodge WC series was introduced in 1942 to supersede the earlier ¹/₂-ton models which dated back to 1936, and had proved to be too light for many of the anticipated roles. At the time of its introduction, the US Army had not recognized the ³/₄-ton payload as a standard vehicle class, but the design changes which the Dodge engineers introduced resulted in a vastly improved vehicle. The chassis and bodywork were redesigned to give a 450mm/18in reduction in profile and there was increased power and better tyre flotation on soft ground. This was one tough and enormously capable tactical truck which remained in production until 1945 in a range of variants.

Constructed on a robust steel ladder-type chassis, nothing about the vehicle was innovative or ground-breaking,

which is probably the reason why it was so successful. Power came from a Dodge six-cylinder side-valve engine producing close to 100bhp. This had a special tip-proof carburettor which prevented flooding or fuel starvation when the truck was operated at extreme angles and a high-efficiency oilbath-type air cleaner. A four-speed gearbox and single-speed transfer box were fitted, allowing two- or four-wheel drive. The wide-track axles were suspended on semi-elliptical springs and provided excellent stability off-road, particularly when compared to the ¹/₂-ton model which the T214 was replacing. There was a choice of two wheelbase lengths, the longer version being reserved for a telephone maintenance truck. All of the mechanical components were common across the range. A percentage

RIGHT: **The WC64 was known as the "ambulance collapsible, ³/₄-ton 4x4". It was designed so that the body sides and top could be dropped down into the lower part of the body, together with the cab and windscreen. This made it easily transportable by air. Introduced in January 1945, 3,000 were built.**

LEFT: The T223/WC63 was the 6x6 version of the Dodge 214, and was rated for 1¹/₂-ton loads. Without the winch it was the WC62. Mechanical components were basically the same as those in the T214. The T223 was widely used after World War II by the armies of France, Greece, Turkey, Israel and Portugal.

of weapons carriers and command cars were fitted with a front-mounted Braden horizontal winch driven by a power take-off on the transmission.

Manufactured at the Fargo Motor Corporation's Mound Road plant in Detroit, standard variants included the weapons carrier (WC51, WC52), carryall (WC53), ambulance (WC54, WC64), 37mm gun motor carriage (WC55), command car (WC56, WC57), radio command car (WC58), and telephone installation and maintenance truck (WC59, WC61). There was also a rail conversion of the WC51, by Evans Auto-Railer, where the truck was equipped with hydraulically raised and lowered railway wheels. A larger 6x6 variant (WC62, WC63) of the weapons carrier shared many components with the 4x4.

A version of the weapons carrier was also assembled by Dodge in Canada, as "truck, 15cwt, 4x4, GS, APT", with a slightly modified engine.

A total of more than 255,000 of the WC series of all types had been built by the time the model was discontinued in 1945. More than half of the production total was of the weapons carrier variant, which was nicknamed "Beep" – commonly believed to mean "Beefed-up Jeep" or "Big Jeep" which rather superbly describes the machine.

The vehicle saw service with all of the Allies, and thousands remained in service, particularly in Europe, until well into the 1970s and later. In US military service, the truck was replaced by the M37 in 1950. A civilian version was also made available under the name Power Wagon.

ABOVE: The WC56 command car was originally intended for use by officers in the field. However, it was soon discovered that the distinctive outline of the vehicle made it an easy target for enemy artillery and anti-tank gun crews. Similar variants included the winch-equipped WC57 and the WC58 radio command car.

Dodge T214 WC series

Type: Truck, ³/₄-ton, weapons carrier, 4x4; WC51, WC52

Manufacturer: Chrysler Corporation, Dodge Division, Fargo Motor Corporation; Detroit, Michigan

Production: 1942 to 1945

Powerplant: Dodge T214; six cylinders in-line; petrol; water-cooled; 3,772cc; side valves; power output, 92bhp at 3,200rpm

Transmission: 4F1R; part-time 4x4

Suspension: Live axles on semi-elliptical multi-leaf springs; lever-arm shock absorbers (telescopic shock absorbers on WC64)

Brakes: Hydraulic

Electrical system: 6V, 12V, according to variant

Dimensions: Length – without winch, 4,242mm/167in; with winch, 4,470mm/176in
Width – 2,108mm/83in
Height – tilt in place, 2,159mm/85in; minimum, 1,702mm/67in
Wheelbase – 2,150mm/85in, (WC59, WC61), 307mm/121in

Weight: Unladen – 2,563kg/5,650lb
Payload – 204–226kg/450–500lb

Performance: Maximum speed – 87kph/54mph

LEFT: **Model T cargo trucks were used by both British and US forces during World War I.**

Ford Model T

In 1896, Henry Ford began manufacturing motor cars in Dearborn, Michigan. With backing from Thomas H. Murphy, in 1901, he founded the Detroit Automobile Company, but this was closed three years later. The Henry Ford Company was established in 1901, but Ford resigned within a matter of months and the company was reorganized as the Cadillac Automobile Company the following year. By 1903, Ford had established the Ford Motor Company, his first product being the Model A. The Model C was launched in 1904, and in the same year Ford established a plant in Canada. Other models followed, but

BELOW: **Model T ambulances, with female crews, in service with the Royal Navy at a shore-based hospital.**

real success did not come until the development of the Model T, or "Tin Lizzie" in October 1907. By 1909, the vehicle was in volume production and, although the scuttle and wings were redesigned in 1916, it continued virtually unchanged for the next 20 years.

The Model T was a simple, reliable vehicle, designed for the mass production techniques that Ford pioneered. It was powered by a four-cylinder 2,901cc monobloc engine with a detachable cylinder head. Drive to the rear wheels was by a two-speed epicyclic transmission; some Model T trucks had a two-speed rear axle. Suspension was by transverse semi-elliptical leaf springs. The main brake was described as an "engine brake", and there was also a separate "emergency brake".

During World War I, the Model T was one of the vehicles standardized by the US Army in the "light" class. The first truck, using a long-wheelbase chassis designated Model TT, was launched in 1917. Although Ford himself was a pacifist, he was also an astute business man and he was happy to supply the US Army with more than 12,000 of these vehicles, some 7,000 of which were shipped overseas. There was no civilian production of the Model Ts between 1917 and 1918.

Total US and Canadian production of the Model T amounted to more than 15 million vehicles by the time production ended in 1928. From 1911, the vehicle was also assembled at Ford's Trafford Park factory near Manchester, where some 250,000 were built.

The Model T was widely used by the US and British armies during World War I as a staff car, ambulance, van and cargo truck, even as an artillery tractor, for which application the truck was fitted with twinned rear tyres. Many remained in service into the 1930s.

Ford Model T

Type: Truck, light, cargo, 4x2
Manufacturer: Ford Motor Company; Dearborn, Michigan
Production: 1907 to 1927
Powerplant: Ford; four cylinders in-line; petrol; water-cooled; 2,901cc; side valves; power output, 20bhp at 1,800rpm
Transmission: 2F1R; 4x2
Suspension: Live axles on transverse semi-elliptical multi-leaf springs
Brakes: Mechanical, separately operated "engine" and "emergency" brakes
Electrical system: 6V
Dimensions: (Model TT van variant)
    Length – 3,480mm/137in
    Width – 1,702mm/67in
    Height – 2,108mm/83in
    Wheelbase – 2,550mm/100in
Weight: Unladen – 544kg/1,200lb
    Payload – 410kg/904lb
Performance: Maximum speed – 56kph/35mph

LEFT: **A Ford GPA (General Purpose Amphibian) in service with the US Marine Corps after landing at Anzio, January 22, 1944. Many GPAs were supplied to the Soviet Union, where it was copied and produced as the GAZ-46.**

Ford GPA

Type: Truck, amphibian, ¼-ton, 4x4
Manufacturer: Ford Motor Company; Dearborn, Michigan
Production: 1942 to 1943
Powerplant: Ford GPA-6005 (licence-built Willys Go-Devil); four cylinders in-line; petrol; water-cooled; 2,199cc; side valves; power output, 54bhp at 4,000rpm
Transmission: 3F1Rx2; part-time 4x4
Suspension: Live axles on semi-elliptical multi-leaf springs; hydraulic double-acting shock absorbers
Brakes: Hydraulic
Electrical system: 12V
Dimensions: Length – 4,875mm/192in
Width – 1,625mm/64in
Height – 1,727mm/68in
Wheelbase – 2,134mm/84in
Weight: Unladen – 1,660kg/3,660lb
Payload – 290kg/640lb
Performance: Maximum speed – 88kph/55mph

Ford GPA

In 1941, marine architects Sparkman & Stevens designed a small amphibious vehicle using components from the Jeep. By December, Marmon-Herrington had built a prototype, with a second from Ford in February 1942. Following trials by the US Quartermaster Corps the Ford prototype was chosen for production. Designated GPA – or "GP Amphibian" – the vehicle had a lightweight steel hull together with the Jeep engine, transmission and axles. Propulsion in the water was by a three-bladed propeller. Steering was by a boat-type rudder.

Although similar to the DUKW, it was not a success. On the road, the increased size of the body made the vehicle unwieldy. In the water there was insufficient freeboard when loaded, which reduced safe usage in choppy water. Production ended in June 1943 after about 12,785 vehicles had been built. Many were supplied to the Soviet Union.

Ford GTB

Dating from 1942, the Ford GTB was a low-profile forward-control truck developed for the US Quartermaster

Ford GTB

Type: Truck, cargo, 1½-ton, 4x4
Manufacturer: Ford Motor Company; Dearborn, Michigan
Production: 1942 to 1944
Powerplant: Ford G8T; six cylinders in-line; petrol; water-cooled; 3,703cc; side valves; power output, 90bhp at 3,400rpm
Transmission: 4F1Rx2; part-time 4x4
Suspension: Live axles on semi-elliptical multi-leaf springs; hydraulic double-acting shock absorbers
Brakes: Vacuum-assisted hydraulic
Electrical system: 12V
Dimensions: Length – 4,597mm/181in
Width – 2,184mm/86in
Height – tilt in place, 2,540mm/100in; minimum, 2,083mm/82in
Wheelbase – 2,921mm/115in
Weight: Unladen – 3,289kg/7,250lb
Payload – 1,500kg/3,307lb
Performance: Maximum speed – 72kph/45mph

ABOVE: **The Ford GTB was developed to a specification issued by the US Quartermaster Corps in 1942.**

Corps for use in combat zones. During 1942, prototypes had been produced by Dodge, Ford, Chevrolet and others in the ¾ and 1½-ton weight classes. Despite testing continuing into 1944, the Ford GTB was the only vehicle to enter production.

The GTB was based on a commercial truck, and the low silhouette was achieved by placing the driver alongside the engine, which was offset to the right. The engine was a Ford six-cylinder driving live axles through a four-speed gearbox and two-speed transfer box. Both single and twin rear wheel variants were produced. Some were equipped with a front-mounted winch.

Total production was 15,274. The US Army and US Navy took 8,218 cargo vehicles (GTBA), and 7,066 of a Mk II variant were supplied to the US Navy.

FWD Model B

The Four Wheel Drive Auto Company (FWD) started building trucks in 1910 and launched the Model B 3-ton 4x4 truck in 1912. The truck was standardized for its class by the US Quartermaster Corps and remained in production throughout World War I.

A 6,375cc Wisconsin four-cylinder engine was fitted under the cab and was connected to a mid-mounted three-speed gearbox via a belt or silent chain. A locking centre differential with shafts connecting the drive was fitted to the front and rear axles. The axles were located by radius rods, and suspension was by semi-elliptical springs. Although originally using solid tyres on spoked or disc wheels, many were converted to pneumatics in the early 1930s. More than 16,000 were supplied to the US Army, many sent to Europe. The trucks were also built by Kissel, Mitchell-Lewis, Premier, and Peerless, the latter destined for Britain.

RIGHT: **An FWD Model B in World War I US camouflage as part of a display in London to encourage people to buy War Bonds. The vehicle was built at the FWD plant at Clifton, Wisconsin, between 1912 and 1919.**

FWD Model B

Type: Truck, cargo, 3- to 5-ton, 4x4
Manufacturer: Four Wheel Drive Auto Company (FWD); Clintonville, Wisconsin
Production: 1912 to 1919
Powerplant: Wisconsin; four cylinders in-line; petrol; water-cooled; 6,375cc; side valves; power output, 36bhp at 1,800rpm
Transmission: 3F1R; full-time 4x4
Suspension: Live axles on semi-elliptical multi-leaf springs
Brakes: Mechanical
Electrical system: None
Dimensions: Length – 5,640mm/222in
Width – 1,930mm/76in
Height – tilt in place, 3,200mm/126in
Wheelbase – 3,150mm/124in
Weight: Unladen – 5,534kg/12,200lb
Payload – road, 4,990kg/11,000lb;
cross-country, 2,994kg/6,600lb
Performance: Maximum speed – 24kph/15mph

International M-5-6, M-5H-6

The International Harvester Company was one of the contenders for the US Army's standardized 2¹/₂-ton 6x6 chassis of World War II. The first prototype was produced in 1940 and the M-5-6 went into production the following year. The company built around 40,000 in both long- and short-wheelbase form. Most were supplied to the US Navy and Marine Corps.

The engine was a 5,912cc International RED-361B six-cylinder driving through a five-speed gearbox and two-speed transfer box. Suspension was by semi-elliptical leaf springs, with a Hendrickson-type rear bogie.

Early production vehicles were fitted with an all-steel cab, but this was eventually replaced by the typical canvas-topped open cab. Standard variants included cargo, workshop, fire-fighter, recovery vehicle, dump and fuel tanker; there was also a tractor for semi-trailers. A 6x4 variant was also produced, designated M-5H-6.

LEFT: **The International M-5-6 was produced in 1941, the majority being supplied to the US Navy.**

International M-5-6, M-5H-6

Type: Truck, cargo, 2¹/₂-ton, 6x6
Manufacturer: International Harvester; Chicago, Illinois
Production: 1941 to 1945
Powerplant: International RED-361B; six cylinders in-line; petrol; water-cooled; 5,912cc; overhead valves; power output, 126bhp at 2,500rpm
Transmission: 5F1Rx2; part-time 6x6
Suspension: Live axles on semi-elliptical multi-leaf springs
Brakes: Vacuum servo-assisted hydraulic
Electrical system: 6V
Dimensions: (cargo vehicles)
Length – 6,452mm/254in
Width – 2,337mm/92in
Height – tilt in place, 2,388mm/94in;
minimum 1,930mm/76in
Wheelbase – 3,785mm/149in, 4,293mm/169in
Bogie centres – 1,143mm/45in
Weight: Unladen – 6,078kg/13,400lb
Payload – road, 4,536kg/10,000lb;
cross-country, 2,427kg/5,350lb
Performance: Maximum speed – 72kph/45mph

LEFT: **The DUKW was essentially the mechanical components of the GMC CCKW truck. The vehicle was designed by Sparkman & Stephens, a firm of marine architects based in New York, from where they continue to design yachts.**

GMC DUKW-353

Dating from 1942, the GMC DUKW is probably the most successful amphibious military vehicle of all time. It was designed in 1941 by New York-based marine architects Sparkman & Stephens working to a brief drawn up by the National Defense Research Council. It was to be built by GMC's Yellow Truck & Coach Division.

The first prototypes, which were successfully trialled in June 1942, were based on the components of the AFKWX-353 forward-control truck. Following the trials, an initial contract was placed for 2,000 vehicles, now using components of the CCKW-353. By the time production ended in 1945, a total of 21,147 had been built.

Power came from a GMC (Chevrolet) six-cylinder overhead-valve engine driving either all six wheels, or a propeller, through a five-speed gearbox, with an overdrive top gear and two-speed transfer box.

The axles were suspended on semi-elliptical leaf springs, inverted at the rear. A rudder was fitted at the rear to provide directional control in the water. Late production models were fitted with a "Central Tyre Inflation System" (CTIS), which allowed the tyre pressures to be set from the driver's position to suit ground conditions when leaving the water. A mechanical winch was installed at the rear.

The welded-steel hull included seating for a driver and co-driver at the front, combined with a spacious cargo area at the rear, over which a full-length canvas cover could be erected.

The DUKW – the name was simply the manufacturer's chassis code indicating the year of development, the drive-line, wheelbase length, and the type of body – was first used in amphibious landings in the Pacific and on Sicily. Although a scheme to use DUKWs equipped with fire escape ladders to scale the cliffs at

Pointe du Hoc was unsuccessful, the DUKW was used very effectively to ferry supplies ashore in the days following the D-Day landings, before the Mulberry Harbours were operational.

The DUKW was used by all of the Allies during World War II and remained in US Army service into the 1960s. It was also used in the post-war years by France, Britain and others. The British Army still retains a small number of DUKWs at the Amphibious Trials & Development Unit (ATDU), Instow, North Devon.

LEFT: **The hull provided seating for a driver and co-driver and had a large open bay at the rear, which could be used for cargo or personnel. A full-length canvas roof could be erected over the cargo bay. Early DUKWs can be identified by the upright windscreen.**

GMC DUKW-353

Type: Truck, cargo, 2¹/₂-ton, amphibian, 6x6

Manufacturer: GMC Yellow Truck & Coach Division; Pontiac, Michigan. After 1943, GMC Truck & Coach Division; Pontiac, Michigan

Production: 1942 to 1945

Powerplant: GMC (Chevrolet) Model 270; six cylinders in-line; petrol; water-cooled; 4,416cc; overhead valves; power output, 92bhp at 2,750rpm

Transmission: 5F1Rx2; part-time 6x6

Suspension: Live axles on semi-elliptical multi-leaf springs, inverted at rear

Brakes: Vacuum-assisted hydraulic

Electrical system: 6V

Dimensions: Length – 9,450mm/372in
Width – 2,515mm/99in
Height – tilt in place, 2,690mm/106in; minimum, 2,286mm/90in
Wheelbase – 2,921mm/164in
Bogie centres – 1,118mm/44in

Weight: Unladen – 6,750kg/14,880lb
Payload – 2,268kg/5,000lb

Performance: Maximum speed – 80kph/50mph

GMC CCKW-352, 353

Known as the "deuce-and-a-half" or the "Jimmy", the GMC 2½-ton 6x6 was probably the most significant US truck of World War II. And, with a total of some 562,750 produced, it was also the second most numerous vehicle of the war, beaten from the top spot only by the Jeep. The "Jimmy" served in every theatre of the war and with all of the Allied armies. It was produced in a large number of variants.

From 1939, GMC had started supplying a range of lightly militarized, but essentially civilian, 2½-ton 4x2 and 6x4 trucks to the US Army from 1939. However, the vehicle for which the company became known worldwide was derived from the 6x6 ACKWX which had originally been intended for the French Army. When France fell to the Nazis in 1940, the trucks were diverted to Britain. In January 1941, the ACKWX was modified to produce the standardized CCKW (initially designated CCKWX). The all-steel Chevrolet civilian-type cab

of the original was retained, but the bonnet and radiator grille were replaced. The enclosed cab, with a V-shaped top-hung screen, survived until 1944, when it was replaced by a standardized open military cab with a canvas top and flat, folding windscreen.

The truck was powered by a GMC (Chevrolet) six-cylinder overhead-valve engine, driving all wheels through a five-speed gearbox, (with overdrive top gear) and two-speed transfer case. The front axle drive could be disengaged when not required. Suspension was by semi-elliptical multi-leaf springs, inverted at the rear. During the production run, two types of axle design were used, described as the Timken "split" axle, or the Chevrolet "banjo". The latter was less susceptible to catastrophic failure through over-loading.

Production took place at GMC's Yellow Truck & Coach Division, although after 1943 the company was renamed

RIGHT: Up until 1944, the truck was fitted with a militarized version of the manufacturer's standard civilian cab fitted with the simple military bonnet and mudguards. Later production vehicles had a canvas-covered open cab designed to save materials and reduce the shipping height.

as GMC Truck & Coach Division. The model code CCKW indicates that the truck was designed in 1941 (first C), was fitted with a normal-control cab (second C), front-wheel drive (K), and rear-wheel bogie drive (W). The "X" suffix, which indicated a non-standard wheelbase, was dropped soon after manufacture began. The vehicle was produced in two chassis lengths, the "353" having a wheelbase of 4,166mm/164in, and the "352" measuring 3,658mm/144in.

The long-wheelbase (CCKW-353) cargo truck was the most numerous in production and while most cargo bodies were of welded-steel construction, timber bodies were also fitted. Both types had fixed sides and a drop tailgate and had folding troop seats fitted in the rear. Five removable hoops were provided to support a canvas cover. There was a multiplicity of other variants, including fuel tanker, water tanker, stake truck, compressor vehicle, workshop vehicle, bomb-service truck, dump truck (tipper) and van body. The

truck was also supplied as a chassis-cab unit for the fitting of specialized bodies. A number of vehicles were fitted with a Gar Wood or Heil 5-ton capacity winch installed on chassis extension ahead of the radiator. One out of four trucks off the production line was fitted with an anti-aircraft machine-gun mount above the passenger seat.

The truck remained in service with the US Army into the 1950s. After the war, thousands were passed to the armies of the liberated European nations, where many remained in service into the early 1980s.

BELOW: **A GMC CCKW-353 mounted with a Le Roi Model D318 air-compressor for road repairs.**

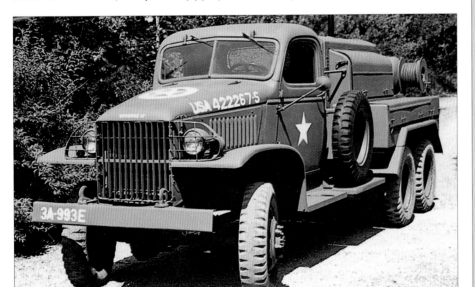

GMC CCKW-352, 353

Type: Truck, 2½-ton, cargo, 6x6
Manufacturer: Yellow Truck & Coach Manufacturing; Pontiac, Michigan. After 1943, GMC Truck & Coach Division; Pontiac, Michigan
Production: 1941 to 1945
Powerplant: GMC (Chevrolet) Model 270; six cylinders in-line; petrol; water-cooled; 4,416cc; overhead valves; power output, 92bhp at 2,750rpm
Transmission: 5F1Rx2; part-time 6x6
Suspension: Live axles on semi-elliptical multi-leaf springs, inverted at rear
Brakes: Hydraulic with vacuum servo-assistance
Electrical system: 6V
Dimensions: (cargo vehicles)
  Length – (CCKW-352) 5,842mm/230in; (CCKW-353) 6,477mm/255in
  Width – 2,261mm/89in
  Height – tilt in place, 2,770mm/109in; minimum, 1,880mm/74in
  Wheelbase – (CCKW-352) 3,658mm/144in; (CCKW-353) 4,166mm/164in
  Bogie centres – 1,118mm/44in
Weight: Unladen – 4,370kg/9,635lb
  Payload – road, 4,536kg/10,000lb; cross–country, 2,427kg/5,350lb
Performance: Maximum speed – 72kph/45mph

Jeep CJ10A

The Jeep CJ10 was introduced in 1981, and remained in production until 1986. It was available with a choice of diesel or petrol engines, coupled to a four-speed manual or three-speed automatic transmission and two-speed transfer box.

In the mid-1980s, PSI Mobile Products produced 1,500 examples of a CJ10-based short-wheelbase tractor for the US Air Force. Designated CJ10A, it was intended to be used to tow ammunition trailers or as a tug for towing small aircraft and helicopters. The wheelbase was reduced to 2,032mm/80in and there was a minimal, short, rear body incorporating a large fuel tank, and fitted with a stepped towing bumper with three pintle hooks. The centre pintle was designed to telescope and to swing from left to right.

The CJ10A was powered by a Nissan SD-33 six-cylinder diesel engine driving a four-speed manual transmission, with the transfer box locked in the low ratio.

Jeep CJ10A

Type: Air Force aircraft tug, 4x4
Manufacturer: Jeep Corporation; Southfield, Michigan. Modified by PSI Mobile Products
Production: 1985 to 1986
Powerplant: Nissan SD-33; six cylinders in-line; diesel; water-cooled; 3,246cc; overhead valves; power output, 95bhp at 3,500rpm
Transmission: 4F1R; full-time 4x4
Suspension: Live axles on semi-elliptical multi-leaf springs
Brakes: Hydraulic
Electrical system: 24V
Dimensions: Length – 3,683mm/145in
Width – 1,730mm/68in
Height – 1,780mm/70in
Wheelbase – 2,032mm/80in
Weight: Unladen – 2,722kg/6,000lb
Payload – 436kg/1,000lb
Maximum drawbar pull – 1,814kg/4,000lb
Performance: Maximum speed – 40kph/25mph

LEFT: **The Jeep Corporation's CJ10A was used by the USAF as a light aircraft tug.**

Jeep Wrangler TJ-L

Produced in Egypt by Arab American Vehicles (AAV) for the Egyptian Army, the Wrangler TJ-L was a joint-venture project between Daimler-Chrysler and the Egyptian Government. The vehicle was initially powered by a 3,958cc six-cylinder petrol engine, mated to a five-speed manual transmission. From 2005, a VM Motori four-cylinder 2,800cc diesel engine was also available. The pick-up bed was suitable for mounting a heavy-calibre machine-gun or could be fitted with two rows of seats to carry troops. Production began in August 2003 at the AAV Cairo plant and is running at approximately 1,500 units a year. The Egyptian armed forces' initial order was for 1,000 Wrangler TJ-Ls.

Jeep Wrangler TJ-L

Type: Truck, utility, 4x4
Manufacturer: Arab American Vehicles; Cairo
Production: 2003 on
Powerplant: Daimler-Chrysler Power-Tech I-6; six cylinders in-line; petrol; water-cooled; 3,958cc; overhead valves; power output, 181bhp at 4,600rpm
VM Motori; four cylinders in-line; turbocharged diesel; water-cooled; 2,800cc; overhead valves; power output, 120bhp at 3,800rpm
Transmission: 5F1Rx2; part-time 4x4
Suspension: Live axles on dual-rate coil springs; locating arms, track and stabilizer bars; telescopic gas-filled shock absorbers
Brakes: Power-assisted hydraulic
Electrical system: Dual 12V/24V
Dimensions: Length – 4,420mm/174in
Width – 1,694mm/67in
Height – tilt in place, 1,763mm/69in
Wheelbase – 2,931mm/115in
Weight: Unladen – 1,520kg/3,350lb
Payload – 907kg/2,000lb
Performance: Maximum speed – 113kph/70mph

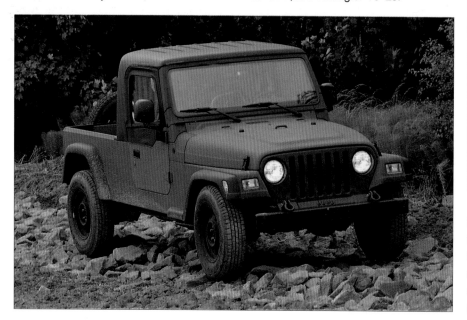

LEFT: **The Jeep Wrangler TJ-L is in service with the Egyptian Army which placed an initial order for 1,000 vehicles. Although derived from the civilian Wrangler, the TJ-L has a lengthened wheelbase and is fitted with uprated suspension and a heavy-duty rear axle.**

Jeffery Model 4017 Quad

Thomas B. Jeffery started building the 2-ton Quad truck in 1913, and the US Army and Marine Corps were among the first customers, with many seeing service during the Mexican War. The Quad drove, steered and braked on all four wheels. Despite the use of cast-steel wheels and solid rubber tyres, this represented a considerable improvement in mobility when compared with other manufacturers' 4x2 trucks of the period.

ABOVE: **A Model 4017 Quad fitted with solid tyres. Note the chains on the front wheels for extra traction.**

A Buda four-cylinder petrol engine was installed ahead of the driver, and transmission was by a four-speed gearbox driving the wheels through ring and pinion gears. Suspension was by semi-elliptical leaf springs. By 1919, four-wheel steering feature was not installed

on the military Quad. More than 11,500 examples eventually entered military service.

The trucks were renamed Nash-Quad in 1917, and were also manufactured by Hudson and National and during the latter years of World War I, by Paige-Detroit.

Jeffery Model 4017 Quad

Type: Truck, 2-ton, cargo, 4x4
Manufacturer: Thomas B. Jeffery; Kenosha, Wisconsin, later Nash-Quad
Production: 1913 to 1928
Powerplant: Buda; four cylinders in-line; petrol; water-cooled; 3,785cc, 4,719cc; side valves; power output, 32–36bhp at 1,800rpm
Transmission: 4F1R; 4x4
Suspension: Live axles on semi-elliptical multi-leaf springs
Brakes: Mechanical
Electrical system: None
Dimensions: Length – 7,544mm/297in
   Width – 1,880mm/74in
   Height – 1,956mm/77in
   Wheelbase – 3,150mm/124in
Weight: Unladen – 3,590kg/7,900lb
   Payload – 2,000kg/4,400lb
Performance: Maximum speed – 20kph/12mph

Mack NO1–NO7

Mack NO1–NO7

Type: Truck, 7¹/₂-ton, prime mover, 6x6
Manufacturer: Mack Manufacturing Company; New York
Production: 1940 to 1944
Powerplant: Mack EY; six cylinders in-line; petrol; water-cooled; 11,586cc; overhead valves; power output, 170bhp at 2,100rpm
Transmission: 5F1Rx2; part-time 6x6
Suspension: Live axles on semi-elliptical multi-leaf springs
Brakes: Air-pressure; wired for electric trailer brakes
Electrical system: Hybrid 6V/12V
Dimensions: Length – 7,544mm/297in
   Width – 2,591mm/102in
   Height – tilt in place, 3,099mm/122in; minimum, 2,388mm/94in
   Wheelbase – 3,962mm/156in
   Bogie centres – 1,473mm/58in
Weight: Unladen – 13,436kg/29,620lb
   Payload – 7,031kg/15,500lb
Performance: Maximum speed – 52kph/32mph

The Mack NO was a heavy 6x6 tractor designed to tow the US Army's 155mm and 240mm howitzers. The first example, NO1, was launched in December 1940. This was followed by the NQ of which there was no series production. Subsequent modifications produced the series NO2, NO3, NO6 and NO7. Models NO4 and NO5 were long-wheelbase heavy wrecker variants, but there was no series production.

All variants were powered by an 11,586cc six-cylinder petrol engine driving through a five-speed gearbox and two-speed transfer box. The triple-reduction elevated front axle used bevel gears and revolving kingpins as the final-drive. Suspension was by semi-elliptical springs.

Models NO2 to NO7 were fitted with an open cab and a fabricated steel body

ABOVE: **The Mack NO series was fitted with a large mechanical winch at the front of the vehicle.**

with seating for 12 personnel plus stowage for spare wheels, parts and ammunition. A chain hoist above the tailgate was used for lifting the gun trail.

LEFT: **Introduced in 1944, the soft-skin variant of the "Dragon Wagon" was designated M26A1. The differences were confined to the cab, the vehicle being powered by the same 17,861cc Hall Scott 440 engine, and Knuckey chain-drive rear bogie. The Fruehauf M15 semi-trailer was the standard unit.**

Pacific TR1 "Dragon Wagon"

Better known as the "Dragon Wagon", the Pacific Car & Foundry TR1 was one of the largest vehicles of World War II. Unhappy with the Diamond T Models 980, 981, which had been produced for the British, the US Army developed the TR1 as a replacement. The armoured cab made the TR1 suitable for use as a battlefield tank recovery vehicle.

The TR1 was prototyped by the Knuckey Truck Company of San Francisco in 1942 but, lacking manufacturing facilities, it was produced by locomotive builders Pacific Car & Foundry. However, even the production version of the vehicle retained Knuckey's huge chain-drive rear bogie.

Aside from massive size, the most striking feature of the original M26 variant is the angular armoured cab with distinctive armoured shutters for the radiator and windows. Later the M26A1, a soft-skinned variant, was produced in October 1944, retaining the angular shape. Both variants were powered by a 17,861cc Hall Scott six-cylinder petrol engine, with a capacity of almost 18 litres, driving all six wheels through a four-speed gearbox and three-speed transfer box. The front axle was suspended on semi-elliptical springs, while at the rear the walking-beam chain-drive bogie was oversprung. Two huge winches were fitted behind the cab to assist with loading disabled tanks.

A folding A-frame allowed the truck to be used as a recovery vehicle.

The standard trailer was the Fruehauf M15, a 45-ton eight-wheeled rear-loading unit. The tractor and trailer together were designated "M25 40-ton tank transporter truck-trailer". The vehicle was produced between 1943 and 1945, with 1,372 tractors completed. The M26 remained in service with the US Army throughout the 1950s. Many were left in Europe after the war and became a popular conversion for heavy-haulage operators.

LEFT: **In its original armoured form dating from 1943, the "Dragon Wagon" was intended to be used for recovering tanks under fire. Two winches were installed behind the cab and an A-frame was fitted to allow the vehicle to operate as a recovery vehicle. The rear brakes on the tractor could be operated individually to allow accurate positioning. Front brakes were not fitted.**

Pacific TR1 "Dragon Wagon"

Type: Truck-tractor, 12-ton, 6x6; M26, M26A1
Manufacturer: Pacific Car & Foundry Company; Renton, Seattle
Production: 1943 to 1945
Powerplant: Hall Scott Model 440; six cylinders in-line; petrol; water-cooled; 17,861cc; overhead valves; power output, 240bhp at 2,100rpm
Transmission: 4F1Rx3; part-time 6x6
Suspension: Live front axle on multi-leaf semi-elliptical springs; walking-beam rear bogie without suspension
Brakes: Air pressure, rear wheels only
Electrical system: 12V
Dimensions: Length – 7,721mm/304in
  Width – 3,810mm/150in
  Height – 3,480mm/137in
  Wheelbase – 4,369mm/172in
  Bogie centres – 1,600mm/63in
Weight: Unladen – 19,051kg/42,000lb
  Gross train weight – 60,329-64,865kg/133,000-143,000lb
Performance: Maximum speed – 42kph/26mph

Oshkosh M1070

Type: Truck-tractor, heavy equipment, 8x8; M1070
Manufacturer: Oshkosh Truck Corporation; Oshkosh, Wisconsin
Production: 1992 to 2003
Powerplant: (M1070) Detroit-Diesel 8V92TA; eight cylinders in V configuration; turbocharged diesel; water-cooled; 12,061cc; overhead valves; power output, 500bhp at 2,100rpm. (M1070F) Caterpillar C18; six cylinders in-line; turbocharged diesel; water-cooled; 18,100cc; overhead valves; power output, 7,00bhp at 1,300rpm
Transmission: automatic 5F1Rx2 (M1070), 7F1R (M1070F); part-time 8x8 (M1070), full-time 8x8 (M1070F); differential locks on rear axles
Suspension: Live axles on semi-elliptical tapered-leaf springs at front; live axles with Hendrickson air suspension at rear
Brakes: Air-pressure
Electrical system: 24V
Dimensions: Length – 9,195mm/362in
Width – 2,591mm/100in
Height – 3,556mm/140in
Wheelbase – 5,461mm/215in
Bogie centres – 1,524+1,524mm/60+60in
Weight: Unladen – 20,058kg/44,220lb
Gross train weight – 99,792–117,936kg/ 220–260,000lb
Performance: Maximum speed – 80–85kph/50–53mph

LEFT: **The Detroit-Diesel powered Oshkosh M1070 was originally designed as a transporter for the US Army's Abrams main battle tank.** BELOW: **Fitted with the Caterpillar C18 engine, the Oshkosh tractor was selected by the British Ministry of Defence as a replacement for the Scammell Commander.**

Oshkosh M1070

In 1990, the Oshkosh Truck Corporation delivered the first prototype to the US Army of the M1070 "Heavy Equipment Transporter" (HET) which was intended to replace the company's earlier M911 tractor. Production began in the spring of 1992 and a total of 1,600 examples were completed.

The M1070 was a massive tractor, rated for a gross train weight of up to 99,792kg/220,000lb and easily capable of carrying an Abrams main battle tank or two smaller armoured fighting vehicles, such as the Bradley "Infantry Fighting Vehicle" (IFV), on the standard four-axle semi-trailer. Power was by a 12,061cc Detroit-Diesel V8 diesel engine driving through an Allison automatic five-speed

transmission and two-speed transfer box, which incorporated a front-axle disconnect. Live axles, with hub-reduction gears, were used front and rear. The front axle was suspended on parabolic tapered-leaf semi-elliptical springs. Hendrickson air suspension was used at the rear. Inter-axle and intra-axle differential locks were fitted. Axles one (front) and four (rear) are used for steering the vehicle.

Three winches were installed behind the cab, above the first of the three rear axles – two 55-ton two-speed hydraulic winches, together with an auxiliary single-speed 1-ton winch used for paying out the steel hawser from the main winches. A "Central Tyre Inflation System" (CTIS) was fitted, with preset

selections for highway, cross-country, mud/snow and emergency conditions.

In 2001, a Caterpillar-engined variant, designated M1070F, was selected by the British Ministry of Defence to replace the ageing Scammell Commander tank transporters. Designed for use with a seven-axle King semi-trailer, the M1070F is rated at 72-tons. A total of 92 of these tractors were built, with deliveries completed by October 2003.

Stewart & Stevenson FMTV

Prototypes for what the US Army was describing as the "Family of Medium Tactical Vehicles" (FMTV) were produced by three companies towards the end of the 1980s – the Tactical Truck Corporation (a consortium formed by General Motors and Bowen-McLaughlin-York), Teledyne Continental and Stewart & Stevenson. Following extensive trials, the Texas-based Stewart & Stevenson company received a five-year $1.2 billion contract to produce 10,843 trucks. Production started in 1991, and further contracts followed requesting a total of 85,000 vehicles.

The FMTV is a forward-control all-wheel drive truck, designed to replace the ageing 2½-ton and 5-ton "M Series", the origins of which date back to the early 1950s. The truck is being produced in two basic variants with an 80 per cent component commonality. The range now encompasses some 14 chassis versions.

The "Light Medium Tactical Vehicle" (LMTV) is a 4x4 design rated for a payload of 2½ tons, while the "Medium Tactical Vehicle" (MTV) is a 6x6 rated at 5 tons. Both vehicles are powered by a Caterpillar six-cylinder diesel engine, with full-time all-wheel drive through an automatic seven-speed gearbox and single-speed transfer box incorporating a torque-bias lockable inter-axle differential. Suspension is by live axles on parabolic tapered leaf springs. An upgraded "A1" variant was introduced in September 1999, with increased engine power and anti-lock brakes.

An electronic "Central Tyre Inflation System" (CTIS) is standard, and a number of vehicles are fitted with a 5- or 7-ton winch. The cab roof can support a machine-gun ring mount.

The LMTV has been procured in cargo and van variants. The MTV is available in four wheelbase lengths, and standard variants include cargo, crane-equipped cargo, expansible van, tractor, recovery vehicle, dump, flat rack load-handling system and fuel tanker vehicles. The MTV has also been used as a transporter-launcher for the US "High Mobility Artillery Rocket System" (HIMARS). Purpose-designed 2¼-ton and 5-ton trailers have also been produced.

ABOVE: **Rated for a 5-ton payload, the 6x6 "Medium Tactical Vehicle" (MTV) is produced in four wheelbase lengths. Standard variants include cargo (with optional hydraulic crane), expansible van, tractor, recovery vehicle, dump, flat rack load-handling system and fuel tanker.** LEFT: **The 4x4 "Light Medium Tactical Vehicle" (LMTV) is rated for a payload of 2½ tons. Shown here is the latest upgraded "A2" variant.**

Stewart & Stevenson FMTV

Type: Truck, cargo, 2½-ton, 4x4; M1078A1-M1081. Truck, cargo, 5-ton, 6x6; M1083A1-M1096A1

Manufacturer: Stewart & Stevenson, Tactical Vehicle Systems Division; West Sealy, Texas

Production: 1991 on

Powerplant: (LMTV) Caterpillar 3126 ATAAC, (MTV) Caterpillar 3136 ATAAC; six cylinders in-line; turbocharged diesel; water-cooled; 7,200cc; overhead valves; power output, 275–330bhp at 2,400rpm

Transmission: Automatic 7F1R; full-time 4x4 or 6x6; inter-axle differential lock

Suspension: Live axles on parabolic tapered leaf semi-elliptical springs; hydraulic double-acting shock absorbers

Brakes: Air-pressure

Electrical system: 24V

Dimensions: (typical)
Length – (LMTV) 6,420mm/253in; (MTV) 6,960–9,305mm/274–366in
Width – 2,438mm/96in
Height – tilt in place, 2,845mm/112in; minimum, 2,680mm/105in
Wheelbase – (LMTV) 3,900mm/154in; (MTV standard) 4,100mm/161in, (MTV long) 4,500mm/177in, 5,300mm/209in, 5,500mm/216in
Bogie centres – 1,525mm/60in

Weight: Unladen – 7,978–10,287kg/17,589–22,678lb
Payload – (LMTV) 2,268kg/5,000lb; (MTV) 4,536kg/10,000lb

Performance: Maximum speed – 93kph/58mph

Ward LaFrance Model 1000

The US Army's first heavy wrecker was produced by Marmon-Herrington in 1935, with small numbers supplied by Corbitt from July 1937. The design was standardized as "truck, wrecking, heavy, M1" and Ward LaFrance and Kenworth received contracts for 69 and 300 vehicles respectively. Similar in design and appearance, the vehicles featured a Continental petrol engine, Fuller transmission and Gar Wood hand-operated crane. Some 2,030 examples were built, with most coming from Ward LaFrance, before production was halted in favour of the M1A1.

Introduced in 1943, the standardized M1A1 had improved lifting equipment and featured an open cab. Both companies were now producing what was effectively the same vehicle, with a total of 3,735 M1A1s produced before 1945. Ward LaFrance were again responsible for the majority.

The vehicle was assembled around a Continental-powered 6x6 heavy-duty chassis. Ward LaFrance used the same Model 1000 chassis as had been developed for their M1 wrecker, now designated the Series 5. Kenworth's chassis was the Model 573. Transmission was by a five-speed Fuller gearbox and remote-mounted Timken two-speed transfer box, driving both front and rear axles. Suspension was by semi-elliptical springs, inverted at the rear and located by means of radius rods. Brakes were air-pressure operated. Brake-line connectors at front and rear, as well as a double check valve in the brake lines, allowed the vehicle to be braked by a towing vehicle.

The Gar Wood US 5A crane of the M1 was replaced by the fully powered US 6A unit. Winches were fitted at the front and rear. A massive V-shaped front bumper, and V-shaped tow bar, was fitted which could be used to tow or push a light or medium armoured vehicle. The crane could be slung through 180 degrees to lift at the rear or side. Maximum lifting capacity was 7,276kg/16,000lb. Jacks and triangulated braces were used to support the vehicle during lifting operations.

Production began in 1943 at Kenworth's Seattle plant – production was moved to Yakima, Washington, in 1944 – and at the Ward LaFrance truck factory at Elmira, New York. In 1945, Kenworth was purchased by Pacific Car & Foundry and production was moved back to Seattle.

Ward LaFrance Model 1000 (M1A1)

Type: Truck, wrecking, heavy, 6x6; M1A1
Manufacturer: Ward LaFrance Truck Division of Great American Industries; Elmira, New York
Production: 1943 to 1945
Powerplant: Continental 22R; six cylinders in-line; petrol; water-cooled; 8,210cc; overhead valves; power output, 145bhp at 2,400rpm
Transmission: 5F1Rx2; part-time 6x6
Suspension: Live axles on semi-elliptical multi-leaf springs, inverted at rear; hydraulic shock absorbers at front
Brakes: Air-pressure
Electrical system: 12V
Dimensions: Length – 8,840mm/348in
   Width – 2,540mm/100in
   Height – 2,970mm/117in
   Wheelbase – 4,600mm/181in
   Bogie centres – 1,320mm/52in
Weight: Unladen – 14,152kg/31,200lb
   Maximum weight on crane – 7,276kg/16,000lb
Performance: Maximum speed – 72kph/45mph

ABOVE: **Produced by both Kenworth and Ward LaFrance, the Continental-engined M1A1 was the standard US Army heavy wrecker during the last years of World War II. The recovery equipment was manufactured by Gar Wood and featured a power-operated crane.** LEFT: **The M1A1 remained in service throughout the 1950s. This vehicle is with the US Air Force in West Germany.**

153

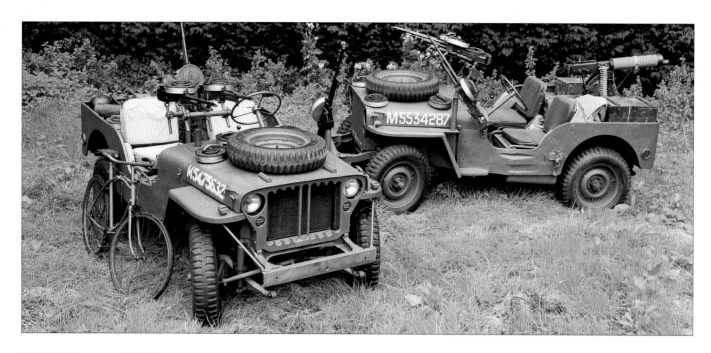

Willys MB

ABOVE: Cut down and loaded with weapons and essential supplies, the Jeep made an excellent special operations vehicle and was quickly adopted by David Stirling's SAS Regiment for behind the lines operations in North Africa.

In 1940, Willys-Overland, American Bantam and Ford had all contributed prototypes to the US Quartermaster Corps (US QMC) project to develop a light reconnaissance car. In late 1940, following trials at Camp Holabird and elsewhere, officials at the Army and the US QMC appeared unable to make up their mind as to which of the three vehicles offered the best combination of performance and reliability. Each manufacturer was awarded a contract to produce 500 vehicles based on the respective prototypes. This number was subsequently increased to 1,500.

Unsurprisingly, since all three had been based on the same specification, and Willys and Ford engineers had apparently been able to inspect the Bantam prototype before developing their own, all three of the prototypes shared design features. The simple, open-sided four-seater body was provided with a folding windscreen and a removable canvas top. The body was generally assembled from flat panels which would simplify

repairs in the field. A four-cylinder water-cooled petrol engine drove the rear wheels through a three-speed gearbox. Drive to the front axle could be selected via a two-speed transfer box, which allowed all-wheel drive through a set of low-ratio gears. Live axles were suspended on semi-elliptical multi-leaf springs in combination with hydraulic telescopic shock absorbers. A towing pintle was provided at the rear, and a circular plate designed to support a machine-gun pedestal was welded to one of the chassis cross-members.

Once the contracts were issued, staff at the US QMC started to draw-up a specification for a "standardized" Jeep which would embody elements of all three designs. Trials had shown that the Go-Devil engine of the Willys MA offered the best all-round performance. In July 1941, Willys was asked to produce a further 16,000 MA Jeeps.

With this work underway, representatives of the US QMC and the user arms met at Camp Holabird to discuss further changes and improvements to the design. One important aspect of this work was the standardization of components with other US military vehicles of the period. The standardized Jeep, which employed a version of Ford's front end, was designated MB.

By October 1941, it was obvious that Willys lacked the production capacity to keep up with the enormous demand for the vehicle. It would have been the obvious solution to involve both American Bantam and Ford but, for some reason, there was still a reluctance to order further vehicles from Bantam. The Quartermaster General, E. B. Gregory, arranged a meeting with Edsel Ford at which it was agreed that the company would

LEFT: The US Seventh Army in Alsace fitted a number of Jeeps with 4.5in rocket launchers; the 12 rockets could be fired at two-second intervals. Note the steel roof designed to protect the crew.

ABOVE: **Such was the versatility of the Jeep that the US Army used the vehicle in a variety of roles. Several attempts were made to build an armoured reconnaissance vehicle on the Jeep chassis. All were to fail due to the poor power-to-weight ratio.**

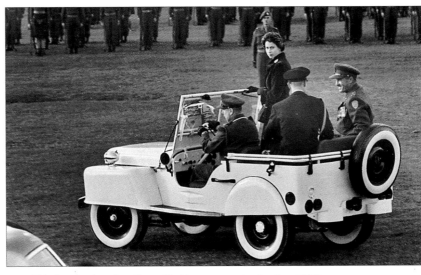

ABOVE: **This Jeep has been heavily modified to serve as a royal review vehicle. Note particularly the whitewall tyres and the addition of stylish front and rear mudguards and extended running boards. The occasion was the inspection of Canadian troops by the, then, Princess Elizabeth in January 1951.**

produce Jeeps according to the specification of the Willys MB, with every part interchangeable. Ford received a contract for a further 15,000 Jeeps which the company designated GPW.

Although the two vehicles were effectively identical, and all parts were indeed interchangeable, the products of the two manufacturers can be identified by the radiator cross-member, which is in the form of an inverted U section on the Ford and is circular on the Willys. The modern-day Jeep cognoscenti claim that the GPW was a better product, but it is doubtful that there is any practical difference. However, Ford did make subtle changes to better suit their mass-production methods, and stamped a script "F" on as many components as possible, including bolt heads, to indicate that this was a Ford product.

The needs of mass production, combined with shortages of components and materials forced myriad small changes during the production run. Early on, the welded slat grille, used only by Willys, was replaced with the familiar pressed-steel

grille. The manufacturer's name, which had been stamped into the rear panel, was omitted, and a jerrycan holder was fitted. In late 1945, the original Willys Type 441 engine was replaced by the improved Type 442, which featured a redesigned oil pump and a gear train in place of the former timing chain set-up.

No further changes were made to the design and by the time production ended in 1945, some 639,245 MB/GPW Jeeps had been completed. Willys built 361,349 and Ford was responsible for 277,896. Jeeps served with all of the Allied armies during World War II and the design went on to be copied by many other manufacturers.

The Ford GPA amphibian was built using the same engine, the same automotive transmission and suspension. There were also experiments with armoured, half-tracked and 6x6 variants.

ABOVE: **Jeeps were successfully equipped with both .30 and .50 calibre Browning heavy machine-guns as an early exponent of the "shoot and scoot" philosophy. This vehicle carries both weapons.**

Willys MB

Type: Truck, ¼-ton, 4x4

Manufacturer: Willys-Overland Motors; Toledo, Ohio. GPW produced by Ford Motor Company; Dearborn, Michigan

Production: 1941 to 1945

Powerplant: Willys Go-Devil Type 441, 442; four cylinders in-line; petrol; water-cooled; 2,199cc; side valves; power output, 60bhp at 4,000rpm

Transmission: 3F1Rx2; part-time 4x4

Suspension: Live axles on semi-elliptical multi-leaf springs; hydraulic telescopic shock absorbers

Brakes: Hydraulic

Electrical system: 6V

Dimensions: Length – 3,353mm/132in
Width – 1,575mm/62in
Height – tilt in place, 1,772mm/70in; minimum, 1,322mm/52in
Wheelbase – 2,032mm/80in

Weight: Unladen – 1,113kg/2,453lb
Payload – 363kg/800lb

Performance: Maximum speed – 105kph/65mph

Willys, Ford, Kaiser Jeep, AM-General, M151

In March 1951, the Ford Motor Company started design work for a new Jeep-type vehicle, initially known as the XM151. It was intended to offer reduced weight when compared to its predecessors, combined with maximum cross-country capabilities, high flotation, air-drop capability and ease of maintenance. The production vehicle, introduced into service from 1960, was ultimately manufactured by Ford, Willys, Kaiser-Jeep and AM-General, as the M151.

It was designed on a radical low-cost "throw-away" principle using a unitary chassis-less construction. Conventional live axles were replaced by independent suspension using swing axles and coil springs. Power was provided by a 2,319cc Continental overhead-valve engine, giving the vehicle a respectable speed and excellent off-road performance.

However, the combination of swing axles and a relatively high centre of gravity also led to difficult handling

and a roll-over problem that was never satisfactorily resolved despite two modifications. The M151A1, introduced in 1964–65, had stiffer springs, firmer mountings and an extra rubber bump stop to reduce rebound. This was replaced by the M151A2 in 1969–70, which had a completely redesigned suspension at the rear using semi-trailing arms, which allowed the wheels on each side to assume different angles. Although this improved the handling considerably, it did not entirely eliminate the problem. In 1986, the US Army started installing a "Roll-Over Protection System" (ROPS) to reduce injuries. There was also an M151A2LC variant built in small numbers, which used live axles and semi-elliptical springs.

Despite a lower profile, in appearance the vehicle was not unlike the original Jeep, with an open-sided body and folding windscreen. Alongside the basic cargo variant, it was produced as a front-line ambulance (M718); as a communications vehicle with rear-facing passenger seat (M107, M108); as a platform for the 106mm M20 recoilless rifle (M151A1C and M825); and as a US Marine Corps "fast-attack" vehicle. There were also experiments with extended wheelbase 6x6 and 8x8 variants.

Production continued until 1985 and was resumed briefly in 1988. Around 100,000 M151 and M151A1 vehicles were built, and 332,000 of the M151A2. Some early examples were

ABOVE: **Military vehicle enthusiasts in a restored M151A1 originally produced in 1964.**

assembled by Willys, but Ford was the primary supplier until late 1970, when contracts were awarded to Kaiser-Jeep and AM-General. All of the variants were fitted with bodies built by Fruehauf. The M151 saw service with around 100 countries worldwide.

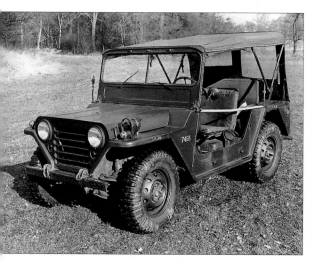

ABOVE: **Designed by the Ford Motor Company in 1951, the M151 was intended to replace all the US Army's existing Jeeps. The suspension of the original M151 was modified in an attempt to improve the handling.**

Willys, Ford, Kaiser Jeep, AM-General, M151

Type: Truck, ¼-ton, utility, 4x4

Manufacturer: AM-General Corporation; South Bend, Indiana. Ford Motor Company; Dearborn, Michigan. Kaiser Jeep Corporation; Toledo, Ohio. Willys-Overland; Toledo, Ohio

Production: 1960 to 1988

Powerplant: Continental L-142; four cylinders in-line; 2,319cc; petrol; water-cooled; overhead valves; power output, 72bhp at 4,000rpm

Transmission: 4F1Rx1; except model M151A2LC, 3F1Rx1; part-time 4x4

Suspension: Independent suspension using coil springs and swing axles front and rear; except model M151A2LC, semi-elliptical springs

Brakes: Hydraulic

Electrical system: 24V

Dimensions: Length – 3,510mm/133in
Width – 1,650mm/65in
Height – tilt in place, 1,800mm/71in; minimum, 1,321mm/52in
Wheelbase – 2,159mm/85in

Weight: Unladen – 1,066–1,089kg/2,350–2,400lb
Payload – road, 340kg/750lb
cross-country, 250kg/550lb

Performance: Maximum speed – 105kph/65mph

TAM 110T7BV

In 1947, Tovarna Automobilov Maribor (TAM) started manufacturing Praga trucks under licence at Marburg, in the former Yugoslavia. By 1957, TAM had become the largest motor manufacturer in Yugoslavia, and the Praga had been phased out in favour of a range of TAM-designed civilian and military 4x2, 4x4 and 6x4 trucks using licence-built KHD (Deutz) diesel engines.

The high-mobility 1½-ton 110T7BV was launched in 1976 and is effectively a version of the German-built Magirus-Deutz 130T7FAL under licence. Power was by a 5,880cc air-cooled four-cylinder diesel engine driving both axles through a five-speed gearbox, together with a mid-mounted two-speed transfer box which included a front-axle disconnect. Live axles were fitted front and rear, suspended on semi-elliptical leaf springs. Both were fitted with ZF self-locking differentials for improved mobility in difficult conditions.

The steel forward-control cab was open-topped and the windscreen could be folded forward to reduce the profile.

Unusually for a vehicle of this size, the cab was designed to tilt forward to allow improved access to the engine. At the rear, there was a steel drop-side cargo body with a drop-down tailgate. Collapsible bench seating was provided for 12 personnel. A 2½-ton capacity front-mounted under-floor mechanical winch was fitted and driven by a power take-off on the transfer box. There was

also a 6x6 variant (TAM150T11BV), rated at 3 tons and fitted with a V6 diesel engine.

Export sales were handled through SDPR, the Yugoslav Federal Directorate of Supply and Procurement in Belgrade. Following bankruptcy in 1996 the company became MPP Vozila, but the TAM name is still used on vehicles.

ABOVE: **The high-mobility 1½-ton TAM 110T7BV was launched in 1976. It was effectively a version of the Magirus-Deutz 130T7FAL built by Tovarna Automobilov Maribor (TAM) under licence in the former Yugoslavia. There was also a 3-ton 6x6 variant fitted with a more-powerful engine.**
LEFT: **A tilting cab is unusual in a vehicle of this size, but clearly allows improved access to the engine.**

TAM 110T7BV

Type: Truck, 1½-ton, cargo/personnel, 4x4
Manufacturer: Tovarna Automobilov Maribor (TAM); Marburg
Production: 1976 to 1996
Powerplant: Deutz licence TAM F4L-413R; four cylinders in-line; direct-injection diesel; air-cooled; 5,880cc; overhead valves; power output, 115bhp at 2,650rpm
Transmission: 5F1Rx2; part-time 4x4
Suspension: Live axles on semi-elliptical multi-leaf springs; hydraulic double-acting shock absorbers
Brakes: Air-assisted hydraulic
Electrical system: 24V
Dimensions: Length – 4,850mm/191in
    Width – 2,270mm/89in
    Height – tilt in place, 2,470mm/97in;
    minimum, 880mm/35in
    Wheelbase – 2,850mm/112in
Weight: Unladen – 4,500kg/9,921lb
    Payload – road, 2,500kg/5,511lb
    cross-country, 1,500kg/3,307lb
Performance: Maximum speed – 90kph/56mph

Index

ABOVE: **Beijing Jeep BJ212.**

ABOVE: **MZKT 74135** *Volat*.

Acknowledgements

Picture research for this book was carried out by Pat Ware and Jasper Spencer-Smith, who have selected images from the following sources: JSS Collection, Warehouse Publications, Getty Images, Tank Museum, Imperial War Museum, Archives of Canada and Ullstein Bild.

Much of the colour material has been supplied by the following (l=left, r=right, t=top, b=bottom). Every effort has been made to acknowledge photographs correctly, however we apologize for any unintentional omissions, which will be corrected in future editions.
Mark Barnes: 80b.
John Blackman: 19t; 19b; 58b; 81t; 87t; 88b; 100t; 111t; 115b; 120b; 121t; 121b; 124t; 128t; 129b; 132b; 139b; 143b; 154b.
Phil Royal: 18t; 18b; 60t.
Simon Thomson: 13b; 17t; 25t; 28t; 29tl; 30b; 37b; 48t; 48bl; 48br; 49t; 49b; 52tl; 52tr; 53t; 54t; 58t; 61t; 62t; 71br; 79t; 83t; 85t; 86t; 95t; 96t; 97t; 99t; 102b; 106t; 110t; 113t; 113b; 114t; 118t; 119t; 133t; 136t; 138t; 140t; 142t; 145t; 147b; 148t; 150b; 152b; 153t; 156t.

ABOVE: **Timoney 8x8 truck.**